BAD INFIDEL

Copyright © 2019 Natividad Ruiz. All rights reserved. No part of this book may be scanned, copied, uploaded or reproduced in any form or by any means, photographically, electronically or mechanically, without written permission from the copyright holder.

"Do Not Go Gentle Into That Good Night"
By Dylan Thomas,
from THE POEMS OF DYLAN THOMAS, copyright ©1952 by Dylan Thomas.
Reprinted by permission of New Directions Publishing Corp.

The events portrayed in this book are all true.
Some names have been changed to protect the guilty.
Some identities have been hidden to protect those who may still be serving.

ISBN 978-1-943-492-51-0 (hardback)
ISBN 978-1-943-492-52-7 (soft cover)

Book and cover design by designpanache

Elm Grove Publishing
San Antonio, Texas, USA
www.elmgrovepublishing.com

BAD INFIDEL

A BLACK SHEEP SERGEANT AND THE DEADLY POLITICS OF THE WAR IN AFGHANISTAN

NATIVIDAD "SHEPHERD" RUIZ
MASTER SERGEANT, US ARMY (RET.)

"I met the then SFC Ruiz at Joint Base Lewis McCord in Sept 2010. Always direct, with a great sense of humor. I liked him immediately. I found *BAD INFIDEL* to be a fantastic account of his life. The good times, and some disturbing incidents involving leadership at high levels. I highly recommend *BAD INFIDEL*. It's a wonderfully honest account of a soldier's wartime experiences."

– GREG COUMAS
PROUD FATHER OF SPC KYLE A. COUMAS
KIA 21 OCT, 2009. AFGHANISTAN

"One of the best memories of serving in the military (is) the people I have encountered and the lifelong friendships. Working and deploying with Natividad was no exception. Not only is he a soldier I would want in my foxhole, but he is someone I have called friend for over a decade and a brother for life. His leadership, conversation, and banter are qualities I know I can count on and look forward to every time we talk."

– JESSE J. HENNAGE
SERGEANT FIRST CLASS (RET.)
U.S. ARMY

Contents:

FOREWORD – *Dr. Elizabeth M. Stanczak Clinical Psychologist*	7
Do Not Go Gentle Into That Good Night	11
Kandahar, 2010	13
Alpha Company 1-17 Infantry	34
Any Means Necessary	45
The Flock	59
So, You are Perfect	76
Listening, Learning, Growing	87
Going Up River	102
Nothing Good Lasts Forever	113
The Men From the Mountain	132
The Platoon Status	143
"Mad, I Tell You!"	151
Do Not Go Gentle	168
Gotta Find The Key	192
"Who Did This?"	219
Respect Goes Both Ways	253
Guns, Ghosts, Bullets and Bombs	274
How About Them Apples?	294
Afterword	321
Military Terms and Abbreviations	324

Foreword

DR. ELIZABETH M. STANCZAK
CLINICAL PSYCHOLOGIST

I have known the author for several years now and I have found him to be honest to a fault, honorable in every sense of the word, and holding a plethora of military knowledge, skills, and abilities. As I read his book, I became aware of his ability to put his knowledge of the military into print in an easy to read and understand manner. He clearly operationalizes the current challenges of our military. He has not only provided those challenges but also provided possible solutions to those challenges. Some of those solutions are traditional in their military conceptualization, but other possible solutions are less traditional and rather focused on a more modernized battlefield to deal with current mechanized combat challenges. Ruiz talks about challenges that he has direct knowledge of, issues that have cost military men and women their lives, as well as innocent lives often referred to as "collateral damage."

Over the years, I have watched Ruiz work to move from his Non-Commissioned Officer (NCO) or military stance to that more like a civilian. With that said, he will never be a civilian. Rather, his experiences have forever changed him and his perspective on life. He is now hypervigilant, attempting to protect those who look to him for assistance, and he will train and educate anyone intelligent and focused enough to listen and learn. Many active and retired military will tell you that they "...do not suffer fools..." but they can't stop themselves from protecting those fools, despite their ignorance. Ruiz has far too much compassion to allow others to suffer in the manner that he and – most importantly to him – his men, have suffered. Ironically, the very experiences that may lead to deep moral injuries will prompt him to take action. This book may not accurately reflect his compassion, but I assure you it is there, along with his desire to help save the lives of future service members who serve long after he is gone.

The author is a military man who has fought the good fight, though many civilians have no idea what that may mean. Civilians often get a sanitized version of what military combat experience is all about, but Ruiz shares those little known facts with his readers. He provides information that may open the reader's eyes to things that will change their view of war as well as their experience of civilian privilege. Ruiz once told me "...you have unicorns and rainbows coming out your ass..." and he was right. I was once foolish enough to think that military and civilian lives were very similar except for job titles and job descriptions. However, after my very minor stint in the military I learned that was not even close to the reality of military service. I have further learned that my non-combat, non-deployed military experience was nothing compared to those who have risked their lives in poorly-planned and hastily pulled together efforts to mobilize units for deployment without focus on unit cohesion and good military training. My greatest wish would have been that when my son was deployed to Afghanistan he would have had the training and unit cohesion necessary to avoid some of the losses he experienced. I wish that Ruiz had been my son's NCO. My son's military experiences would have made sense to him, his mission would have been clearer to him, and he would not likely have lost so many battle buddies during his year-long tour.

Some who read this book may not feel it respects the military enough or recognizes the work our military does. Ironically, that is far from what the author is trying to communicate. I believe his intent is to improve our military's training efforts, better define and respect the hierarchy by which our military once thrived, and in so doing, better identify the mission, vision and goals of our military. He is a patriot who is attempting to uncover the politics that is seeping into and damaging our military at every level, but predominantly at the level involving the officer corps. It seems to me that he is also trying to get someone to listen to issues related to the training of our young recruits. Ruiz identifies that the United States has the best-trained military in the world, but he is also focused on appropriate, time-tested training methods that will save lives. Better training will allow for less loss of American lives and fewer incidents of collateral damage. Better training might help us send a message to the world that we are the most focused and mission-ready military in the world. It might also lessen the need for our young men and women to die. One never knows what possibilities exist until one listens to the wisdom from someone who has the knowledge, skills and abilities to back up their lessons. I'm listening MSg Ruiz, I'm listening!

E.S.

Do not go gentle into that good night,
Old age should burn and rave at close of day;
Rage, rage against the dying of the light.

Though wise men at their end know dark is right,
Because their words had forked no lightning they
Do not go gentle into that good night.

Good men, the last wave by, crying how bright
Their frail deeds might have danced in a green bay,
Rage, rage against the dying of the light.

Wild men who caught and sang the sun in flight,
And learn, too late, they grieved it on its way,
Do not go gentle into that good night.

Grave men, near death, who see with blinding sight
Blind eyes could blaze like meteors and be gay,
Rage, rage against the dying of the light.

And you, my father, there on the sad height,
Curse, bless, me now with your fierce tears, I pray.
Do not go gentle into that good night.
Rage, rage against the dying of the light.

– Dylan Thomas

Kandahar, 2010

Getting out of bed was tough. As I got older, there was something about those last minutes of sleep that made everything in the world seem pointless and worth missing. At that time, I had become used to the pre-alarm to the real alarm. In the final minutes between the two, I always seemed to get the best moments of rest. Not only did it come with more rest, it also came with a personal sense of accomplishment. That is hard to imagine, being that I am in a tent in bum-fuck Afghanistan, a tent packed with soldiers doing their morning rituals. They were moving around, listening to music, the occasional electric razor in the background. Regardless of the sounds there, even with the lights on, I lay in comfort, relaxed, and in peace.

One would think, given where I was, it would be tense: the whole picture of vehicles rolling around, motors running 24/7, people coming and going in and out of the tent, people talking here and off in the distance, the shitter truck outside, beeping. It would make the rounds in the morning, stopping at the shitters outside. It would suck up the frosted brownies, resupply the toilet paper, and pressure wash off the dirty, nasty crap that sticks everywhere—the nasty crap that just flies in the air. Even with all of that going on, it all can be drowned out by the next C-130 landing. Once she hits the ground, as if to let everyone know that the bitch is there, her engines rev up as she slows down and jogs to her directed spot. Then again, I am not talking about every sound you ever heard being in the army, or being on an airbase, or even the sounds that Afghanistan makes. All of that crazy bullshit is normal noise in my environment. I was talking about the noise in my head. I usually had thoughts and ideas that were speeding around not allowing me to get to sleep. I looked back on past events and wondered if that shit really happened. *Why did it happen?*

Was I a dick?

Was it me?

No, it had to be something else.

And it would go on and on and on. Finally, at some time in the night, my mind would tire out and fall victim to the darkness. My body relaxes in the cool tent and I slowly fall asleep. That moment is more fragile than any china. In that sleep I am drifting away from where I was. It's cool, dark, and silky smooth, so quiet that the silence feels heavy.

What an awesome place to be. To feel safe and warm. To have nothing. Everything has melted and with it all your pain and stress. To feel nothing, yet never be so complete and focused.

As I get comfortable in the mighty silence of peace, bam! That fucking first alarm goes off. At that moment, I do the one thing that seems to be frowned upon in theater. I slap the shit out of the alarm. Ah! Fifteen minutes of bliss. In that short span of time I get what I want; I do what I want to, and I don't hear shit out of anyone. That moment is mine, the second I slap that alarm. It's fucking perfect.

Everything good comes to an end though. I lie awake in my little bed looking at the springs on the top bunk. I can only describe waking up as similar to starting a computer. The screen is on. Buttons are blinking, fans are going and there is a hum. It is another damn day and I should be happy. I have been dead for over six months. No matter what I do, where I go, I keep waking up in Afghanistan. I lie there thinking of all the checks and tasks I have to do to get up and running. Life at that time was basic, and it was boring. At night, I re-examined events from different points of view, morally, tactically, from the other side of the fence, and in the other person's shoes. It was only right to give others the benefit of the doubt, so I did. Problems were cheap, magnified, joined with red tape, and lacked common sense. The military I grew up in was a fighting force. Back then, warriors carried weight, were smart, spoke with authority, and were leaders of men. Now, it wasn't that. As with everything else, now the military was about scratching and fighting for the next best move up the ladder, "a career path." This ignored the decisions, actions, and deeds, the soul and spirit of those who had paved the way, paved it in lives, blood, body parts, sweat, nightmares and tears. I had long known about the army and its mission. As a grunt, you know the price. It was very simple. You were sent in to fight for a town, hill, valley, or airfield. We were trained to win, to capture and hold, but these days we seemed to fight only to give it back.

Then again, I don't know shit. I don't want to know shit, unless someone else wakes the fuck up who can change things. Perhaps it was a misunderstanding due to a lack of communication. Whatever the case may be, shit had changed, and I was as lost as a lieutenant doing night land navigation. During the day, I was trying to make sense of simple stuff. After all, I'd had years to see and learn what to do and what not to do. I didn't know what was going on and nothing was how or what I had learned. In order to stay sane and not get lost in politics, favorites, and coffee clubs, I had to do some self-analysis. I tried to make sure I was doing what I was supposed to, be the person I wanted to be, and maintain my worth and values. I tried to keep my moral compass and knew this to be the hard road. Maybe I thought about it too much? But I had time on my hands, and I felt it was important. I'd been put in a corner, had no responsibility anymore. I was doing minor tasks here and there. With such a change in the new military society, I was doubting myself. Everything that I'd experienced and been taught didn't mean shit. That right there, well that is a hard pill to swallow. Does a crazy person know he is crazy? Maybe I needed to take a step back? Was I over-thinking, or just paranoid? I didn't have a fucking clue, and even just typing this shit is giving me a headache. But it was real and there was nothing I could do to find myself again. I had nothing tying me to the ground. I was simply floating in space, and I was trying to remember who I was.

Some things I knew. I knew I was in Afghanistan. I knew I was a soldier, but what kind? I didn't know anymore. The politics, loyalties, and pursuing personal interests were new products of the military business model.

I moved over and swung my legs off the side of the bed and sat there. I felt like I went ten rounds in the ring, off a cliff, hitting every damn rock down, only to land into a pile of shit. I sat there and thought if I was drunk, life would have made more sense. I had changed over the last few years. As a private, I waited for first call. Up and at em! I ironed my uniforms and spit-shined my boots. My vocabulary used to consist of five words: yes, no, roger, that, and sergeant. Now, the new me? Well, he had more of a confrontational attitude. However, I was not going to *be* what others wanted. Not today or tomorrow. I thought of myself as being the gap between two different generations. In the past, I had superiors who were harder than woodpecker's lips. Old Sarge, Mr. "I have more jumps in green fatigues than you have days in the Army" line.

There were superiors that would hurt you bad, might even make you disappear, better known as The Hard Side. Today, I was in the smarter, faster, corporate, micromanaging, backstabbing, do-as-I-say-not-as-I-do, double-standard, PT belt-wearing, straight edge, hippie, educated, cloned, freeze-dried, sun-bleached, paperwork, PowerPoint, fully programmed Army, with I-know-a-better-way-to-do-everything officer, and sniveling fake-ass sergeants who have never fired a round in anger. The Mr. "I'm going to go get a desk job for this deployment" fuckers.

Now, I looked in the mirror and all I saw were two black holes. I had taken the hardest route to be a soldier. I wanted to be like my leaders, no matter what I had experienced. Their value to the unit and army was immeasurable. Yet, they were simple and down-to-earth people. So, during my upbringing, I lived the life and saw the politics. No matter what had happened, there was a higher purpose. People gave the best of themselves and you saw it. You witnessed it and despite ideas or opinions, it felt right in your bones. That gave you your example of leadership. Now as I looked into my own reflection, I peered into those holes to see if there was anything good left inside me. I was the product of one generation, and when it came time to do the job, everything had changed. It hadn't happened overnight, but it had happened. I took my time washing up and enjoyed the cool water on my face and head. I pulled out my razor and ran it across my wet face. I rinsed my face and poured water over my head again. I wanted to feel it as I poured it onto my scalp and then used my hands to wipe the excess away. I wanted to remember it and I wanted to be sure I took every second to make this memory stick.

I reached for the razor again. This was a task I had done millions of times. I had done it in the early mornings and late at night. I had shaved in the barracks, billets, a sleeping bag, in the rain, and in the snow. I knew my face and the movements were like a battle drill. One side of my brain was feeling and seeing with my hands, and the other side of my brain was looking into the eyes of my reflection. I'd seen younger days. I once was with others who were living the same life. Sure, I was a number, but I was not alone. I was years from there, and wondered what kept others going way back then?

I had been smart enough to stay off the radar. I wanted to be near the top, but far enough down to not get picked for shit. I had stood by others who were physically superhuman, people that made you wonder why the hell they were in the ditches. On the other side were people who made you think the same damn thing. Why the hell were they there? There was no damn reason that the little bastard should have made it this far in life. I didn't play well with others. I had tried but if I knew shit to be stupid or a waste of time, I tended to speak up. I was no private anymore and had earned my right to voice my concerns. I was a SFC/senior sergeant and was tired of making simple shit harder than it had to be. I was always told to keep it simple. As my leadership used to put it, "K.I.S.S." – *Keep It Simple Stupid*. That type of attitude and thinking got me tarred and feathered. I was a round piece trying to fit into a square hole, and that does not work. You try to be a team player, and just end up getting walked all over. You try so much that you get to the point where you no longer recognize yourself as a man, soldier, or anything like any leader you ever knew. By trying so much to be a team player, did I make life worse? Did I end up causing more confusion, lack of respect for the grade and position? What about loss of authority to the other leaders in the unit and the NCO corps? So what do you do?

I resorted to doing what I knew, what was simple and had been done for years before, long before I ever got any stripes on my collar. In the new corporate system, I shot myself in the foot. Put it however you wanted, doing things how I learned was way better than making it up as I went, but I knew I no longer belonged. I thought of those that could quit and never did. I would like to think I was as good as them or as tough. The truth? I was too damn dumb to quit. I remember those little bastards hanging tough, and figured I would do the same.

Maybe it was a fluke or just luck. It would take me time to learn deep down in my bones, that you never knew, until you knew (if something was right, if someone was honest, hard, or a quitter). You never judged a book by its cover. Looks didn't have shit to do with anything. All that ever really mattered was what was inside that one person. It was about what made him do what he did. It was the drive and fire inside him. It was his will to fight and win. In short, it all came down to heart.

I looked in the mirror and wondered if I was empty or spent. The day was off to another start and I dragged on one task after the other. Life wasn't too shabby for being dead, huh? Well in case you were asking, yes, I said dead. That, I'll explain later, and it's a whole different ball of bullshit.

I headed to my tent and threw my shit into my 24-hour bag. I am careful to not rush and forget anything. Today I was leaving the mega camp and I didn't plan on ever coming back. I accepted I was old and out of place. I was just out of date and different. I was now a part of a new social experiment in the army. I knew my time was up, and something had to give. I believed so much in what I grew up and knew. Nothing was left for me in the modern, better army. I knew I wasn't going to change again. That would make all I did and had come to believe in, mean nothing. It would have all been for nothing. If that was going to happen, the end of my time in the military, I'd rather it be in a scrap instead of being choked to death by paperwork and politics. I preferred to have some say. I wanted to end my career in a fight, not sitting on my hands and being scolded and thrown to the newer "snowflakes." Being mean, stubborn, and too dumb to quit, I chose to go back. While others were moving up the ladder, I decided to go down. Once again, I volunteered to go live and do what I was taught to. I had no reason to. They threatened to send me to the worst and most dangerous place and I said, "Okay." Others feared it, talked about it like it was the end. So, when I volunteered, they took it upon themselves to put me down for something others wouldn't do. You see, I was not in any ordinary tent. I was in the Senior NCO's tent, and was the youngest in the crowd. Some had been there the whole time we were in-country, working at their desks or making sure tasks were completed to keep operations going. Days before, I had just arrived from being out close to the Pakistan border. I walked in and threw my shit next to the first empty cot I found. After a talk with one of the brigade sergeant-majors, I returned to start packing. I was formally told that units were short leaders. I was to get ready and move out in hours. So much for blending in and POG-ing out (People Other than Grunts).

I remember walking in and getting my bags. I took out the things I needed to get cleaned like my uniform. Then I started to repack. This seemed to be quite the attraction for the evening. Soon there were other senior sergeants gathered around and asking questions. "What are you doing?"

"What's going on?"

"Didn't you just get here?"

"Where do you think you are going?" I already knew the outcome. Some of these "leaders" were on the line and came back to take some time. I had been deployed before and had never seen such a thing. I grew up when this shit didn't happen. The platoon sergeant stayed as long as the troops. As a matter of fact, his was the last boot to leave the ground. So, I figured I would drag this out and see what kind of reaction I would get. I started off by saying the one thing I knew everyone cared about. I told them I was going to go back to the line and take a position as a platoon sergeant. That went off like a shit in an elevator. "Huh? Why are you going?"

"When did you get promoted?"

I answered and told them my date of rank. It was quickly pointed out that they all out ranked me. So again, that kind of pissed some off and got a few shitty with me. I then decided to take the high road and offer my position up.

"Well if you want a position for a promotion, ask to go get one. If you want one, you could have mine." I was then asked where I was going and I answered, "1-17 Inf."

I didn't think their responses would shock me. I kind of expected them.

"Well, I came here early, and I don't want to get too close to the men." Or, "I came here early and I'm going to go home early."

Others said, "Oh, okay. Good Luck!" and that was all she wrote. Since that time I wondered if they had heard stuff I didn't.

Why the fuck did I get all the poopy attitudes? And then, "Later dude!" I sat there and kept trying to run things in my head.

Since I was so "out of date," and not part of any group or club, I thought surely this would be my end. I put my stuff away and then reached into my laundry bag to pull out my clean uniform. I had it turned in and recently picked it up from the locals who were employed at the local laundry stand. I remembered the feel of the somewhat fresh, supposed to be clean, uniform. As I put it on I knew that it was only a matter of time before it was drenched with sweat and salt stains. I sat on the edge of my bunk, reached for my boots. I looked at the stains and checked out the tread. I saw them as being worn and used, like me. I thought of the miles these boots had gone, and the places that they were going to be. I dusted them off, and dropped them on the floor. I began to put them on slowly and carefully. Again, something simple like this only required muscle memory and my mind wandered off. As I'm putting on my boots, I remember being told to tie a knot in the middle of your boot strings. Then it was right over left. Why? I didn't know at the start of things, but I learned quickly. Like everything else, the answer came by pain, or mother-fucking misery. It wasn't about the boots, but knowing why things were done. I was now going to have to remember a lot and depend on the things I was taught, to do my job and maybe prove my point. From an ambush, to a raid, a trench, danger areas, knots, security, and even how to take a piss. You didn't know a damn thing, till you were taught. *Don't piss on or near the trees!*

That's an example, but now common sense. If shit hit the fan, you would be going to the nearest tree to take cover. In training, sometimes you learned the harder way. That method literally stank. I was taught that way, and it stuck. Even years down the line. That was then, and now all of it was for nothing.

I felt cheated and pissed. Everyone went through some shit to earn your place in life. Now it was about liking one more than another. It was about the individual relationship. That guy is cool, he gets the spot. It was not about what was due or deserved. Yet, in a fucked up way, it was perfect. The days of picking and choosing were a continent away. I bypassed the hoops and slipped into the need at the time. Yet, it was still about choice. Some just didn't want to choose to take a job or position because we were in Afghanistan. I said, "fuck it!" My opinion about things, how I felt about working to get to where I was, all the bullshit, and how I wanted to go out—this was it. All the stars were aligned and a straight path to the suck was now in front of me. I had my rest and was up and moving. Now I was at another task and getting ready to move out. I kept thinking about my first time here and there. How every time I got scuffed up and smoked was for something. The old sergeants would fuck you up. Either I didn't know, or, at times, I was known to fuck some shit up. Hey, it's the infantry, we do that.

Lessons were hard, but now remembered with fondness. So, why right over left? Well that is a good question. It cost me, but this is free info.

In some jungle, in some country, the locals would sneak up on the people and kill their ass in the night. Of course, it would be dark as fuck, dark enough to not be able to distinguish friend from foe. So the locals reach for the boots and feel the person's laces. Right over left was the deciding factor to kill or be left alone. Now in Afghanistan I have laced up my boots. Pulled out the slack from the strings. Wrapped the excess around my lower calves twice. Tied a square knot and tucked the ends into the tops of my boots. I stand up and tie a bow knot at the bottom of my pants and tuck in the strings. This of course is done in defiance and seen as being a maverick. Yup! That's infantry style and just my thing. I reach for my uniform top and think, *right over left*? If the fuckers are getting that close to me in my fucking sleep, we have one hell of a problem with our security. Really? Right over left? We are years from any jungle conflict. I'm in Afghanistan! It's a fucking desert and not any jungle. As I finish buttoning up my top, I run my hands down the front of my uniform and look at my boots. *Damn right. Right over left, motherfucker! You ain't got to tell me twice.* Like I said, oh to be young again. No matter how painful or hard, you got the point. You learned the lesson and laugh about it now. I make quick work of all my gear and put it all in a pile. Even as life is going on all around, I am on my own. The days of being part of any team or even a platoon are far from where I am. I fell in love with the army as a young soldier. No matter what happened to me or where I was, I was still in love with it. This was only because in my time I lived to see the right way, see the best in soldiers. I knew people but really, very little politics compared to today's standards. I liked the ceremonies and traditions carried on. I liked the fact that it was actions and deeds that mattered, not empty words. I thought I knew the reasons for being made into a soldier. With that came honor, integrity, trust, and loyalty to each other. If I was able to live by the words that were written in black and white, I honestly thought I would be a good man. Sure, there were others who wanted this or that, people who would do things for some other reason than the group or men they were with. I had seen it before and those people stuck out, and were often not around too long. I spent a life going up and down hills and mountains, running mile after mile and getting smoked in the rain, snow, and smoke pits from here to Fort Benning, Georgia. All the hours of training and doing to be smarter and better. Now, we have digital learning. Your position and authority is decreased. You, as a leader are no longer the trainer or mentor. Your ass is now sitting in a seat next to a private in class. So, you become unneeded, overlooked, and marginalized.

"We don't do things the hard way anymore. We do it like this." Everything was all tap and type here. Knowledge from a program is spot on. It is perfect for getting one message out to large amounts of units and soldiers. The only problem I noticed was the execution. The training didn't allow for hands-on learning. Grunts belong in the field, living and thriving in unfriendly conditions, practicing and doing the drills, new or old. Leaders in the units were reduced to the status of privates and all trained by civilians. To me, that meant losing the lessons that taught loss and humility, the agony of defeat, the morals and values that breed winners and, most importantly, heart.

Instead of my role as a leader, I was expected to go back to a vocabulary of five words. The new army was kind enough to add an additional one at no cost whatsoever. Yes "sir!" So that really made six.

Before too long, things started to backfire. I think it was due to the loss of a chain of command, the castration of the NCO corps. Of course, once things began to go wrong the responsibility fell firmly and solely on the shoulders of the unit's leadership, the company leader ship, the platoon leadership, and then the Sgt in charge of the guy. It was a light switch being turned on. One minute you are a leader, then you are not. Believe me, that was no way to make real leaders with values, certainly none that would stand the strain of war. That then left another problem. Now you have whiny-ass sergeants that don't know shit, using the guidance and ideas of an officer to punish a soldier, to make him an example for others. However, everyone's lack of leadership means they don't know enough to do it right, most importantly when enough was enough. I for one had stepped on my dick so many times I piss like a pressure washer. Growing up, punishment or corrective training was exactly that—training. It wasn't pretty and at times embarrassing as fuck. You were going to get the fast version of the lesson but you knew it was deserved. You manned up and knocked it out. Then, it's done. I firmly believe that in one's education, it is important to add fear and pain to the lesson. If not, it would simply be forgotten and that leader becomes as much of a soup sandwich and his soldier. Using that method builds your knowledge muscles as well as your physique. As a bonus, you become a little more squared away and believe it or not, confident. In today's Army, once you are labeled a shitbag, you are a shitbag for life. Around every corner, every floor, or in your own room you will get smoked by a bitch-ass sergeant who is following the new digital program's definition of a leader. Years later, here I was. I had been told that war was bad. Well, yeah, it is. Then again, anyone can go. Some go by force. Others because of the guy standing with them. As far as I was concerned, I was not happy with all I had done. Your saving grace was to get in a group or unit where you had a mean and hard son of a bitch in charge that knew what he was doing. That would get you to be what you needed to be and through the ordeal. That and a little bit of praying and guts.

I had been scarred and taught to do my part. Some call it duty, pride or honor. It was just doing the right thing. I seemed to be the last of my type: grouchy, pig-headed and still holding on to old ideals and values, myths and tales that were common, once upon a time. There are always tickets to the show for the brave, stupid, dumb ass, and wannabe hero types. I was probably seen as being one of the stupid ones. I had been shunned, cast away, labeled a fool, and called a shitbag. There were times that I hated myself for not being political. I could have played nice and been a puppet. Life would have been easier, but it went contrary to how and what I had experienced. The words and actions of others haunted me without rest. The moment I decided this life to be a good thing and worth the price, I committed everything. I wanted to become half as good as the old timers. Never could I imagine something that started out as being good and right, evolve into micromanaged madness. My last unit had a formation and all of us were told that the minute we left, we were all dead. "What the fuck, over?"

"Can you say again?" "You are coming in stupid and unbelievable!"

Yes, we were told that we were dead the moment we had left and I thought, *this motherfucker is on drugs.*

What a fucking thing to tell the entire unit? Did they think it was a psychological advantage to fuck someone up in the head? This retarded motherfucker then goes further and said it was going to be bad. I, or the vehicle I was in, was going to get blown up and I was going to burn. I had been here and there. I swear, I'd done some shit in my time and seen worse. I had never, ever, ever, heard or seen anyone give a speech to a unit that told everyone, "You are fucking dead."

I knew that moment was special. It was one of those things that you wouldn't believe if you were told. You wouldn't believe it unless you were there. It could be argued as one of the most significant and fucked up things to ever happen in this military till the end of the century. The guy, our first sergeant, First Sergeant T-Anus, was a scared-ass, nasty, dirty, bastard, willing to tell everyone they were going to die because he would be staying behind to tell the tale. At the time, I thought of a saying I once heard, "There is a thin line between hard and stupid."

I looked at my feet and didn't see a line, but right then, I knew exactly on which side of the line I was standing. I was now taking time to look at the past and learn from the whole enchilada. I took a good look at the last company and thought about what made it so bad, then what made my piece of the pie fucked up too. It came down to communication and teamwork.

There was none. It made the platoon's leadership void. It was so controlled by the company commander, there was no reason for any position.

So we were run by our captain, the company commander, ole Ginger himself. This left a taste of shit in my mouth, but moving on to a new company and platoon, I hoped life was better. As far as my old company, who gave a shit? It was in the good hands of the commander, till the altar required a sacrifice.

It took me two years of fuck-fuck games to just say, "Fuck it!" I wanted to go to war just to get away from the pair. It was a bad place to be physically and mentally. I felt useless and shit on. Finally, I broke and I let them have it. This led to me bouncing around in Afghanistan for a while till I could get to an infantry unit. I did what I could and stayed busy. I did it until someone, somewhere was in need. The newer version of the army's leadership and training was beginning to be reaped. I was packed up and ready for the next *hoorah* and I couldn't wait to get away from the flagpole.

Now back to real time in my tent in Afghanistan, I just sat there. I sat waiting for the arrival of transportation to shuttle me out to the helipad. After that, it was a ride to the worst there was to offer.

I recalled my lessons and those who shared knowledge, how the world I knew had changed to the refined and more modern soldier. There was a time when soldiers would be lined up to take the hardest or most dangerous tasks. Never did I think any had a death wish. I do think that they were just that good. Soldiers used to compete for the hard jobs, if not for winning among their peers, then to see if they could face the challenge. It was about competition, and wanting to be first in the door. To be the main effort, to lead the charge, to be number one. Now, it seemed to be about the classroom. The more bells and whistles, the better to get you out of stuff. Instead of the use of knowledge and skills, people used it as a get out of jail card. No one wanted to test fate. I really didn't give two shits about anything. Between the candy-ass pretend war and the real war being fought by simple men, I'd rather be out in the almighty suck. I hoped things were as they used to be. At least, I hoped that operations in the field were not as different as everything else had become (working in any operation hub is not being out in the field, it's having a 9-5 job). Maybe, just maybe, I still had a little fight in me. There was no real way to find out unless I took the challenge. If so, I was the only one in my crowd. That was my crazy world. I didn't like it and didn't understand it. Therefore, I didn't belong. I accepted my possible fate. I knew it all when I raised my hand and chose to stick with it. I didn't have any one sugarcoat it or church it up. I felt like I was keeping my oath, not hiding out, and doing the right thing. I had been here months. Despite the doom and gloom, I was still alive. Maybe not for long.

I'd probably get it sooner or later. We all have the same outcome, sooner or later. We all have that coming. Despite the warnings and failed attempts to scare me into a better soldier, I was doing exactly what others were not going to do. My transport arrived. I got onto a small local-type bus. My bags were packed and this was all it came down to. The flagpole was not like the Army. I never thought I would push toward the fight. Not when I had checked all the blocks. I thought that this was exactly the kind of story someone tells you about a dumbass who got killed for nothing. Despite playing it safe for years, it was funny how things were turning out. I used to be the guy waiting to get out of the rain, mud, and back to garrison. Now, I couldn't stand being in civilization and that includes the military and civilians. As I sat down on the minibus, I thought about my life. I was reminded of life in the 173rd. Back then, we were always taking buses somewhere. I thought about my brothers and myself. It was a period where I had experienced reality and learned things I still considered important. I was younger and meaner in those days. Yet, I remembered it as if it was someone else. The bus pulled up, and I got out. I was a little bit early. I sat there waiting for my ride to arrive and it was getting hot. The sun lit up the sand and made it almost impossible to go without glasses. As I contemplated my life and my actions, I thought it was funny. It would have been a whole lot more funny if it happened to someone else. Since I thought of it like that, I knew this was hilarious. Everything that had transpired put me right under the brightest sun I had ever known.

    I made myself comfortable and prepared for the wait. I was already sweating in the clean uniform, but the day was just starting. It was still early and it was going to get hotter. I figured I might as well get used to it. I had officially fucked shit up good this time. I looked around and wondered what the fuck was wrong with me. I came to the conclusion: nothing. It's exactly how I remembered my leaders being. How they stood up for something, and that it was something they required out of the young. You had to make your decision, good or bad, right or wrong, and go with it. A bad decision, in time, was better than a good decision too late. It's the choices we make that put you where you are today. Some have a path or an idea to get to where they want to be. I didn't have that. I did get to a point where there was an idiot doing stupid shit at a higher rank, so I figured I couldn't fuck it up worse than him. Here I was. This is where all of it had got me. I figured life was now going to be easier. I was going to have to get back in the groove of things. What I was doing now, wouldn't work on the line. I'd better get it out of my system, because shit was about to get real. It was all going to start this morning, and now I was sitting right in the middle of the desert. It had begun. I found myself down from an open sewage pond, waiting to hitch a chopper ride now. As I was waiting to get on the bird coming in, I committed to my idea of how to finish up the year. I had made my choice a long time ago, and that was to get back in the fight. While others were toning it down for the final months, I figured I might as well piss off some bad guys too. I once had questions and none of it mattered. My last company would stay in my head. Just as I had thought, once there, First Sergeant T-Anus dug in on post. He was as happy as a pig in shit. For someone who was always a subject matter expert in everything, someone who refused to delegate a task or mission, it had now become funny. Old First Sergeant, T-Anus himself, went from one extreme to another. It could have been from his message of death, perhaps? He went from leading a simple mission or micromanaging to popping smoke/disappearing. I swear he had more smoke than the Chemical Corps (the Chemical Corps has the ability to create screens and provide concealment on the battle field, you know, Smoke Screens). He walked up to me on the first mission and told me how I was awesome. How I was this and that, but I knew exactly what was going on, and who it was coming from. Looking at that man, watching him explain why he was not going to go out, made me better than him. He gave over everything he used to do, for settling to be in the rear. Then and there, my opinions and thoughts about him came to light. I guess

I knew a thing or two after all.

It had changed me. It was also all gone now. I had no more problems from before, and if I died, then no more problems ever. I kept being troubled and confused. I had never before seen anything that bad, but I knew what it was. It was a unit running on the greed of one man and supported by fear from another.

Well, that bad experience taught me to not stray from what you have experience in, to trust in what all of us were trained on over and over. I was no longer the young bushy-eyed, greenhorn, waiting for scraps from any table. If anything, the time in that company made me into a harder man. Slow to trust, and when in charge, I was going to be in charge. I accepted the fact that life on the big base was not living. It was more comfortable and pleasing, but would fill many with regret. As for my morals? They were not only mine, but something that had been passed down from generation to generation. Taking time to see things, and realizing that helped me find my way onto the right path. No one was with me, but I no longer felt alone. I felt more like an inductee into the infantry's Big Balls Club.

My decision to separate and leave my last unit cost me plenty. It was also a strain on my family, knowing I would become the hunted as well as being a hunter. Looking back on everything, doing what I was fixing to do made perfect sense. I had to be an idiot if I thought trying to play politics was somehow going to change anything. The system was not for me, and broken when it did work. So I did what wasn't normal. It was fucked up, but so was everything else. I let my high school education convince me it was simply two negatives. You put them together, and it should be a positive? Damn, is that right? I was not without fear. I was a little worried. After all, I am human. I was fixing to do what I wanted. I laughed as I remembered getting to slap the shit out of the clock earlier. Now, I felt calm, clear, and focused. I felt sure of myself and was actually starting to feel as if I was living again. I was on the right track. I felt like I was moving to where I belonged. The unit didn't matter, nor the location.

As my ride finally showed up I finished my bottle of water and placed the empty bottle in my pocket. The civilian helicopter landed and began to load some supplies going to different places. As for me, I put on my gear and put in a pinch of Copenhagen. I put on my gloves and grabbed my helmet and made my way to the best looking helicopter I had seen. I sat in a nice leather seat, and looked out the window as the dust kicked up and we began the trip. My next post would be in the most dangerous place that our units were deployed. I had nerves, but that was normal. The time I took to do my self-evaluation set my mind and heart at ease. I reached down for my pocket and pulled out my empty water bottle. I pulled the cap off and sat there on the evergreen flight and used it as a spitter for my chew. As we flew, I looked out the window and watched as we went over the villages. I'd had a lot on my mind, and now just tried to enjoy as much as I could of the flight. Looking out the window, I knew down there was where I was going to be. I might never get a good look at the land like this. Maybe, this would be my last trip? At least it was comfortable. Soon enough I was told that my stop was next. That stop, was Frontenac. I was joining the Mighty Buffaloes of 1-17 Infantry.

Sunrise over Kandahar, 2010. Stryker in foreground.

Off to a new start? Maybe I just needed to get out and back into one job and one task? Whatever, I needed to shake it up and roll the dice. At this point I'd been treated like a red-headed stepchild and was basically talking to myself. I was set on trying to prove to myself it could be done the way I was taught. Everyone was so concerned with modernization and coming up with new ways to do anything. The simple fact was the bad guys over there wanted to kill you. However way they tried wasn't gonna matter if you were dead like me. In return, by saying, "Look at me, I'm a bad guy," it was simple training. Targets up! Bam! Bam! Bam! Targets down. Then again, I'm old, crazy, and my time had passed. Still, I wanted to fight, and do something. I wasn't going to let my last company be my end. I refused to go out like a dying flame. I had the chance to go out with a bang. Doing something I learned to like. I had one last chance to do the things I learned the hard way. I had the ability to live, or die in that way. I was not going to be micromanaged and put in a corner. I also knew that where ever I was going, I hoped to beat my bad reputation.

Alpha Company 1-17 Infantry

I remember landing after one of the best helicopter rides I ever had. I got off and I know I had gear to stow, but as soon as I landed, I went straight to the battalion TOC (Tactical Operations Center). I knew no one, but knew enough that I had one person I had to talk to. I went and found the Battalion Command Sergeant Major. We talked a bit and there was nothing really important said. Someone like me coming in is known. Sometimes no one says anything just to see if you know what to do. As a matter of fact, I do not ever remember having a discussion with him after that. He did let me know I was going to Alpha Company. Oh, by the way, they were not there. I would travel to them the next day with one of the other company's platoons. On the ground by the Stryker vehicle. *Hmmm, okay.*

By the time I was done, it was pitch black outside and nothing like Mega Tent Central. I would be there the night and then travel by ground to the company. Unlike the larger base, here they were setting up two-man trailers. One of the good things was that getting better living conditions to the units in the field was the priority. It was beautiful and amazing. Wow! Years of seeing these things and never had I not been in a tent. We either slept under the stars, the roach motel, or tents. So that night, I did not stay in a tent, but a small room for two. I had a couple of soldiers from the company helping me out. As we were moving my stuff I was just listening to what they had to say. Finally, the platoon sergeant came by and we sat there for a while. He was in the same company, but from first platoon. I came to find out that they were there in Frontenac. They were also going to transport me out to the company's location.

He was filling me in on the area and some of the fights that had happened. He filled me in on the events that transpired and confirmed some of the stories and things that I heard before. I sat there and heard some of the same miserable bullshit that used to come out of my mouth. It sounded like my old company, and I was not planning on dealing with this again. We talked late into the night but I knew I had to see things for myself. I had lived with others that were told about me and that was not good. If I didn't like it I would be a hypocrite to do the same. So I believed in the whole benefit of the doubt thing and making a decision for myself. He told me what he thought was wrong, and told me what to look out for.

I remember him saying that he felt sorry for me. I was in the worst company in the battalion and taking over the platoon no one wanted. Their platoon sergeant* left them to go work in the Battalion TOC. After that a staff sergeant took over till he got blown up. It was currently being run by another staff sergeant and an okay officer. I told him I didn't care. I was looking for a fresh start and, after my last experience, this would be a cakewalk. I would do the work,

---

*The head NCO in a Plt is the Psg/platoon Sgt. His rank is a Sergeant First class/SFC. His paygrade is E-7. Staff Sgts/SSg are the usual rank for the Squad leader/SL position in charge of an infantry squad. His pay grade is E-6. There are 4 Squads in an Infantry rifle Plt. A Squad is made of 2 Infantry teams. Those teams are led by the lowest level of Sgt. He is a Sgt/pay grade E-5, and that is the hardest Fucking job in the Army. To make it easy I have to use the rank system. But be known the Platoon Sgts can be called E-7s, SFCs and even mother-fucker at times. Staff Sgt's are also referred to as E-6's and Squad leaders. Sgts are used for them all. But mostly used between Sgts to Sgt's and unless specific, meant to be E-5's. Also called team leaders and hard fuckers. We are all supposed to be NCOs.

and wanted to handle my own shit. After hours of talking, we said good night. We agreed to link up in the morning to have some chow before we rolled out. Morning came early, because I froze my ass off. I got up and kept turning the AC down till it was sun-up. I was really excited about sleeping in a room that had lights and a bed. I didn't count on the fact that I was going to freeze. As the morning moved on, no one was beating on the door. No privates were there to call me to a meeting or tell me I was needed by "Your Majesty." I got up, cleaned up, and linked up with the other soldiers for chow. I met one of the guys from the new platoon I was taking over. He was injured and there for recovery time. I was actually surprised and in shock with what he said. He told me he didn't want to go back and was spending time with First Platoon. All of the company was somewhere else, except for this platoon. The platoon wanted to stay here and be away from the company, so they were the battalion go-to guys. They were used for running missions and they filled in the areas or positions when others needed to come in for refit. It didn't sound like too much fun but they liked it that way. They thought it was way better than being with Alpha Company. I didn't know what to think. Usually it takes a long time for people to get to the point that they don't want to be with their unit. For me it was over two years in the last company. Here, they were willing to do all the go-for work. They were willing to be away from the company and on their own. They didn't have the company to filter any bullshit, and chose to deal with it on their own. They were willing to be sent everywhere and do all different kinds of crap just to be away from their own company. Well okay. I for one just wanted to get to my platoon.

All I wanted was to just get there and get started. Seeing and getting all this information and knowing soldiers were not wanting to return was not going to give me any bad perception before I actually got there. I was thinking of this soldier and he had some shitty things to say. I told him things were going to change one way or the other. I told him to get well and come back; he already belonged to a platoon and we needed him.

We did whatever we had to do and it was time to pack up and get on the road. I had been on movements before and this was nothing new. What was new was that this was the first time that I had been moved from one place to another, a platoon tasked to take me there and pick up mail. I liked to think that they were tasked just for me, but picking up a care package seemed to be the more important and obvious reason. We rolled out of the small camp, took a turn and down the road we went. It wasn't pretty and basically, we were moving from point A to point B. After hearing all the stories and events of where not to go and what not to do, this was it. This was where everyone was worried about, out on the road was where danger lived. With every story told, it had seemed to convince everyone that being in any vehicle going over land was a death sentence. To me, I was in the back shooting the shit and looking for a spitter. As we went along I couldn't help but notice things were done a little differently here. The Stryker looked used and dirty. It was not like the super clean vehicles I was in before. It had everything that they needed and it was all there to be used. They did things the way it made sense for them, something that had come from experience and knowledge gained in operations. I was no longer in a company that had never seen bad guys or much less been in a fight. I sat in there with a dip and one soldier handed me a spit bottle. Then he began to share his stories. I was hearing about all the contact and events that had happened since they arrived in country. This company lost their CO in a fucking IED as well as others. As we were talking I remembered a soldier named Coumas that was transferred without his company knowing. I am now in the same company that he ended up in. It was with the platoon I was going to take over, who he was with when he died. Coumas, he was a Soldier. With that title used to come responsibility and duty. However, he was different. Straight out of basic, he went to work for the paper-pushers in Brigade. He crossed an awesome Master Sergeant Festus.

Old Festus didn't like him and gave him shit to do. He was placed on running the mail. That was way above his pay grade, but who's gonna say shit anyway? That was usually one officer, an NCO and a clerk or two. Festus had him doing the job by himself and he did what he could. Maybe Coumas was too friendly with Festus' little private who was a female? Either way Coumas was threatened with being sent to the line where he would die. Festus made it happen, and before his company command would find out he had been moved. They found out he died in Afghanistan on his mother's birthday. Yeah, like I said, the new 'virtual' training was reaping the fruits of weak labor. That was where I was headed, to the bottom of the pit, and that was fine. To me the leaders at the top of the barrel were way more rotten. Plus, at the bottom, you have no place to go but up.

After a while we get to the location and I know things are going to change me forever. Up till now it was all talk, and now it was time to put up or shut up. I had been other places and other times, but this time, I was going to be the platoon's Old Man, the crusty fucker that others looked up to. No pressure. Everyone expects me to die, again! Get hurt and/or fuck shit up and die. So I said, "Fuck it, let's get it on and get started."

I got left off, and the platoon did not hesitate to get back on the road. I think they went to the chow hall, picked up their mail, and got the fuck out.

It was a little tense with the first sergeant and the First Platoon's Platoon Sergeant. They bounced out and I stayed there and talked to the First Sergeant first.* He asked me straight out, "Are you the one here to replace me?"

He was smiling, but he was serious. He asked if I was in Bri-

---

* *The highest NCO in an Infantry Company holds the position of the "First Sgt" he is usually senior to all the other Sgts in the company and is the Company Commander's Right hand. He is usually at the E-8 pay grade and is a Master Sgt. The only difference is a Master Sgt has no company to run and a First Sgt does.*

gade, and I said yes. He asked if I was a first sergeant before, and I said yes. Then he asked me who sent me. I told him I was in one place, came back and was told to come here. He gave me a speech and during it, I started to remember some stuff. Now even at the top level there were problems in the Brigade, low and high ranking soldiers that were thought may need to be replaced. We talked and I answered his questions. I remembered, from a conversation I had a month ago, that there were some people who were not doing so good. They were going to possibly get relieved. I started to try to remember any specific that would allow me to figure out if this was one of those soldiers. Then things started to click: names, stories, places, and here I was. I didn't know what to do, because yes, this was one of those soldiers that was to get the boot. I'd landed on Turd Island, but, to be fair, I had to give him the benefit of the doubt. If he was this high, I knew that the shit had a bigger radius than a team leader or lieutenant. After he let me have it the way it was going to be, which is usually the end of the conversation, I responded and let him know who I was. After getting an earful, I figured it was my turn.

So, I began to tell him about *my* expectations. First of all, I said, I am an A-type person. I am loyal till it's time to not be. I am not here to take over the company, regardless of what you may or may not think. I am there to be the platoon sergeant and what is mine, is mine. I will do my job, and that's all I want to do. He got up and said a few words and that was it, he walked away. I talked to the CO next.

He was doing his thing and asking questions, and then it was my turn. I told him the same thing I told the first sergeant. He was quiet for a bit and then we talked about the area. I asked where Second Platoon was. He said that they were out on mission, but would be back soon. I got to learn a couple of new things and where certain things were located. While I had some free time I turned in my old weapon and signed for a new one. I made some small talk and then I asked to be shown to the tents. The one fucking time that I actually got to sleep in a room and on a bed, I froze my ass off. Now, I was going to be living in a tent again!

I made my way across the rocks that were put down for something (mostly it was to screw up your ankles and lose important parts in). I found the tents for the platoon. No one was around so I took a peep. I went in and found the lieutenant's little palace. He had a large area and everyone else was doubled up. I believe that I was supposed to be his bunk mate, but I was going to get a place of my own. Some great people decided to make a hallway down the center of the tent and put rooms on both sides. When I had walked in, there on the left was a storage place, maybe? There seemed to be stuff and equipment in there. I grabbed the bags that seemed to be left there, and put them outside. I made a little home and was met by some guys coming in. They asked me who I was, and I responded with, what platoon were they in? They said the Second and I told them that I was their new platoon sergeant. I met the staff sergeant in charge of the platoon, as well as the FO (Forward Observer) and the lieutenant. They told me that guys were going to move where I was, and I said yup, they were. Not now though. We cleaned up and I wanted to talk to the lieutenant. The staff sergeant, who was the platoon sergeant, and the FO tagged along. They were the platoon leadership and I wanted to answer any questions and hear what they had to say.

We made our way to the chow hall, which was basically a freaking big white tent in the middle of the small base, and had our dinner. We sat down and began to talk. It was basic questions and small talk. A lot was about the company's first sergeant. He was First Sergeant Dicks. There were concerns and stories from the night before that were matching with what I was being told, again. We continued to chat and I told them to let me worry about him. That was my job now and I had talked to him earlier. We talked about the platoon and I wanted to know what the problems were. Lieutenant Osborne, Staff Sergeant Brinkley, and Staff Sergeant Woods said nothing. The platoon was good except First Sergeant Dicks. Finally the lieutenant asked about me. Who was I? I had thought about this for a while now. I decided to be straight with him and let him know I was a dick. I figured if you are going to make an impression, now is the time.

"I don't like officers, and I really don't like West Point officers," I said straight off.

It sounds hard, but that was it. I wasn't being a dick, as much as there was a reason. The old unit had two, and that left a bad taste in my mouth with ole CO Ginger and lieutenant Needles. The ring-knockers were greedy bastards and they were in it for themselves. They were dirty and acted like they were better than the fighting men.

Brinkley and Woods started to laugh and the lieutenant sat there. "Well, I am both," he said.

I had to laugh.

"Well you aren't off to a good start," I said.

The ice was broken, the first funny moment, and others would follow. No matter what my plans were, or the logical reason for me to treat these men tough, they had nothing to do with all I had seen and experienced at the hands of others. The lieutenant let me know that he was screwed right off the bat. I had to say something. I had set him up, he flopped, and I had to lighten it up with a joke. I couldn't be the ass I felt I deserved to be. So, we laughed. We sat there and bullshitted. I told them I was from Texas and what is mine is mine. I didn't like to fuck around and do stupid shit. I had a company that did it so much, my stupid meter was broke. They sat there and said it was about time. The staff sergeant and the one before him were getting raped. They were getting bullied by the other platoons and even First Sergeant Dicks. Third Platoon were First Sergeant Dicks' babies and the CO had a pulse and was breathing. Second Platoon had been trying to make things better, but it was not working. I told them I talked to First Sergeant Dicks and told him the same. From now on, that was my problem, and if anyone talked shit, or wanted anything, it came through me.

They were glad. They'd been waiting a long time for anyone to show up. They were shit out of luck, because they'd been sent me. They were getting so much shit, they told me that they were called the Black Sheep. The lieutenant was known as Shepherd Six, and I would be Shepherd Seven. How fucking funny is that? We stayed late into the evening there, for many nights to come. Later in the days to come we would talk and make plans for the platoon. Despite my doubts and past experiences, this lieutenant was looking good and off to a good start. He would talk to me and later admitted that he never wanted to make a career out of the army. All he really wanted to do was to be the lieutenant of an infantry platoon. He didn't care about making rank. All he wanted was to be in charge of men. I responded and told him I was never going to make this a career neither. I just wanted to be a buck sergeant, a team leader. It is the hardest job in the army. Everything after that, it was all extra credit.

It actually looked like we were going to get along well. He asked me stuff, and that shocked the shit out of me. I was grateful for being asked my opinion or ideas. So I went with the flow. I am not a tyrant, just wanted to have that dynamic relationship. That meant working together and getting it done. The staff sergeant and FO were right across from me in the tent, and those boys were crazy. After the first night, I was going to have to meet the men of the platoon and get to know them. It was the beginning of who knew what? I thought that if the lieutenant and me could stay together, we would be okay. Right now, my first thing was to see how bad things were in the platoon. I would get them what they needed to do their job, and fight for them, too. I understood the position that they were in—I'd been there myself. Most of the crap was unnecessary and at the whim of First Sergeant Dicks. It sounded to me that he demanded tribute for respect. I didn't know when or who it was going to be, but I knew before too long, someone was going to check/test me.

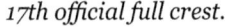
17th official full crest.

Above: Lt. Osborne aka "Shepherd 6." A good man and one hell of a Soldier.

Left: This wall stood in front of the entrance to the Bn. Opposite was another wall with the names of those who paid the ultimate price (see page 320).

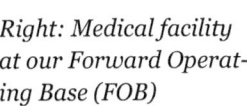
Right: Medical facility at our Forward Operating Base (FOB)

I had seen people come and go in my time. I knew the things that some had done that I wanted to do in my time. I also seen what others did that I was not going to do. Right off the bat, if I was going to do my job, I was going to need for the leaders to open up to me and trust in me. This wasn't any field exercise or training event. It was war. I needed to make sure communications were not what I had in the past. Some would say that my position and rank required people to do what I told them to do. Well, it also meant for others to do the job as well. I tried to learn what I could and build trust. It was only a matter of time before something happened. I had to be ready by then. I was not going to go anywhere, and I was going to be in the fight. I was going to show them, and expect them to do the same thing. You can't do that without trust and communication.

NATIVIDAD RUIZ

Any Means Necessary

So here I was in a new area. Things seemed to be a little different and that was not really a bad thing. Sure, there was some stuff to be getting used to. This included the manner in which operations were conducted. For the most part, you usually get there and basically observe. I had experienced it differently and knew what I didn't want to do. Unlike another leader I had, I knew what to do and how I was supposed to ease into the position. Thankfully I had other leaders who not only showed the right way, but explained it as well. Having a good mentor and peers helped you grow and become full of good knowledge and experience.

I had my own plywood section of a tent. It was not great, but it was mine. I got my hands on some spray paint and put a huge Longhorn symbol on my door. I noticed the men seemed to be beaten and tired. They were not the cream, but they were what I had to work with. For a long time, most kept to their squads and didn't come by. They didn't want to see me or hear from me. When they did, they were courteous and would acknowledge me. Like most, I am pretty sure that they were wondering who I was, or what kind of person I would be. Without time to sit down or get to know things, we were off on a mission. How about that for OJT (On The Job Training) motherfucker? OJT was a cruel joke for me. I was a buck sergeant when I arrived in Italy. I was doing the in-processing, and that took like two weeks. One of the other soldiers that arrived with me wanted to be high-speed and on his off time went to the company. Fuck that! There will be years of me being there on the line and time to get fucked with. He was an over-achiever, and I just wanted to take all the time to adjust. For the most of my career, I did as he did. My plans were ruined when he ratted me out. Next thing I knew I was front and center with my platoon sergeant, SFC Grant.

I happened to be a reclass, to 11B. He had his doubts about me and off I was, to prove myself again. I said the wrong thing to the wrong person and my life changed forever. All I said was that this is OJT. He had a real serious face when he looked at me.

"What's OJT?" he said.

"On the Job Training," I said. Boom! Fucking nuclear.

"Do some mother-fucking pushups, fucker!"

I got dropped and didn't recover for over a month. You do a lot of thinking in the front leaning rest/push up position, and you become strong.

I linked up and met the crew that I would be working with. That includes vehicle crews and those on my vehicle. I had around six dismounts and that is usually a squad minus. I didn't know what to expect at first, but I just went with the flow. These guys were off and doing a mission like most would get into a car and go off to the local store. Their process was simple and worked like clockwork. On day one we were off and doing a presence patrol to the south of our camp. On this particular day we were off and out in the middle of the open. I guess there was something in the desert, or it just looked out of place. We got the call to stop and we dropped off dismounts to go and look at the thing. I was in the back and listening to the traffic on the radio and heard something that seemed weird. A call came over and it was simple: try to detonate it with a burst of the weapons system. I sat there and realized that despite the difference of companies, things here were a little less restrictive. I didn't know what to think at first. I didn't get a chance to when there was another call. A vehicle was off in the distance and they were driving out in the middle of nowhere. Two vehicles, one of them being mine, were off to get in contact with it and do some random questions. Off we went making a bee-line to cut the vehicle off.

At first we were going slow, we were trying to stay off small piles or what seemed like ant hills out there, a random hole here and another one there, things that you would not think of twice in the States, riding in a field or the woods. These were things that seemed normal, but out here were off. Imagine walking in the forest and seeing a fully laden Christmas tree out in the open? That would be an attention getter even if it was freaking December. Here we were off and swerving here and doing this and that.

Finally, I just told the driver to hit it and we went from a single file line to a full out race to get to this car. The way we were moving, and at that speed, we would not have caught it. So we kicked it into high gear and I asked the driver if he knew what to look for, what to avoid. I got a "Roger" and I said, "Okay, let's go." That was all I needed. If it was our time, it wouldn't have mattered if we were out in the desert or at home, it was our time. Slipping and falling getting out of the shower at home or chasing a car in the desert, either way, fear or caution was keeping us from getting it done.

I'm sure my driver was getting shitty gas mileage, but we soon caught up to the car and were able to cut it off. We dismounted some of the men and with the help of a terp (interpreter), they asked what they needed to ask. After a quick search they were sent off on their way, no harm, no foul. We remained in communication with the other vehicles and sent up the info we had collected. We then simply turned around and began to head back to the others. It seemed that everyone was in good spirits. We had a little adrenaline rush thinking about the chase and what dangers were out there. To most, it seemed a lonely and desolate place. To the men that were with me, they were aware of the opposite. Some had ran into IEDs out there. It seemed that there were enemy out there making holes in the desert and putting pressure plate IEDs out to get the vehicles and crews. The initiation devices were simply pots or metal bowls that you would use to whip up frosting or beat up eggs for an omelet. They were using them because our vehicles were way heavier than the locals' cars.

They would not crush the bowl to make a connection, which in turn would blow up the charge. The enemy had adapted, and even though their method was crude, it was selective to their target. The others told me this as we made our way back, how the enemy did things. We just took it slow, following the same tracks we made out to our current location. Once we got back and had the platoon whole, it was time to "Charlie Mike" or continue mission. And what was our mission? Mostly to be seen and to monitor the traffic in the area. Sometimes we were on the look for specific things, and would intercept possible targets just to stop them and get any info. If you look it up somewhere, it was described as prohibiting the enemy's freedom of movement. It wasn't the kind of glamorous shit you see on the TV, but that was our deal. There were times we would sit out there for hours. I took what time I had and I got to talk to the men in the vehicle.

I talked to the gunner and the weapons guys in the back. I was told how they were the "Black Sheep" and life was just shitty. I learned about the history of the platoon. They talked about how they had been without a senior NCO for some time. They thought I was crazy when they heard I volunteered for the job. I had thought about it before as well, right before I left. Put in the same position, they didn't see themselves volunteering for what I had now.

Adding to the misery from their point of view was working for someone else. The company was attached to another battalion. Belonging to someone else, they felt that they were getting whatever came down the line. It seemed normal for shit to roll downhill. In this company, I was told that we were at the bottom.

Surely this was just a theory, and I sat there to listen. I was told that missions would be given or directed to the battalion. Then, they had their choice on what to keep or pass down. What was not taken or given to their own, sifted down through the company. Then plop, to the bottom of the shit pile.

I listened to it all and focused on learning from them as well as their personalities. I tried to get to know the men and did not try to make them like me. After all, I had seen several leaders that used what they had to intimidate and make people do as they wanted. As a leader, getting someone to do something is your job, but it's different when it isn't business and it's personal. At first it could work for a while, but not without negative results. However, to get someone to do something that could possibly get him killed, well that's leadership.

I ended up telling and sharing my past with the men. I tried to answer any question that was asked of me. I did not want to have these guys be afraid of me or think I was there to just be a shit-bag leader. It seemed that everybody, especially those that get shit on, have their own little things that they hold and do. They have a way of measuring and calculating your worth. Others had come and then left, so I knew it wasn't about what was said. All that mattered was if you were going to be there and share in the experiences, or leave. Not many people get to have a second or third chance in life to change, maybe a chance to make up for your past sins, or become the person that you wanted to be. To me, this was that chance. Especially after I felt like I was chewed up and spat out.

While coming up in the army, everything is, "Do this and prove you are this good." I never thought of doing something just to do it. If it would change my life and the way I was living in the army, okay. I would do it because I believed in it. I didn't fall for going to some school only to come back to where you were before. For what? It didn't change a thing and these others were freezing their ass right there with me. I had also been around long enough to know there was no instant credibility in the infantry. With unit after unit and leader after leader, you had to prove yourself all over again. It isn't the preferred technique but it is a technique. Having to always prove you are good enough for this or you could do that, was how it was for me. I had made my decision and was where I felt there was actually something special to do. It wasn't to be found in a crest or motto, but in the men who did all the stupid shit no one ever hears about. I was right there, and I was all in. All I heard was that this was the most dangerous place to be. With no one really in the running to get here, I guess I was the dumb fucker that actually won something. The weak side of my brain thought that this just might be the dumbest shit I'd ever done. It might just get me killed. All of this to prove a point, that all those before me were right. I had only been there a very short time and even I felt that the platoon was alone. Other people would come by and fuck with the men and tell them how they were pieces of shit, smoke them (make them do push-ups, or some dumb routine), and harass them for just being whatever kind of soldier that they thought they were. At this point in the war, they were confused, and to tell you the truth, I didn't blame them. Shit usually ran down hill, but were these guys in a fucking valley or what? These guys were getting it from every direction. Their battalion sent them to be with another battalion. They would get the crap and bullshit that others didn't want. The company command was second place. First Sergeant Dicks had a target on some of the guys. He was either in the process of kicking them out or giving them an Article 15.* He would also take turds from any other platoons and put them all in a single pile. Despite all that, these guys had something that I had not seen in a long time. Believe it or not, they were still motivated. Call it personal pride or fake motivation, but if they were going to get it done, it was going to be right. They did what was asked of them and rolled with the punches. The platoon was a freaking mix of just about everyone you could think of. We had country boys from the south, rich and poor. We had educated kids from the city. We had white, black and brown. Guys from California, Idaho, New York, Georgia, Arkansas, and everywhere in between. Tall guys, skinny guys, buff guys and chunky ones too, brainiacs, nerds, history buffs and heathens. We were all crammed in tents that were separated by plyboard and handmade walls. Everyone had a freaking hole that they would go into and hibernate. When there was a mission it was game on and these boys worked. They did their job and came back to their home. There was not much room in their little areas, especially when you have tons of equipment everywhere. Add your clothes and boxes of stuff and basically all you really have is a cot, a TV and Xbox.

It was home, not like any home anyone else ever knew, but it worked. Everything that you do normally in your home, here, was always a walk to another tent or building. The chow hall was where we would all go and eat, usually in buddy teams. There were trailers set up where we would go and shower up. Some camps had a chapel set up or service was in the chow hall. In another place, there was a gym or rec tent. Every tent was different and it just seemed that after whatever they did, it was off to do your own thing. Now that isn't bad, but we like to keep everyone together and stay in their teams. After being there a bit, I wanted to meet and talk to the leaders of each squad. In First, I had Fairchild. He was a veteran out of the 82nd. In Second, I had Briola who was from the island of Guam. Third was Brinkley, who was trying to hold the fort down and was the acting platoon sergeant. In charge of the crews was Sergeant Roesch. The FO was Sergeant Woods, who was a pain in my ass and a little guy, but he was cool as shit and he made me laugh. We were it, and I know that you should never judge a book by its cover, but it didn't look promising. Most of the time you like to see soldiers that are tall and statuesque.

The Uniform Code of Military Justice forms the rules of being in the military. Article 15 is the specific one used to bust your ass, take your rank, and money.

They all have broad shoulders and small waists, look clean cut—basically your picture book definition of a soldier. The only one who fit was the lieutenant. He was over six feet tall and a runner. I was five-ten and taller than Briola. He was older and they claimed to have pictures of him in Vietnam. Brinkley was shorter and I think Roesch was too. But what these guys did have was surprise. They knew their shit and trained their men like leaders were supposed to. By staying busy with all the bullshit missions it kept them on their mother-fucking toes. Staying active and knowing what was actually going on built experience, and that was how they made their money. I sat there and talked to them. I told them about me and that I was not like everyone else. We were going to fight and my job was to make sure they got what they needed, and to protect them from anyone else. The lieutenant was a good guy and we were a team. I talked to him and we were going to fix things. I was always there for anything and so was he. The platoon was mine and what was mine, I protected. In turn each man talked about themselves and I listened. I knew I was behind the power curve and that meant learning by actually hearing what they had to say. For the most part, it was plain and generic. Like most fucking things new, talk is cheap and they did what I would have done. They welcomed me to the platoon, and kept their mouths shut. I was going to have to prove my worth again. At this point they did share that they did arrive with one platoon sergeant and he left to go to the battalion. Another staff sergeant took over and he tried to keep them from getting shit on, but he was quickly reminded that he was an acting platoon sergeant and got shot down. He did stay in the platoon till he was injured in a blast that sent him home, leaving Brinkley to step into the position. I sat there and remembered how hard it was to get a platoon sergeant position when I first went to division. Everyone had the job and at times there were even staff sergeants getting the spot. Coming from the main post I couldn't help but think about all the senior sergeants that were there in that tent back on the main post.

They had questioned me about where I was going to. I told them to get another platoon, and they fought back. I noticed openings when I was out and about doing battle field circulation and going to places. It was easy to see that there were some positions open. The fact was that some just didn't want the job that bad after all. I couldn't help but think that there were probably some people that were out there that were happy because I was in my current fucking predicament.

The men continued about all the things that got them to where they were at the time. One of the old commanders was in the battalion and looking out for them. They used to be one of the best platoons in the battalion if not the brigade. They had worked and won favor in others, but they were no longer in the company.

Everything seemed to change when the command did. It was as if the new leaders were jealous and wanted to build their own precious team. You have a strong unit and it makes sense to build upon success. There are times when everything changes. Systems are changed and everything is started anew. That includes the way business is done. Just like soldiers have to prove their worth, squads and platoons have to prove theirs too. A whole squad, platoon, or company can be shat upon or pampered because of the relationship of two people: the commanding officer and the lieutenant, or the first sergeant and the platoon sergeant. Despite anything that had ever been done or how successful a unit or team is, can all be erased if one person rubs another the wrong way. It is that simple. It is really bad to say, but ass-kissers can become superstars overnight if there's someone who wants to be given respect and support, to be held on a pedestal as if they were Patton reincarnated. In return, the small unit becomes the new favorite and gets the best. That includes getting taken care of. Then the gulf between the platoons grows into resentment and hate. As they talked I listened, and I remembered doing the training to get the company certified. My buddy Bobby Sampson and I did work training our own company, and we did pretty good. The Brigade

Command stood there and told us we were one of the top platoons, along with one in the 1-17 and 4-23. Where I was standing at the moment, I figured and hoped that this was that platoon, the one they had mentioned being from 1-17. Two and two added up. The places and time were apart but the stories were the same. What I had heard and what they were telling me months later was all the same. I was sitting there listening to the men that made that platoon back then. Months later in Afghanistan, I found out this is where they were. Now I'd come to be with them. Their history and mine seemed the same story. We were together in some shithole in Afghanistan. I imagined someone out there looking for some artifact or following the leads to some lost and forgotten place, someone looking for something, working and tracking to find the past. Just like that, I found the lost city of gold. Of course, it was beat up and covered with shit. Let's just say it was chocolate covered, but to me, it was pay dirt. I didn't mind it being beaten up and felt I could work with that. They used to be good, but time and individual relations seemed to have broken them down. Because of the good reputation and job, people thought highly of these men. Unfortunately, their company didn't see them that way. The new leader picked another platoon to love. Even with such good performance in the past, Second Platoon were chosen to do the dirty work.

Since they were good before, it made it easy to be put on the difficult missions. Portray the shitty mission as a dangerous one and boom, you have the reason to send in your best. Plus, having the battalion command fond of the soldiers was one of the causes to dump on them, even if it was from their own company. They had earned their respect, and that was not given to First Sergeant Dick. Hence the question when I got there, if I was going to replace him. It all started to add up.

I had heard of a couple of first sergeants possibly getting relieved. All of it seemed like some freaking political game that had nothing to do with winning any damn war. I kept the thoughts of that live fire in my head. Sampson and I stood there and First Sergeant T-Anus took all the credit. We stood there in the AAR (After Action Review) hearing and they glorified the magnificent job done. We were one of the best, but what we did better than anyone else, is we were the fastest. Fast, violent, accurate, and done. Me and my old friend Bobby Sampson stood there and listened how that was the typical training that T-Anus was known for. We stood there as he took all the credit and thanked them. He was nervous and didn't say a peep. It had happened to me in front of the company and brigade, so it wasn't too hard to believe for me.

I was listening to all the shit that they have gone through, and it made my blood boil. I had gone through it believing that there was some kind of good to come out of it, and it never came. I lost it and I left to get out and do my job. Well, careful for what you wish for, because you might get it and more. Here in front of me were normal men who were not far from the point that I had reached. They were becoming the products of a piss-poor command and I did not want what happened to me to be their fate as well. Out of all the danger and the losses in their time there, these men were still holding on for that hope.

It wasn't much, but it was hope that someone would give a shit about them and treat them with a little dignity is all. It's hard enough to go out and get the shitty missions, to be able to see the guy shooting at you, that wants to take your life. Then, to come back and be set on fucking duty (fancy way to say chores), for the next three days, or shit on by your own team. That was bullshit, and it was not going to happen so easily if I was able to stop it. I am no hero, and I don't think I am better than anyone else, but the least that these guys deserved was to have some peace and some respect. I let them know that all that was over. I had my job and if I got my ass chewed, well it was okay. After all, that shit grew back at night. I didn't give a shit what they did after we did our jobs. That being said, when it was time to work, it was work. They could all bullshit when we got back, but then again we were all infantry men. There is always something that comes up or things to get done. Also, stay away from the POGs. I told them that whatever happens to tell me the truth. I just wanted them to be straight up and forward with me. Do that and tell me the truth, and I would fight for their ass. The way I saw it was that we were all in the same boat. I was going to fight as well, and if anyone was to try to hurt any of us, we would wipe them off the fucking face of the earth. We would open the biggest can of whoop-ass known. We were not running from a fight, and we were not going to stop. We were going to take to the fight, and do the job that we were supposed to do–close in and destroy the enemy by any means necessary.

Handing out free stuff.

I had been introduced to the platoon and settled in. I was taking in as much as I could, trying to absorb the events and tactics that they had seen. I was trying to get to meet and know soldiers. I was fucking up names and not doing too good of a job. I was also trying to get a handle on everything that the platoon had been through. Life couldn't have always been as bad as it was now. It started and came from somewhere. The men were efficient and productive. They completed the things they were told and were effective. I couldn't figure what was the deal. Problems used to come from a lot of places, and now, it was from the top. No one was fucking up too bad. There wasn't a reason to be treated like they were. It could have been simple. One person just hated them, or maybe the first sergeant just sucked at his job? He had forgotten what it was like coming up. He didn't know why he got smoked and chewed out. Now, he was trying to be like his leaders were. It never clicked for him, and he thought this was how to be awesome.

The Flock

The stories that I had heard all sounded very similar. The actions and excuses the seniors gave me. The greeting and way that I was talked to by First Sergeant Dicks and the CO. How the first platoon sergeant talked to me the night before he drove me out there. Add to that the demeanor of the men. There was definitely something there and within hours, days, or weeks, I was going to be living it too. On the first day, I was busy. I finally got to the rack and got a little quiet time for myself. I had taken in so much information I was now trying to settle down and unwind. Like normal, I lay there in a plywood box looking at the top of the tent. It was time to try and forget all the stuff of the day and those I had met, try to forget about all the bullshit that I had dealt with, and what was coming. I had to isolate myself to try and find some rest. I laid there and realized again, I was alone. It sounded like I was going to have my hands full. I didn't feel like there was going to be a good end to this. I hoped that all I had done and everything that I was going to go through was the right thing. I hoped it would also keep me in the good graces of God. Then again, all these locals are praying to God that we leave, die, or deliver us into their hands so they could fucking chop our heads off. With all the events that surround you, and everything on your mind, it's just you. You are alone and when no one is there, well, I just hoped that I had the strength to do the right thing. I wanted to be a good man, not a hypocrite. I wanted to give a damn about the soldiers and not fuck shit up too bad. I guess, all that shit about *This is your last day and we're all going to die* stuck in my head. Did I think that I would one day come home? No, and I didn't want to get my hopes up either. I had enough shit on my hands. I could do without thinking about home right now. I didn't want home to be a distraction. No shit, I thought I was going to get fucked up. Good enough to send me home, or it was going to be the one time I was going to get it and die. To tell the truth, I wanted it, too. I didn't want to come back and walk around and be lost, dead to the world and only reliving the good times in war. I did however, want to go out fighting and dying like a man. That way, well that was honorable to me. It was a fitting end to a soldier, the way a fighting man should go out. All I had at that time was an old saying, "Live by the sword, die by the sword," and that was just fine. As long as I had a chance to fight for my life. I was not planning on giving up, so they better bring it, 'cause this shit was not for free.

On other nights, I laid there thinking about all that I learned and how it was almost identical to the life that I had hated. Was I now the newest member and going to fall to the same fate? How was I going to keep these guys from giving up or giving in? I lay there in my plyboard cubical. I tossed and turned and had so much going through my mind. People, places, and memories from the past, mixed with the information just given to me. I lay there on my back with my hands behind my head wondering if this was it? Is this the new military life?

As I began to get to work in the new company, I had rolled right into doing daily patrols. We had a sector and it went from the hardball road that ran east to west as the northern edge, and went due south to a water obstacle. It was said that the enemy used the low ground as their way to move freely in and out of the area. It was their stronghold, and that was a hornet's nest. This was the same thing told to us days after the entire brigade got there. To the northwest of Kandahar was the Taliban stronghold. They had been there as long as anyone knew. We were told that it was the badlands, but we went in and it went down anyway. There were soldiers lost and even more once patrols started to go out. I guess we just gave them bigger targets and better things to shoot at and blow up.

Most people would like to think that having an armored vehicle was a good thing. That all you had to do was stay in the vehicles. No, it is not. Yes, there are things that will blow you up, but on foot is where you make your money. On the ground is where you find all the tell-tale signs that things that are out of place. Through time and experience on the ground you notice the people, how they react and where they go. You notice debris and stuff that you would see as normal trash on the ground, but it was different. It's like in Vegas. There are all these guys handing out cards for call girls and people just drop them on the sidewalk and keep going. It looks like shit, but everything in the environment tells you it is the normal thing. You see where it comes from, what is done with it, and where it ends up. In Vegas, that there is normal. Here cans, bottles, wrappers, animals, or maybe washed up stuff was normal.

It took you and your ass at pucker level ten to go out there and get the feel of the area. Now if you saw a hooker card there in Afghanistan, kiss your shit goodbye. It is going to take you out for sure. After months of doing this over and over, at the first sign of trouble, we would dismount and begin to operate. For me, I simply observed the platoon and tried to see as much of the picture as possible. I was in the learning phase and the teachers were my soldiers.

Despite all the history and bad events, the new platoon worked like clockwork. The methods used were ingrained in each and every guy there. They had adapted from experience and to make sure, there was a good NCO there to apply a little purpose and motivation. Prior to me arriving these men were in several fights, close fights, like within hand-grenade range. They were in the small villages, fighting when others were doing other "important" things. They were patrolling the orchards and roads that were booby-trapped, while others were at Taco Night on the big FOB.

Time and time again they adapted and learned new ways to defeat the bombs that were hidden and waiting. In the orchards they crossed where everyone else did, until a present on the other side of the wall hurt someone. After some bad success they just ended up breaking a section of the wall down. The enemy were putting bombs at all the known and used crossings. There were even starting to place them at all the lower places and any avenues of approach. So they adapted and kept the fight going. I was still getting to know all the men and doing a poor job of it. Most of the times I would butcher their names and come up with a nickname. One of the next people I met was a young sergeant. His name was Colunga. To me he looked straight up Mexican, but I was wrong. He was actually adopted by an Irish family and he was Irish.

Colunga was an athlete and played football. He didn't like the fact he had to learn stuff there in college, and one day, decided to enlist in the army. No big contract, just to be a soldier, and he was going to basic to be an infantryman.

One day as I was coming back from the chow hall I saw Colunga. I had not really talked to him or gotten to know him yet. It was a little early and I remembered that he came up to me. Like I said, I didn't know too much about him at the time, but I did know someone wanting help. He seemed to be on First Sergeant Dicks' shit list and I didn't know why. I was told that both he and I were called up to the company and there was going to be some formal business. As his platoon sergeant, I didn't have a clue what was going on and told him to tell me the story from the start.

We talked a little and I got some of the intel and I told him that whatever it was, it didn't seem to be worth much more than an ass-chewing. I told him that we have tact and candor. If it is the truth, say it and be respectful. I also let him know that at times, you will get called in, and end up taking whatever they want you to get. Just because you don't like to be in trouble, does not mean that you are not going to get shit on. I told him to fight for his shit. I would go in as well and get caught up on what was going on. For no reason would I allow for someone to screw someone over. If it was right, so be it. If it was wrong, I would stand up for him. All I wanted was the truth, and his word. As I entered the company area things seemed off. For one, it was called the company area, but no one was allowed in there. They had the big screen TV and some weird cable, but it was all for show. The minute someone was caught in there, crap started. First Sergeant Dicks didn't want anyone there. I sat and talked again to the first sergeant. He said Colunga was doing this and that and the other. He was injured in an event, or might I say "blown up" twice in one day and sent up to Germany. While there he was treated and somehow ended showing up back in Afghanistan. I am listening to this being told to me and I am thinking to myself, "Fuck yeah!"

First Sergeant Dicks was getting heat; something had come down about the way people were getting treated. Go fucking figure. It was something that I had heard before which let me know again, I knew the person I was talking to. In order to get payback or just to fuck the guy over, he wanted him to get reprimanded. He assumed that Colunga had talked to some people up there. This was the cause of bad times and the reason heat was coming down from the top. The first sergeant was getting his balls squeezed, and he didn't like it. I'm sitting here listening to a guy who has been doing some fucked up shit. Now he is feeling the burn. I think I just had a conversation with one of my soldiers who was going through the same thing. I told him he might get screwed if it was true, and if it wasn't, to stand up for himself. Now, this guy Dicks is basically trying to fuck someone because he himself had been doing fucked up shit.

At that time, there were a lot of rumors about the company. It was heard up at Brigade that the command was doing something wrong. After what I had heard just being there, it was obvious that First Sergeant Dicks was not taking care of soldiers. I was told that big wigs were asking questions and the company was on the radar. People were out there telling the truth about others not going out, letting the little guys do all the heavy lifting. Generally speaking, no one was taking care of the men, and it all came back to First Sergeant Dicks. I don't know if there were any investigations, but now I was reminded why there was a position for me in no-man's land.

First of all, it was rumors or first sergeant's word. There was nothing saying that Colunga or anyone did anything. Second, First Sergeant Dicks had the paperwork all written up and there was no one else. I had been around the block a couple of times. So, being that there was no officer, especially the company commander, it was evidently First Sergeant Dicks trying to shove an Article 15 up Colunga's ass. He couldn't do what he wanted to because he didn't have the authority and I was not going to let him. Yeah, it was a dirty thing, and I was getting checked like I thought I would. If it was because this soldier came back to be with his comrades, I would not allow him to get fucked. So we sat there with a document that accused him of hearsay. I listened to what first sergeant had to say, and I guess he thought I was going to let him do what he wanted. Colunga of course was fucking nervous, and therefore hit me up beforehand. I had seen some dirty shit before, and thought Colunga probably had too. I also think that he thought this was what was done. Well, it was not going to end good for me either way. I was damned if I sided with First Sergeant Dicks, and fucked if I supported Colunga. Well, that's why we get paid the big bucks. When Colunga reported in, he was shaking and shit. Dicks kicked him out and made him do it again. Once he came in and sat down, Dicks read the statements against Colunga. I looked at Colunga.

"No, first sergeant," he said, "I did not do this. This is wrong. I came back to be with my men and be a part of the team. How can I get in trouble for coming back and wanting to do my job, in this company?"

Despite all the fucked up horseshit and stories, this man wanted to come back to finish the job. To me, not knowing him that well, I saw a hero. I was also lucky that he was in my platoon and I agreed with him. Colunga and I talked and Dicks was pissed. He ripped up the paperwork and told him to get the fuck out. I sat there and me and Dicks chatted for a bit. I could see he was angry because I didn't back him up. Then again, not only was he not being fair, he was wrong. He wanted to get Colunga to admit to something, anything just to get him to sign a paper. We are at war, and even though this is just my opinion, this is not what we should be doing. He mentioned something about me being there to replace him, and I said that I was a platoon sergeant. *No mas, no meños.* I walked outside and down the row and found Colunga waiting. We talked and he told me the full story. He got fucked up by an IED in a wall. He got out of the blast but got a concussion. He was walking by and saw it, went to get away and boom. He got up, got back into the fight, and off to get some bad guys they were chasing. They came up to a mud hut this time, and they went to kick the door. That was where he got number two. Boom! Afterwards he was left at the battalion FOB and was beginning to have some issues. He was lost, sweating and delirious. They put him on quarters and he was alone and tripping out. What sucks, is that people knew and usually checked up on the injured, maybe the Battalion Commander or the SgM, maybe some buddies, but no, he was found wandering off somewhere. He got shipped out to Germany and wanted to be back with his buddies/soldiers/brothers. After some time there, he was asked about the unit. He was questioned about the specific unit and what was going on, but his concern was for his men. After making some calls, he was sent back to be with the men of the Black Sheep.

We ended up getting to know each other very well. His soldier was almost as interesting as well. He had a guy named Swain. Swain and him were tied at the hip. Yes that was his soldier, but they knew how to fight and did it well together. Swain was a Texas boy and grew up in Houston. He smoked Newports and had a raspy voice. He was a funny guy and had a certain way of telling stories that he did with his whole body. He talked shit better than some, and was a cocky son of a gun. He did two tours back to back in the National Guard and came back to do Afghanistan. He had to go Regular Army, and that is what he did. He was a fighter and there was no question that he liked a challenge. He liked to train his guys and had a wealth of knowledge. He was older, and had been in enough fights that he used caution in things that you would not think of. He had just been around and seen a lot. The actual first time that I got to chat with Swain was at a range. We walked over and he was talking about this and that. I was like okay, I'll get my shit zeroed and then we can put up or fucking shut up. It's about bragging rights and we were both committed to win. So we started shooting and getting the paper hits. We then went off the paper. Then of course, just about anything. We were both from Texas, alpha males, shit-talkers, and competitive. We shot till the range closed. I would like to say that it was close, but it was not. I smoked his ass. My story, my ending.

As we are off and doing things, I begin to fill in all the blanks from stuff in the unit's timeline. I was hearing about others that were great at helping us out. Soldiers did do great things out there and some didn't. When the CO got hit, we had young troops move out without any caution and pull a guy out of the burning vehicle. Some turd-like E-6s/Staff Sgt's were there frozen and crying. He was broke down like a shotgun as the troops did what they had to do. It was a time to act and shit like this was what was happening. Colunga didn't get any of his Purple Hearts. Paperwork was fucking missing and probably flushed. So, I got the guys around and asked for names of those that busted their ass in the platoon or not. I wanted to know of anyone outside that did good by us. I was given a list of names and I had a plan. Shortly after that, we were supposed to go out and get some shit or whatever from the large camp in Kandahar. As people were going to go look at the women, use the phones, and eat a hamburger, I walked to the S1 section of Brigade. This is where paperwork like Colunga's Purple Heart might be tracked down. I knew some of the guys from my days in the other company and was going to go and see what I could do. I was going over the company and battalion, but if it is broke, then adapt. We went in and were able to get his Purple Hearts moving and tracking. He was concerned about them and we got the ball rolling. Colunga was thankful, and I was like, come with me. I walked over to see the deputy commander and I asked him for some coins to give out to the men. He reached into his pocket and pulled some out. We said thanks and then I went to another battalion and did the same. While I was out there, another incident happened that others were talking about. Rumors of different methods that were getting done out in the front lines, adapting to situations that they had heard about. Colunga had all the answers, filled in the blanks and answered questions. We talked and then asked for some spare coins. We picked up more and Colunga got to tell about his three Purple Hearts and the SgMs were eating it up. Here was this little guy whose knuckles dragged on the ground. He didn't look like much, but he had three Purple Hearts. He was in the worst area of the fighting and was on the actual missions, the legends people heard about on base. It made them wonder and think about never ever leaving the wire. Knowing all that was going on out there made people here look at you differently.

    I dragged Colunga with me as I made the rounds and found out that he was as good if not better than me at getting stuff. He had a black book and would put in the people that he helped out in it. Most of the stuff people threw away or didn't care about, he would save. When there was someone in need, he was the one that people would go to instead of a fucked up system of supply. We finished making the rounds and headed back on a four hour ride through the deadliest and shittiest places on the face of the earth, just in time to make it back to get chow. I went ahead and put out that I wanted a formation. I wanted everyone on the list, of those who helped out the platoon, there for me to address the platoon. I had never done it and wanted to get it all out of the way. Shortly after dinner I had the squad leaders tell me they were all there. I let the lieutenant know and he wanted to introduce me to the men. I had only talked to the soldiers on a one-on-one basis, and this was my first time to address the platoon as a whole. He said some things and turned it over to me.

I told them that we were going to fight, that we were a good platoon, and that we were going to get better. I told them that I did not want to wish I would have done this or that when I was old and in a rocking chair. Then I asked for the men on the list I had put together, to come up to the front of the platoon where I was. As they were coming up, I noticed that the head shed had a group out there comprised of the first sergeant, his favorite platoon sergeant, and some others. They were watching what was going on and getting a kick out of it. I made it a point to talk about the men behind me.

They were the reason that we were successful. They are the reason that we fight hard, and the glue and substance that keeps us going. I had heard about the things that they had done. I had never heard of these soldiers as ever being recognized for all that they had done. I wanted to change that.

So on a little porch outside of a tent in hell hole Afghanistan, I opened a bag with all the coins that I had collected, and gave them out to each man. I let them know that the platoon recommended them for their great work and efforts. As for myself, I wanted to say thank you for doing your job the best you could. On behalf of the "Black Sheep," thank you! I then asked for the plt to give them a round of applause and for any comments from the men who received their coin. One stood out from the rest. He said that this was the first time that anyone had ever acknowledged anything that he had done. He never wanted to be special, just to be told thank you. He was emotionally shaken and a young kid. He had experienced numerous traumatic things in the line of combat, including losing vehicles, and this had now been recognized. He then raised his head and said that if there was ever a time that we needed to have personnel to go out with us, all we had to do was ask. He would go anywhere with us. We all shook their hands and we finished up. I saw the amazement and disbelief from the peanut gallery and walked away to the tent. Everyone's spirits were high and everyone was just rejuvenated. The lieutenant and I talked and I don't know if he was amazed, happy, or grateful that I was there, but it was something that they had been waiting for. To me, it felt good to show appreciation for his efforts to someone that did well. After all, isn't that what awards were for? The truth is, somewhere inside it finally started to feel like we were on the right road. I did not want to be a dictator. All I wanted was to get to a place that I belonged, and that was here. I hoped to help out and not be ridden like a fucking mule. It seemed that so many others were too busy doing for themselves (then on top of that, stuff for extra credit, just to be on the good side, or in someone's good graces). Fuck that! I learned since hitting this division that being nice was hard work. I am not like that. I am not out there to try to win people over. I tried to be fair, unbiased, and a normal guy. I didn't want to act like something I was not. I can be polite, but nice just because I want someone to like me, nope. I was done jumping through hoops and just wanted to live a life as a soldier with soldiers. I now felt like I could be settling into something like a home. We are years from the greatest generation that lived. There were probably millions that stepped up to do their part. Right now, and in this place, I was with some of the few of this generation that were at least similar. They signed their ass on the dotted line, accepted the fact that they could come home in a fucking box with a flag on it. They were treated like shit and just run into the dirt. But then again, at times, it seemed like they liked it. They liked the fact that they were sent out and did the dirty shit no one else wanted to. I think that it was because out there, they were left alone. They didn't have anyone trying to frag their ass from higher. No one was out there putting them on shit detail. No, out there all alone in the "dangerous" areas, they lived simple. They were kept busy and they were the masters of their own fate. They were left to do the job, survive, and live to the next moment they would be sent out again.

Out in the desert on a patrol, no one knew them to be shit bags. Out there they were simply American soldiers, often walking and living in areas where Americans were considered to be myths. They were serious and quick to adapt to situations. They walked taller and talked direct. It was business, and yet you could actually see the real relationships that they had with each other. The hard times made them tighter: they cared for each other. They were proficient and that was less to worry about. Now, we just needed to do a little tweaking. We were on our way to becoming more than a platoon, we were becoming "The Flock."

Spc Iglesias (left) and Ssg Briola.

A rollover accident that happened shortly before I joined the bn. No fun in a vehicle this size and weight. Fortunately no one was seriously injured.

Out on patrol. Spc Swain on the left, Sgt Colunga on the right.

Soldiers pose on a Stryker's ramp. This is possibly prior to a mission. Left to right: Spc Lendrum "Lenny," Spc Rosario, Pvt. McDougal "McDookie," Spc Swain "Swainey Poo" and Sgt Burk. In the back, Pvt. Jackson and Pvt. Lazarro.

Three trouble makers in a shed that is made to protect our bottled water from being under the sun. Why are they in there? Who knows? But they are not working. Spc. Swain "Swainey Poo," Sgt Owen, and Spc Fabish "Fabo."

When you run into something like this, you might as well check it out. SSg McDowell.

This looks like one of those moments where we all hurry up to wait. Spc Gutierrez "Gootie" and Pfc Pylant.

Mission is done and it's time to relax and decompress. Left to right: Pfc McKeen, Unknown Soldier, Spc Gutierrez, Pfc Pate. The masked guy could be one of three different men: Rosario, Shaftner or Lounds.

You just have to stay hydrated. These men take time to enjoy Gatorade. Left to right: Pfc Iglesias "Iggy," Pfc Pylant, Pfc Pate and Spc Spence.

As things start to settle the platoon starts to get its own groove. The future doesn't look so bleak. As a matter of fact I have a lieutenant with balls and a brain. He is able to put together things that he sees on the ground, the things he has experienced and what he gets with good intel. The only problem is who is really listening? What about all the rumors and crap I heard? It always seems that things are getting blown up into more than it really is. Am I to think that in a military organization, it is possible to treat people badly without anyone doing a thing?

As events start to add up, I get a good awakening to the hard reality on the line. There are small moments that pass the time, but at any time, danger comes in one manner or the other. Even though this is something you get used to, you are reminded of how easy and simple things can become deadly.

So, You are Perfect

As time passed, there was a change in the air. Soldiers were off doing duties with little or no guidance. They were off doing maintenance on weapons, vehicles, and, of course, off to the gym. It seemed that during times like this, on a deployment, your off time was what you made of it. Some preferred to call home and send letters. Others were committed to staying in their little wooden cubicles and spending their time reading, writing, and playing Xbox. I swear, if you had never been connected to twelve shit-talking grunts, and played a game that you get to shoot people and hover over them, while standing and then crouching repeatedly, don't do it! Nothing pisses you off more than a young kid doing that shit. It looks like you are getting T-bagged. These fucknuts were champions and knew every fucking trick in the damn book. You run to chase someone, three guys take you out and swarm your character and start popping up and down. You could hear them in the other tents. They were over there laughing and talking shit. At that time of course they are getting motivated.

Some nights after a hard week or a long mission, groups would gather and sit out smoking the Cuban cigar. They would sit out there and talk about events that had happened before, all the stuff from the past, before the war and during. As the conversation continued, it wasn't too long before the topic of those injured arose. The injured and others, who were never going to return. You heard the events that described their personalities and the type of character they were, their best or worst achievements that would be the last things they'd be remembered for. Topics would change and out of nowhere someone would ask about a buddy's sister, or mom. Things would lighten up and then stories would begin about the stupid shit that you do in your environment. Guys would talk about people getting sick or having the shits, or times when your life was unknowingly in danger. One of the funniest was while on a mission, they were lying down pulling security. While in their positions, out of nowhere, the fins off an illumination round hit the ground a few feet away. The simple rules of physics come into play. Requesting illumination not only provides necessary light, it also comes with the dunnage. As they burst up above, the components have to come back down. How about that?

There you are, doing your job in the middle of the night and a fucking hunk of metal from a round thumps into the dirt in arm's reach of where you are lying. Really? Now I've got to worry about this shit too? There are times when you have nothing left to do but laugh. It is war, and life in normal conditions is pretty dangerous. In everyday life, people walk by an event or possible dangers without thought. In combat, you plan and train for certain dangers and those are well known. The main dangers are catching bullets, getting blown up, and possibly crushed by a vehicle. In the low 5% you have a chance of getting bit by a spider, drinking some dirty water and now, shit falling out of the sky. That can be planned for by the firing guns, but how about giving a heads up to the troops on the ground? I guess the FDC (Fire Direction Control) were not monitoring the battle like they use to. Things just seemed to look like the failure of "Attention to Detail" was everywhere.

In our tent, I would sit with the lieutenant and talk. He had an idea that there were some bad guys further south. Seemed that he was wanting to go and see what was out there. Up to that point we had been getting good intel from a local national and he seemed to be right on the money. He would come and a couple of the squad leaders would get the info and we would send it up. He had information on the southern area that the lieutenant wanted to take a look at. Regardless of the idea that the lieutenant had, we were pointed in another direction. Since the lieutenant was given his orders we were off to do as commanded, but his idea, if right, would disrupt a lot of the shit going on in the area. However, we had a different problem.

We were having trouble with the locals in the area trusting us. We were in a sector for a short time and not given the opportunity to develop any sources or build any trust with the villagers. Each platoon in the company would do a day in each sector, and bounce to another one the next day. I thought of it as police working their beat. Being on the ground and getting to know the environment and the people developed trust. Willingness to cooperate and trust that officer was built over time.

War is different, I know. With the regularity of working a steady beat, danger is increased. As an infantry soldier the risks are weighed. The reward has to be greater than the cost. Familiar people can get closer to you. If they are not threatening you, they can become a target themselves. Something like that would go a long way in deterring help from the locals. Knowing the enemy and what they have done in the past has to be considered. Violence on their part was not out of the question. Whatever command was doing, it was not working and there seemed to be no input from the guys on the ground. So, it was off to do the regular missions as planned from above. Whatever the information was that was coming down seemed really different from what we were seeing on the ground. So what does it matter what we know? Why are we doing reports and giving all the information that we collect? We get told to go somewhere else, and off on missions we go. One day we were out and about and we got a call to stop. The lieutenant seemed to find something and we were in a 'squat hold' (used in the Airborne to teach a point. Also known as a stress position). All of the sudden we get a call that we've found an IED. From that point on, it's your baby till the EOD arrives to blow it up. The exact grid position was forwarded up. We were off to do this mission and we were going to get it done, no matter what. So, we bounced two vehicles up to continue on and we left one there with another for security. Little Woods, the FO was there and the plan was he was going to call fire on it and blow it up. Uh, okay! I made my way to the location that we were going to operate in. I hear Woods on the radio making the arrangements to do the mission. We of course were going to wait till we were done and do the actual fire mission on our way home. The guys are doing their patrols and we are in support. I decided to dismount and take a look to see what was happening on the ground. The only thing I could remember was that there was a fucking wolfhound, some meaner-than-shit dog there tied up. He was foaming at the mouth and barking and raising hell. Of course, there are children on this ride that do not know how to keep their hands in the fucking car. Yup, and all they want to do is pet the little puppy.

Now, most dogs there like the Americans and follow us around. They get the shit kicked out of them and beat by the locals and they are more than willing to come and pick up residence with the good old US of A. On the other side of the coin, you could be on a normal patrol and a fucking dog comes at you like a damn lion. He will charge you and if you are not careful, bite the fuck out of your ass. At night they cause a ruckus. Doing a patrol and trying to be sneaky is a problem. All the barking takes away the element of surprise. It gives off your position and will keep it up all night long. This dog was a monster and a bad boy. He was chained and it really only gave minimal clearance for you to get around. It was little old Williams who decided he would befriend this dog. He is a good distance away and starts with the "Here, boy" routine. I'm like, "You are fucking crazy. You're gonna get your ass bit." But he is motivated and has some dedication to the task at hand and starts in. This dog is like, "This motherfucker is crazy! I'm a fucking *wolfhound*, barking, hair on end, foaming at the mouth, and this guy is coming in at me?" Then the dog gets serious. "I'm a fucking wolfhound, bitch! Bow wow, motherfucker!" and charges. I'm watching and laughing.

"Told you, bone-head. That fucking dog is T.A.L.I.B.A.N. Fuck that dog."

We continue on and Willy is talking about how he couldn't figure out why the dog didn't like him. He was actually confused. We are on patrol and this is the discussion going on and we are laughing. We reach the end of the mission, and time to mount up and get the fuck out.

Now it's time to go home and play some sticks (Xbox), but first we are going to blow this IED. Everything has been coordinated. The data has been given to the guns and they say they're ready to go. Here we come across the dunes on the way to link up with the other section, and then we are ready to go. Let's blow this shit and get going. I'm monitoring the radio and listening to what is going on. One station is talking about the fire mission coming down, the other is a platoon internal and we are talking about what is going to happen. For some time now, I have been dealing with a freaking asshole who is fucking with me on the net. I am from Texas and love to watch the Longhorns play. When we roll and are moving I listen to some music to pump me up. The first song is *Texan 'til I die* by Kevin Fowler, just to remind myself that we are proud to be from the best country in the world. This heckler is out there and I'm gonna catch this fucker and rip his lips off. We are sitting and listening to the traffic on the radios and he jumps on our net and says "Texas sucks." I know what is happening. Someone is trying to piss me off, but it ain't gonna happen. Then, he does. He is bad-mouthing Texas and I want to triangulate the coordinates to put that round on his ass!

I'm dealing with this verbal altercation and finally, the guns are ready to drop rounds on target and the mission is ready to go. Old Woods gave them the GRID. They have computers and trained people whose job it is to get rounds on target. Modernization makes the job easier and it is basically a plug and play, "Drop that shit and let's go, I have stuff to do" kind of thing.

1. I've got to find that fucker on the radio.
2. It's time I whooped someone's ass on the sticks.
3. I got a fucking turtle head and that guy is holding for the green light. Lets roll fuckers, I gotta go! Now Woods is doing his shit. He has coordinated all the crap and we are supposed to be safe. Here are all the things we've got to do to not get killed by our own guns. Woods called up the grid and moved back 300 meters. Then they called him and told him to move back 500 meters. Then they called him and told him to move back another 500 Meters. Here we are, a fucking click off the round and waiting. Then it comes.

"Shot over! Shot out! Splash over! Cease fire! Cease fire! Cease fire!"

There was a boom and dirt in the air. This mother-fucking round is like 150 meters from the vehicle.

What the fuck? There are rocks and shit landing on the vehicle and, "My bad!" Someone says it's a bad round and that it happens. I know that a bad round does two things. They go short, or too far away. They do not get shot out of a barrel and go 800 meters to the fucking right or left and nearly land on the guy on the fucking radio. I jump on the radio and have a not-so-fucking-polite conversation with the guy on the other end. It was an intense situation and there were speakers shut off because of some of the stuff getting said. I was pissed! Here we were out fucking with dogs and IEDs and we get an *Ooops, my bad!* Seriously, it's bad enough that we are now used to the fact that we may get wounded and injured by the enemy. Now we have to worry that if we do call for help, we might or might not get taken out by our own side! This was bullshit and if there was a reason to get in fucking trouble, this was it. Hell, I might get fired and fucking who knows what else. We are going in and I remember bitching on the radio to someone on the other end. I warned them that I was on the way. I wanted to know what the fuck happened, and who just almost hit one of our vehicles with a fucking 120mm mortar.

We end up pulling in to the FOB and I start walking straight to our company. Of course, the first sergeant isn't there. He was online doing some class or something. The CO isn't there. All that is there is the young fire support NCO, the officer, and the XO. My lieutenant is there and I don't know if he was getting the run around or what, but I jumped in and told them how it was. We were out there and doing our fucking jobs and we are not important enough to get mad over almost getting hit? How about making sure that everyone else does their jobs with a little proficiency? They were calm, or maybe I was too pissed, but the grid to the target was not entered into the computer right. Someone put in the grid location of our observer as a target instead of the grid from the IED. Since it is a time of war, all safeties are removed and it will not alert you to the fuck up. How did I know that? Because I was a safety check computer for the mortars at one time. There are two guys there putting in the same data. One checks the other. Both of those guys put in the information that they were given. Why else would they call him the "check computer?" However, if they were given the grids in reverse, bam! Luckily for us the bitches suck balls and can't hit shit!

After so many years in the military, let's just say that this was not the first time mortars or artillery came close to taking me out. I was madder than shit and we all link up, to go to chow and settle down. I can't believe that it was called an honest mistake and that was it. Woods was raising hell somewhere and not around, so we took off. I am thinking that I just chewed the shit out of two captains, a staff sergeant, and nothing. On our way to chow we link up with Woods and he is pissed. He was told to calm down and shut the fuck up and that was that. Hell, it was his vehicle that was almost hit. Maybe he sent in the wrong data?

I asked him and he was like, "No fucking way!" If he was that fucked up he would have at least hit himself. He said he would not have been where he was, or the rank that he was. I was listening to him and then I thought, *hmmm. Maybe this is the motherfucker talking shit on the radio?* For some reason, just like that, it popped into my head. However, I was distracted and supposed to be cooling off. Then he tells me that the first sergeant said it was an accident. Then he asked Woods, "So you're perfect? You never make a mistake?"

I just about shit my pants. Are you fucking kidding me? Perfect, uh, no! But if I go to the fucking range to shoot my target on lane three, I know I am going to hit the silhouette, not the guy shooting on lane ten! The whole situation just showed me the importance that we had in our company. We could have lost someone, and instead of getting pissed and ensuring that this didn't happen again, it was chalked up as "another day." Loyalty was the question now, if we are to be loyal to ourselves as a company. Should we not expect that our company go to bat for their own? How would you like to have a day like this, be called "Another day?" Nothing was done to ensure it didn't happen to anyone else, or to us again. It was seen as nothing important. As if it was just like pissing on the toilet seat, or using the last paper in the shitter. There it was, it was real, it happened and it was gone. This however sealed old Woods's fate. For some time the lieutenant and I, along with Brinkley and Woods, would sit and talk in the chow hall. We were getting along well. We were making changes, things were getting better, and really getting to the point of having a strong team. Things were going well and the squad leaders were being allowed to do their job. Soldiers were getting the information and doing their job. No micromanagement, but having to sink or swim. We were starting to solidify together as a team. One mission at a time, day by day.

I don't know if it was Woods pressuring the incident of possible fratricide to someone higher that lead to it. Behind the scenes there was movement. Things were getting done. Before too long, he would come to be replaced and taken out of the platoon. He would not be the only one either. The ranks were then filled with minions who were not good enough for the other platoons, but good enough for ours.

Soldiers patiently wait in the cold for their next instructions prior to going out on mission. Back, left to right: SSg Briola, "B" drinking water. Next to him – probably sleeping – is Sgt Colunga. SSg Woods is in the front, freezing, as Spc Barron takes the last drags of his cigarette.

I start to try and become the younger version I used to be. I didn't want my youth back, but the ability to know without question. To be as sharp minded as I used to be. To do that, I had to take time and deal with the past. I had put it off for years. Now in combat I felt a need to deal with issues or fail in my job. It's hard to pinpoint the origin of your traits that bother you. It's even harder to man up and fix that shit. Now, I realize I am surrounded by soldiers that deserve a better leader than I am. In my search I find it all goes back to my brothers. When war started we had each other and knew if we were going to meet our fate, one of us would look out for our families. Nothing had ever been that close again. The politics made me into what I was. I was left a shell and did not care to do that again. Everything I wanted back is right in my grasp. The past has made me fearful of trying to get it back. In this life there is nothing that is free. Everything you want has got a price. I have paid for it. I can feel it in my bones and in the steps I take. I am being told by time that this is my chance. This is the life I wanted and this is real living. If I don't try to live, I might not get another chance.

Listening, Learning, Growing

The lieutenant was a runner and he was a tall guy. His legs were just as tall as me, and I didn't feel like getting run into the dirt. After the morning piss, I would get my shoes on, and go for a run on my own. Usually on the run, I was out and alone. I didn't need or want people with me. I didn't feel 100% and was still living in the past questioning all that had happened. I had given of myself for a long time. It hurt more than anything to work hard for something and give so much. I never thought it would not work out.

Morning time was my time, and I used it to get through the day. It was about more than running. I came to the realization that it was about me and the past. I had been going and it never stopped. I placed my job and responsibilities ahead of my family and myself. I was good at working, waiting, and being a soldier. I changed my emotions or cut them off. I wanted to become a good leader and push through events without feeling, keeping an eye on the prize or the mission at hand. Everyone says that they will deal with it all, once they are back home safe again. I never did. I never took any time for myself. Inside I was packing stuff away and never really dealing with the emotional side of events. I guess normal people have to deal with emotional pain and loss. I never learned to do it. I was thinking of my brothers Weaver and

Springsteen. I remembered the relationships that we had, and that was what I was looking for. Weaver and Springsteen, well, they were my brothers. They were from a time when we were in a bad-ass company. We had bad-ass leaders in the platoon, in our company, and battalion. Back then, we were young, the soldiers who charged forward. Those were great times and we started the war together. Years later, it was still the standard. It was the best of times being "Red Devils" in the 173rd. Those days were different from Afghanistan. Ten years later the world was different. I didn't run for time or distance. I was out there running through memories and pain. I was trying to run away from the past to stay ahead of it all. I didn't know how to confront the emotional garbage, but it was coming out. It was also a release from the daily crap. With time, I grew stronger. I became more confident and kept the dam from breaking.

I focused more to my tasks, and felt I had to do more. I took time alone in the mornings to deal with my issues, to burn off the fog in my head, and get back to who I was. I needed to concentrate on what I was doing. I needed to be better than what I was and dealing with this alone was me trying to get better. Thoughts about bad shit stayed in my head. There are just some things that stay with you.

I again came to a conclusion that I had what I wanted. With that being said, I didn't want to give everything I had and end up losing it all again. The worst thing would be losing what I just got back.

One morning while I was out and about, I ran into the lieutenant. It was a surprise because everyone was usually in the racks at that time of the day. It turned out that he had found out about me running and decided to surprise me. He asked me why didn't I wake him, so we could go together. I told him that I was not a runner and I didn't want to hold him up. I just wanted to get back into it, and it was just a one-time thing. However, another truth was there and staring me in the face.

The years were taking a toll on me and after all the smoke and bullshit, I was pretty beat up. The honest truth is that when there are numbers to fill, anyone will do. The need for a body able to walk, carry weight, shoot bullets, go where you are needed, bam! You're it! Still, at this point, I didn't want to get too close to the lieutenant. We had been off to a good start. Things were looking like they were heading in the right direction, but I was done getting my heart broke. I had seen things get better, and just when you feel like things are going to end well, that's when shit hits the fan. I didn't want to have that anymore. I gave years to my last unit, and it just got worse and worse. I had most of everything that was good in me torn out. I couldn't afford to give what little I had left. Usually I was the one that was the glue to unite the others to have a common task or idea. I was down for the work and was committed, but to be honest, I didn't feel like I was going to make it back. If I was to meet the end of my days there, I wanted to have a little piece of something good left. I still had enough to believe in the pride of an honest day's work. That was doing the right thing with the platoon, and believing that it would pay off. I was still in love with what the military is described to be on paper, with our values and beliefs, something good, and my part of that was coming home to be laid to rest. Oh, and let's be honest, chances are that I was going to be in pieces. Now, I do know that the lieutenant was a good person and had a great heart. He was an educated man and a great example that held the platoon together before I was even a thought. He loved being a leader, he was down-to-earth and a real live person. He was an officer, and was approachable and honest. He was not into the politics that was killing the morale of units in the area. He was, fuck it, he was awesome. I got along with him fine and we talked. He had a plan and actually asked me what I thought. He trusted me enough to handle things that were my responsibility. It is in the shittiest and most dangerous places that you get to find a real person. This guy, he was not on my shit list, but I still was not gonna run with his ass and get smoked. He was wanting to get up and work out together. He was probably trying to find the same thing I was. I however, tended to be very cautious of new people. Like I said before, I didn't want to get my heart broke. To really like someone is personal. Then you find out that they are a fucking cardboard cut-out, only looking like what a leader was supposed to be. That's exactly what I didn't want to have again. The lieutenant didn't seem to be that way. There were no surprises. He was like someone that you met from another place. He had different manners, but still had common factors of a normal human. I didn't want to get too close, but he was likable. I didn't think he would change, but something was bound to happen. It was just my experience talking; nothing good lasts forever. After running, I started to make my way through the tents and checking on the soldiers and their bunks. I would smoke a couple of Newports and bullshit with Swain. I would then sit and bullshit with Briola since he was an old man. He would catch me up on the different places and fights that they had been in. We would talk about the difference in operations and the different tactics that they had seen. Brinkley and Woods were just on the other side of the tent, and we would talk shit till the end of the day. However, in the morning and alone, I would go and drag my ass around the FOB and think. No more about the past, just focus on the future. I thought about stuff like grappling hooks to find IEDs, or using the robot with a piece of rebar. I wanted to have it drag it to pull up the pressure plates. Since I was from west Texas, it was like a tractor breaking the ground.

    I was slowly putting together the information that I was receiving, studying and battle-gaming the different scenarios. Actions on contact and maneuvering the vehicles to increase the damage we can make and increase our survivability. All this was information that I was getting from the squad leaders and a lot of it. It was me trying to get to the point of them feeling comfortable with how we did things. In my experience, this was unheard of, and it was usually more along the lines of:

"This is the way I did it here, and that is how it's going to get done now!" No discussion, no nothing.

Instead of that, I listened and took the information and used the men's experience. Sometimes they won deciding to change things up. If it was a solid way, we would adapt. Then again, if it was crappy idea, we wouldn't change a damn thing. There were some big fights, things and events that were really hard to hear. Even so, all I knew is that I did not want to end up back in the tent with all those seniors. We were all of the mind set to finish the tour. One way or the other, we were not going to go anywhere. When times were bad, we were not alone in the platoon. For me, I had the lieutenant. He was proving all my premature thoughts were not 100% accurate. He was showing me more about good people. I'm sure everyone would have loved to be anywhere else, but no one was going to just give up. Having fear, a bad feeling, and being nervous is something everyone would experience. It was the fact that there was a someone, your brother there, that made you suck all those things up. It was a reason to dust yourself off, and keep getting up every day. That is commitment to your friend. That commitment was made a long time ago and before my time, through their experiences while on some mission, or any task. If it was something needed, having that commitment to each other, anything could be done. It was having all those feelings, and having the courage to ride, walk and stand right where you were supposed to, despite your feelings or fears, right by his side, and him by you.

I started to notice that there always seemed to be some activity on my way in from a run. We operated on timelines and there was a certain time that we were to begin to move around and start hopping and popping. Before I got Colunga and later Briola to start running with me, they were up to something. So after my morning thing, I decided to check out the locals.

I'd noticed that Briola and Colunga were up at that time and both of them were sitting on the deck in front of their tent. Both

Colunga and Briola were either talking on the deck, or Colunga was up and about. This sparked my interest, and I started to ask around and see what the deal was. Come to find out, these guys had a little ritual of their own. In the mornings, they would get up early and go eat breakfast. Now that sounds normal, but on a timeline, you get sleep instead of chow. Usually you have pop tarts and ramen noodles, tuna fish or sardines, something to eat, but you don't stay up all night and then get up three or four hours later and have breakfast. I saw Colunga and he said, "Morning." I asked what he was doing up, and he said, "Breakfast." Now I was not too surprised, but then again it got me curious.

I was like, why? I mean, they could wake up after getting some much needed rest and eat lunch. Nope, not Colunga, and more Colunga than Briola. They had the opinion that there was one item that not only gave them strength and nourishment, but it tasted good too. It was the French bread in the form of sticks, served in the chow hall. Not actual French bread, but French bread sticks. It was like a prescription from the local witch doctor. They swore that it was good and that everything went well when they ate them. Now here I am looking at this soldier of mine, trying to figure out his thinking. French bread sticks? Colunga, the Irish Mexican. Old Briola from the islands. Both swearing up and down about the ritual of breakfast. Not only did it work, but they swore that they were good too.

The whole thought process and reasoning was simple but crazy. The question was, what would happen if they didn't get their French bread sticks for breakfast? Why not eggs and hash browns? How could you believe that if your time was up, it was up? If it was that simple and left to fate, why not this theory on French bread sticks?

There had to be some rules to it. Some yin and yang, right or wrong, up or down. I couldn't argue about the idea and the existence of some rules that may possibly exist. Sure it was not cutting out the hearts of people on some pyramid. That was crazy, but I'm sure back then people thought it was logical.

It wasn't the last word on the idea of fate, but it was a topic of discussion that was periodically revisited. On bad days when bad things happened, there it was. "We didn't eat breakfast this morning. No French bread sticks, see? Told you."

I began to talk to Colunga more and more. He was a little different from the others and was more serious. He was a funny guy but didn't fuck around when it came to his team. Colunga was a team leader for Fairchild, and Fairchild was an ass. Then again everyone has their reasons. Swain was under Colunga, and they were buddies. However, when it was time to work, all that shit went out the window. It was all about work, and nothing was more important than your job and responsibility. When it came to directions, it was short, to the point and brutal. Across the board, that was how it was done. When it came to the men's equipment and performance, all the leaders were the same in that way.

When I got there, I noticed they continued to work hard. People never really looked up, just keeping their nose to the task. It took a while but things were getting better. The lieutenant trusted these guys and swore that they were legit. He was their leader and also their biggest fan as well. He had developed a good relationship with them and was known to do the hard right over easy wrong. Despite the looks, as time passed I started to see what the lieutenant had achieved. For a long time he was the reason for them staying together and moving forward. I noticed that they were serious and worked good on missions. When the lieutenant would brief these guys it was like this. He gave it to them straight. They were on their SOPs (Standard Operating Procedures) and everyone knew what and how they were going to do. To me, it seemed evident that he was not only the lieutenant, but he was an example. Being from the outside, I was left with some blanks here and there. The lieutenant would do his thing and I just tagged along and observed. There was a ton of stuff that was political. It was higher up but tasks would end up in our lap. There are those times when you might get called to charge the bunker out of necessity, for the survival of the others. *Going out in a Blaze of Glory*. Got it? What I am talking about are the times where you are told to do some of the stupidest shit. Having to inspire and sell such a task that usually ends up with getting people hurt, sucks. Doing some unnecessary task that only panders to egos and creates brownie points for the higher ups sucks. War is really simple; it is politics that creates the casualties that we send home with false statements of honor and distinction. I end up walking into the tent one morning and see the lieutenant pondering something. For some time, we were talking about going out for an extended time period. We were wanting to go out and build some trust in the villagers. Our snitch was telling us that there are bad guys in the area and that they are planting IED belts to increase the likelihood of hitting a vehicle. There are also places where they are processing the explosives that they are using to blow us up. Just recently, a vehicle was blown up right outside of our base. Right outside, these guys were getting close and were not afraid to take the risk to get to us. Putting these guys out of business seemed like a possibility. We just had to get approval from the company. The lieutenant tells me that after asking for some time, we were approved to go out and stay for two days or forty-eight hours. I go shit, shower and shave, and I'm really excited about sticking to one area and finding these bad guys. Plus, things were a little tense in the company area and not really getting any better. I tried to bend and give, but it was always at our own expense. I tried to talk and communicate, but then that turned out to be bad as well. Dicks got pissed or whatever and my FSO, Woods, would later be taken out of the platoon. Members that were just transferred into the platoon before I got there were getting reevaluated and getting taken out. The platoon was doing good, we were tight and the men were coming into their own. Maybe that was seen as a threat? Slowly the followers were getting sent to a new platoon. One by one soldiers were being traded out for first sergeant's minions.

One of the biggest things that had happened causing stress, was the BCS Championship. I stayed up to watch my Longhorns lose Colton McCoy in the first quarter. By this time, I was well known for liking my State, and the college team from there. Sports is a competition and it is fair game if someone calls you and begins to talk shit from another team. No, we can't put on that uniform, nor switch places with the players. But we sure as hell can talk shit like we are on the fucking sideline guarding the water. Everyone talks shit when it comes to football, basketball, it doesn't matter. It passes the time. Some take it seriously and that morning I did take it seriously. I was up at like three in the morning and watched my team lose. The last time the Longhorns played for the national title it was against USC, and we fucking won that shit. That time I was in another country taking the extended summer tour. I was not able to get the gear, nor have I ever been the type to spend money on a jersey. So, I did the next best thing, I got a fucking marker, drew a number 10 on my salty, sweaty, dirty nasty shirt and fucking scared the shit out of the Commandoes. I came out hooting and hollering "Texas baby, we are taking it back to Texas!" They didn't know what the hell I was doing and fuck it. Every time there was an election and it was over, those fuckers would shoot shit in the air and scare the shit out of me, so ha! It's my turn, and it's fucking awesome! However, this year, we lost and I was emotionally vulnerable and weak. That morning I was walking to the chow hall with the lieutenant and squad leaders. The peanut gallery is on the stoop or deck in front of the company. In the company area there were TVs and shit for the company, however the platoon was not allowed. It was a bitch every time someone went in there and got harassed by the first sergeant and the rest of them. I was entitled, but the guys stayed away, being that they were treated like a nice warm piece of shit. To me it was simple; they can't go, I won't go. Maybe that was why the other platoon was given their own big screens and we were sucking hind titty. Yeah, I said it. The fucking bitch platoon were given their own TV and sat on their bunks and played fucking games. Oh, and the other TVs? Well they were locked away in a Connex so as to keep them safe. Anyway, here we are walking and I am weak and emotionally hurt. The peanut gallery is sitting in front of the company CP (Command Post or "head shed"). There they are smoking and joking around the first sergeant. He treated his minions well, but kept them in place, near enough to kick the shit out of them when he needed. We are walking by and I hear First Sergeant Dicks talking shit. He then asks me what happened to the Longhorns? So, at this point, people liked to poke the bear. This was one of those times, and I go off. I make a straight line to the stoop, my platoon fucking walks off and leaves me. The stoop clears as I walk up and say, "Why the fuck are you talking shit? To make fun of me? You want to make me look bad in front of others? What is the deal, or do you want the actual information?"

I knew what it was. It was something that I liked and was dear to me. However, at this moment he was using it to embarrass me. Do it in front of the dick suckers hiding in the command tent and demoralize me in front of the men to make me look weak. I stood there in front and said, "What the fuck, you want to talk shit?" He knew what happened and he wanted to take a shot. No, it was not about the team, it was about me. I had just about had it. Listening to the way these men were treated. How I was given the ones no one wanted and left to sink or swim. How we were not even important enough to give a damn about when we were almost hit by our own guns. How people were now getting moved just because. No, it was time and now it was my fight. He claimed to not know anything and we agreed that it was a mistake.

I went to the chow hall and asked, "Hey fuckers, where the hell did y'all go?" They replied that it was a very clear and precise question directed to me, and it was none of their business. I laughed and cursed a little and began to sit and enjoy the time of day where we would sit and bullshit for hours. Most would come and go, but we would stay and enjoy each other's company. Those days are very long ago and far behind. To be able to sit there and talk, joke around and just be people, it is very hard to find. We were an officer, a Texan who's Mexican, another Texan out of Dallas of a lighter persuasion, and a little shit-talking bad-ass from Chicago, Woods. Yes he was black, but not our skin, race, religion, or past mattered. Hell, Colunga was a Mexican Irishman from Idaho. Briola and Swain, hell they fought against each other in 'Nam. We were all different, in the same situation as the other, and no one was better than the other. I knew I could learn from the lieutenant and others. So I listened and did so. They would listen to me, because they had to, and because I am a funny motherfucker. Nothing really mattered. All the bullshit politics you hear on TV, it was there too, but we all respected each other. We would pray before we went out. Yes we did have atheists, but we respected their opinion, and they respected ours. Like I said, something like that is hard to find, and I had found it. More reason to stay talking shit with the guys and spending time with each other. After all, this is war, and nothing lasts forever. It never does.

Members of the Plt. preparing to go out on mission. Sgt. Owen is closest with Sgt. Colunga wearing his neck gator. Standing beside him is Spc. Gutierrez who is looking away. He is talking to Spc. Sellner who is coming into the group.

Two of the Black sheep with their find. On the left is Shepherd 6, aka Lt Osborne. On the right is Sgt. Colunga. I showed Colunga this picture and he doesn't remember it being taken. He was blown up twice on this day.

Pfc Pate on the 240B. He is in the rear guard position of the vehicle. His main purpose is to keep our butts safe. He is wearing a CVC helmet that allows him to talk to the other positions.

It's hot!

Operations being conducted at one of our outposts.

Off we go. After some time the lieutenant gets approved for the idea of camping out. This was his idea and it made sense to me. I wish I could take credit for it. Everything usually has a process, and it's up to who is going out to set a timeline. I thought there might be an opportunity to have a better relationship with our first sergeant. I was wrong. From the start shit hit the fan. My idea to better things, was another's chance to treat others like shit.

I dealt with it, but it just seemed to be one person intent on messing up the platoon, or people in it. We were fine. We could deal with stupid. What was hard to deal with was Dicks getting pissed, taking it out on us, and not even knowing why. Maybe he was bipolar?

Going Up River

The time to plan and go out on our little camping trip was soon to arrive. We came up with the idea, and like all the other things it began to snowball. It was a little bit of a pain in the ass, but to get out and be away from the daily grind was worth all the effort. Coming along with us, we would be graced by the first sergeant in his brand new vehicle, and I was supportive. I asked him to come out. I thought maybe getting out and doing things would remove the stick out of his ass that was creating his hard-on for the platoon. That even meant our own personal radio frequencies to include other things.

We had our SP (Start, or Start Point) time out there and like clockwork we all gathered out by the vehicles for each leader to conduct their PCCs and PCIs.

First, it was at the vehicles that the crews would show up, then the squads and teams. People would then rotate out to chow and we carried on. Any changes would then be put out by the lieutenant at the ramp-side brief. We did the roll-over drills and evacuation drills. We listed and briefed all the medical personnel and equipment, where it was in the vehicles, the pax (passengers) in each vehicle, so on and so on. Of course, this was all done in the same manner as before and it just got better every time. It was no surprise that this was the manner in which we did things. We set up to have all communications with the first sergeant vehicle and Base. This is where things started to go wrong. As our SP time came, we didn't see Dicks' vehicle. So here we were all dressed up and ready to go to the dance, and we are waiting for one person. I was expecting his vehicle to link up in order to begin movement. There was no contact at all, and then comes the call.

"Where are y'all at? I thought we were going to SP at this time and we are late... blah, blah, blah."

I think it was the lieutenant that said we were where we always were, and were ready. We were just waiting for them to show up. Then there is talk about, "That was not what was briefed and this is all fucked up." So we are told that he was headed up to our location and would link up with us there. So, we wait, and wait and wait. For some reason he was thinking we were to go and pick him up.

Then again, we were under the impression that we were going on a mission and figured he would show up, and do what we all do every time. He was bitching about this and that, and every small thing he could find. He was mad that we didn't go to the CP and pick him up and ... fuck it! I still don't know. He wanted us to tailor our stuff to make him feel special. He was special all right, real fucking special. I thought that this would be the opportunity for him to be around the platoon and see what was going on. I didn't think we were going to have to have a red carpet out and be dishing out the VIP treatment. At this point, I knew I was responsible for the crap going on. All I wanted was to better the relations between him and I as well as the platoon. That did not seem like it was going to happen.

Now, we were waiting and after a while he asks, "Where are you?" He took it upon himself not go to our location, but to go to the front gate. So, now we are looking like dumb-asses. He didn't come to us: we needed to go to him. Now, we needed to follow him and go where we were told.

I was livid. I was on our fucking net and going off. What the fuck? Was he just joining us to make our life miserable and be a pain? This was the first time that this person was actually going to go out with a different platoon than his favorite. We thought that maybe it would be a good thing and that we were going to at least be treated differently and seen in a different light. We then roll out to the fucking gate, hauling ass on the FOB in order to jump through a hoop for our guest.

As we are, I'm going off and we arrive to nothing. We are looking for the new highly designed vehicle with its precious cargo, and nothing. We are looking and calling base to see if he left or where he was, and nothing. He wasn't there either. So we are waiting and I jump on the radio to the lieutenant and tell him that this was fucking bullshit. I was gonna leave and drive straight to the company and see what the fuck was going on.

Now, remember there were different frequencies (or stations) people had. This specific conversation we were talking on was ours. I feel the anger and violent nature coming out of my pores. As soon as I began to run off to find this guy, a call comes over the net and says, forget it. He tells us to go ahead and go, and that he was just going to stay and remain on post. I called and told him I was inbound and that we needed to talk. This was messed up and I was going to let him know that all of this was kindergarten bullshit.

He simply told me that he was okay. He was not mad but decided to stay and that we should continue on. It sounded like he was just quitting, and forgetting about the mission. It started to sound like he was scared, not of me, but of being out and about with people he treated like shit. I would have felt bad as well, after all we were supposed to be on the same team and same fight. I never made it back to have that talk.

Most of the time guests operate and are driven by the unit's timeline. This was not the case here, it was about power. It was selfish and done to micromanage and let everyone know that we were seen as being fucked up. We could still be subject to any bullshit that others wanted us to be. It was to take away the respect of the platoon leadership, and destroy their power base. Yes, this was done by someone that took an oath to take care of his men. Good leadership is hard to find. Bullshit was not, and my ability to deal with it was being tested. It felt that piece by piece I was facing the same crap that I dealt with for years.

That day didn't start off too well. We did have a plan, and would now focus on execution and survival. We made our way out of the FOB and headed south. We continued out and turned to the east south east and made our way toward some villages. As you look across the desert, you see the earth as a straight line. The terrain is not like that though.

You do not see the back side of the hills and it is not flat. It looks that way, but there are places that cannot be seen. They are avenues of approach and places to travel from one place to the other. The enemy in the area know this very well and use these changes in the terrain for movement. It's their home, and we are in a constant fight to learn basic things in order to better understand, better protect ourselves, and fight the enemy. Here we were conducting our movement, bouncing and going up and down, looking at the various tracks on the desert floor, at times looking for hills, disturbed earth, ant trails, debris, and 100 million things to give us warning of a possible threat. Our source the snitch was working with the platoon way before I got there. He had been right on the money before, and was full of information. What didn't make sense was that no one listened. It was all about results and caches. He would come up with intel, and it was swept under the rug. We would send it up, and nothing would happen. He would give the platoon the info, and it ended with us. The platoon, the lieutenant, hell, even I tried to get someone to talk to him, but it all fell on deaf ears. For that simple fact, we were the ones to go and execute whatever it was, and we would find pay dirt. For one thing, we didn't want to lose him. That guy gave us the best situational awareness that we could get. Don't be surprised, but sometimes the poop you get at the normal guy level is a little less than accurate. We had access to him and were able to talk to him via Colunga and Briola. They didn't look like the White Devils that the locals talked about. Second, if someone did listen to us, we sure as hell would have been able to clear up that place in a fucking hurry. He would also be swooped away and given to some other unit and we would be out there stumbling around in the dark, doing the fucking sweeping and mopping after the dance. I guess it was a good thing in a way, not having him taken from us and allowing us to be pretty successful.

To develop an asset, it is usually the job of those trained to do so. They can't do it though, if they don't want to use him or listen to us. It's the job that we were not trained to do, but the mopping is what the infantry does for all the cool guys. So much for training for assaults, raids, mount, actions on contact, first aid, and everything else. It's just not what you get to do. Most of the units that end up with great finds, well, it is just good for them.

Now we are moving out and headed to a couple of places. We come upon a dry river bed or a draw. Here is where people like to plant shit. One, they use it to travel, so they fucking plant shit and keep us out. Second, the charges that they set are target specific. No man will set off a charge that only a vehicle would detonate. Third, it is an obstacle. We know that all obstacles are being observed. The lieutenant is in the lead and has a mine roller in front. It is a big hulking piece of equipment and is a fucking pain. It limits the maneuverability and speed of the vehicle, but it in turn helps to save the lives of soldiers. In my mind I am thinking about another incident with a Stryker. It was in C Co. (Charlie Company) 1-17 Infantry, our Battalion. That platoon suffered their loss in a river bed that took out seven of the platoon's leaders. It was a great loss felt across the Brigade. I was working as a battle captain when the news came over the net. As the information came I realized I knew exactly who the people were. It was a platoon I had gone on a mission with. This was a platoon that I visited with others before and I was envious of. I remembered feeling good to just be around them. I remembered making my way to their Stryker and chatting with them. That blast was one of the biggest to date. There were discussions and we were all reminded to not place all the leaders together. I knew that there were certain things that dictate how things are done. I figured that the leader made the call and he had his reasons. It is one of the hardest things that you will have to deal with, for a very long time. Just trying to put myself in their shoes made me ill. We are rolling down and I see the first vehicle make it down into the river bed. Then the second, the third, and here we go. There had been incidents where it wasn't the first vehicle to get blown up. As the enemy adapted their techniques it was necessary for us to change as well. At this point we had all been successful following the lead vehicle with the rollers. As the mission continues, it seems you are doing multiple things at once: watching, scanning, relaying info over the radio. Calculating how to be unpredictable in a way that makes sense. To be in the vehicle at this time as it is going over the edge when gravity begins to pull it down is like a bad amusement park ride. Waiting for the damn thing to hit the bottom and knowing that this might just be your last hee-haw is fucking crazy.

I am reminded of my oath, the oath of the NCO. Not only am I supposed to provide good leadership, take care of the men and do my job. I should not use my position or rank to fucking get over. If they go, we go. And I ain't going nowhere.

I'm in for the ride and going to be there if and when the shit hits the fan. It's what we get paid the big bucks for. I used to think about some young soldier out there having to deal with bad situations (I'm not talking about a loss of water pressure or having to wait for the next pool table to open up). I wanted to be there and make sure that I could help in the decision. A young soldier doesn't have a choice to make like that. He has to do whatever he is told, and pray he learned enough to live. Being on that FOB made me feel like less of a man and soldier. If some had to face the bad guys, I wanted to be in that fight. I had more experience, was older, and if it was time to pay, I would pay that bill.

So, we come down and drag through the sand at the bottom. We follow the lead vehicle upstream and find a good place to come out on the other side. Most people would think that you have this vehicle and that you can climb walls, but it isn't like that. You go through the right type of terrain and try to prevent the thing from flipping over. It's mostly common sense. We knew the limitations, and so did the enemy. That leaves you with an asshole puckered up. You would swear your ass grabbed about two inches of fucking seat, being clinched in between your cheeks.

Yes, you might see the dune buggies and motorcycles in a recruiting video or on display, but that is not normal guy stuff. No, we roll and do so on the ground. The preferred method of travel is air: zip in and zip out. No ambushes, IEDs, or fucking dogs. Taking out most of the risk in traveling decreases the danger of the whole operation. Bullets still fly and aircraft do get shot at, but in a fucking metal box going up and down turning, and tilting? It starts working on your nerves. No matter what the vehicle is, soldiers know the possible outcome. It stays on your mind, and is with you every step of the way as you move. As we travel through the dry bed, we slither our way out of the far side. Again, on the way out you see sky, as the vehicle goes up over the lip and is suddenly brought back by gravity. It's like being at sea. There is the sky and you are going up. Once you begin to come down you only see blue. Your mind is telling you that you are moving but your picture is still the same. Suddenly, along with the slam of the ground, the earth and horizon return as well. You check out the troops, hear no boom, and the vehicle didn't break. It is all good and we continue to go. We snake along and head toward a known field. It looked like it was going to be a homestead at one time, but all that had been built was an 8-10 foot wall around the location. This was one of the possible locations that we were planning on using as a patrol base. We pulled up and decide to take the for sale sign off the front. Nothing really is simple but the occupation of your patrol base could be harder than it has to be.

Everything is important, and I will take most of the load while the lieutenant begins planning for missions. We go and search the area and then get the vehicle with the rollers to roll the whole area. While they are doing that, we begin to identify positions and reports begin to go up. Once the area is rolled out we occupy and begin our priorities of work. Sectors of fire are identified, the FO is setting in targets and locating targets to register and shift from. The medic is finding a good place to put in a trench to shit and piss in. We are also placing out an area for aircraft to land if possible.

The lieutenant is sending in reports and then getting ready to get patrols out. It is a fucking chore. Everybody is out doing all the things that we are supposed to. One squad goes ahead and finishes up, and begins to get chow. They are the first in the chute and out. They stuff the food down and replenish their supplies. I stay and take care of anything unfinished, and make sure we are ready to defend if necessary. The lieutenant surveys the area and we look and plan specifics. We talk about dismount movements, personnel, weapons systems and so on. After he is done, we go over it and gather up the package and set the time for the complete order. The leaders get the basic five W's (Who, What, When, Where, Why) and brief their guys. Once that is done specific work is started. The next step is to give out the poop all in one sitting.

We climb in the back of a vehicle and begin the brief. All questions are held to the end and notes are taken. As soon as it is done all the leaders are off to brief their guys and ensure that all equipment is checked. Back briefs are checked by them and then, spot-checked by us. We get together back in a vehicle and he checks what was put out. From that point we are on a time hack. We have time and in that time, we begin to joke and talk shit.

Of course, the lieutenant comes up first. He is probably one of the youngest and we talk about getting hitched. He talks about a "friend" and we rag on him. What specifically is a "friend?" We talk and joke and I told him that he was going to be hitched up before he knew it. I told him that it was messed up that he started to see her right before deployment. She was out there back at home and to her the clock was ticking, not for her to have children, but the time counted as being in a relationship. I told the lieutenant that he was getting boned and that even though he was not there, the time was going to count. I also said, that as soon as he got home it was going to be time to get hitched. For him it was like knowing her for the past two or three months. For her, hell, they had already been going out almost a year. We sat there and I listened to the stories prior to me being in the platoon, listening and laughing at these men finding a small thing to laugh about. This was where a lot of men would shut down or realize a fear of the unknown. Here were a bunch of regular soldiers that were thrown together for not fitting in elsewhere. I was happy with that, because what they did have in common was a sense of duty and loyalty to each other. It was all held together by the acceptance that we were not good enough to be anywhere else. As time drew near, the element formed up and prepared to dismount to a village. They were going to be there for a short time and return. There was no real time hack because the intent was for the lieutenant to get face time and do politics. They would return around nightfall. Some of the guys were having problems with a couple of dogs chasing them out of the village. I remember seeing the last members having to turn around and try to get the dogs to stop chasing them. Overall the day proved to be successful. I remember the lieutenant talking to these specific people before. We were back as a show of our commitment to help the area. They were not ready to bite off on the idea that we were there to help, not yet. It hadn't helped with the company rotation schedule putting different platoons through that section every other day. As a gesture, we were back and the lieutenant made good on his promise. He had a successful engagement and was even adopted into one local tribe.

They liked him and he was seen as a good person. The lieutenant balanced everything on his plate and he did it well. He knew what the right thing was and he was doing it, all on his own. There was actually nothing I thought he could do better. All I was really needed for was to help out in the management of the platoon. Otherwise, he was everything you wished an officer to be.

They say you can see good in a person's eyes and feel it in their presence. I'm not gonna say he was just young or naïve. It was more like he made you feel like there were no surprises and he was honest and humble. He was not polluted or spoiled. He had a clear conscience and was doing exactly what he wanted. For that, he was happy and it showed in his being.

Politics and negotiations are not a grunt's forté. What we are meant to do is our job, to go out and fight. Then, people want to know what is going on "Out There." Next, you are asked to get info, send up reports, and hand out treats to people who are hurting, or waiting for you to mess up and kill you. In some stuffy classroom you may get a brief on just about anything. It is usually mandatory to say you had sufficient training if something goes wrong. No one wants to be there; it will never be a private who's doing an officer's or sergeant's job. If something is that important, you will see the appearance of some staff officer. Then again, you might find yourself doing something that you never thought you would ever do: someone else's job.

The point is, we shoot shit. We go where bad stuff happens. You wouldn't have a mechanic build you a bird house. You wouldn't have a truck driver as a yoga instructor, and you sure as hell wouldn't want a crack-head in charge of your finances. Different skills for different reasons, and that is what they do. In the infantry, we do shit that others were trained to do. Everyone has an opinion about this and how it's fucked up because the specialists are not there. We do stuff like intel, EOD, medical, sanitation, payroll, and it all adds up. After "Yes Sir" here and there, you are now doing everyone's job but yours. With that being said, you have your own technique. It's not the preferred technique, but a technique. Here is what the guys on the ground figured out. Here is how we do others' jobs. Here is what you get paid the big bucks for. Life sucks, shit ain't fair, and when in doubt, dump it on the infantry.

Nothing Good Lasts Forever

If the "Grand Poobah" elder, or whoever we were talking to said he knew nothing, we had our own way to test if he was telling the truth or not. This is how we ended up getting real information. The preferred technique was to take the lieutenant's team one way, and a second team the other way. Armed to the teeth but more importantly, with a bag of candy, we found that the kids were willing to tell you where the bombs, guns, attacks, and people came from. This verified the story of the parents or not. This time the lieutenant was given intel that there was a student of a bomb maker that was trained by us. He was training others and teaching them to defeat our systems. There was also a cave that held the explosives being manufactured for all the IEDs in the area. We were told that the specific workers could be identified because the palms of their hands were white. This was caused by the reaction of the chemicals coming in contact with their skin. There was also another cache in the area located in a certain compound. Supposedly, weapons were located in a garden, where they were buried. Would you imagine that it was in the compound of an important figure in the local community? An IED factory was also in the area. Of course, it was full of materiel as well as IEDs. They were pre-assembled and ready to go out and be planted. At that specific time, we were also giving out blankets and lamps. The time of year was getting cool, and farmers were often seen walking at night. We were trying to save them from being shot, so we were giving out lights. They were to use them so as to let us know that they were out and about in the middle of the night. It was for their protection, and to let us know they were not bad guys out there planting bombs in the dark. This was a program that was going on and we were told to give these items out, not only for the safety concerns but for political reasons as well. I guess we were trying to work on our image and change the way people thought of us. I did not know what to think about it all and it kind of left me confused. Here we had people that had never seen us before and hated us, or maybe liked us. It is really hard to tell when you are giving away free shit. If it was me, on the receiving end, I would do or say whatever I thought you wanted to hear to get it. We were giving away more than just blankets and lanterns. We were also giving away hard currency, and could not tell with total certainty that these people were good or bad. Someone out there was making bombs, working for the bomb factory, planting bombs, and yet we were acting like everyone was a good guy. If that was so, why the hell were we there, if everyone was good? Let's pack it up and go home. However coming into country, we were told that we were there to fight for the Afghan people? Yeah? Then I'm a mercenary, so pay me!

I just thought that we didn't think it through, things like giving a guy $2,000 for denting his car. This is a place where people make like $200-$300 a year. Yeah, they are going to milk this shit. We were acting like these people could be bought. We forgot they had been through war and were not Americans, not greedy. If we were giving away free stuff, take as much as you can till you can get no more. Then complain how we are mean and cruel. If you are good enough, you can at least get shut-up money. These people were smart, and knew how to use our own rules against us. If we were really concerned about these people, we would not have given them shit. If we did, maybe it should be by a legit organization and not the infantry on the ground. Have we ever heard of humanitarian aid? Are there not organizations that do this stuff?

I once read a board that said, "I gotta be willing to hand out lucky charms and 5.56 with equal enthusiasm." That shit was the most real thing I had ever seen written. Plus, we are now bringing new things into the combat zone. If the bad guys see some of the stuff we are giving, maybe the families might become victims. "Oh you got a nice little lamp there. I'll take that." Now Mr. Bad Guy looks like a farmer but he's planting bombs.

When the patrol returned with the collected info, the men were happy. It was actual work, and the idea seemed to be panning out. I guess it is the little things that count and a potentially big win for the days to come. All information was sent up to the company and we began to prepare to sleep. I slept in the squad leader position and laid in the hell hole for the night. Thinking and preparing for the next day kept my mind going till I was out.

I woke the next day and was greeted by one of the guys. I guess Dicks was pissed and told everyone, on our company's net, that he was through with our platoon. At first, I didn't know if what I was hearing was what was said. I tried to shake off the fog of the morning and put in a dip. I asked Lendrum, who was a driver and on radio watch at the time, to start all over again. I listened to what the soldier said that he heard. I then asked for him to rewind as if he was a tape deck and see what was going on before. If what he was saying was true, I wanted to understand what led to the statement. I don't know what was said or done, and it didn't matter. I didn't think that this fucker was going to talk shit on the net and pout. What he did was wide open and out on the company net. Our first sergeant let my platoon know, the entire company know, that he didn't like the platoon. Looking back, I should have been okay with that. I had never seen or heard of this kind of crap, but it was out. Everyone knew for a long time that my platoon was getting the shitty end of the stick. It can be passed off as rumors or misunderstanding. Some people would point out the silver lining and do what I used to do. I did that, because that is what I thought it was to be a team player. All that was different now. No longer were there rumors and hearsay. The minute he did that, it verified the simple fact that the platoon was hated. Sure, we had different ways of thinking and doing, but I was not out there to make this guy happy. Or, was I worried about making him like me? I was told a long time ago that you should not worry about your evaluation or do things for any other reason than that for the mission and the men. If you held true to what you were taught, all that would take care of itself. I tried to walk a thin line before and make the higher ups try to understand or at least listen to what was going on, and it always came back to bite me in the ass. Some people just want what they can get from you, and will take as much as they can till you no longer have a use. Then a hatchet comes out, you are cut off and a younger and less experienced person takes your place. This was also the time in the units that "yes men" were being bred to be the caterers to those of higher privilege. Instead of a sense of responsibility to our oath, "To provide Good Leadership to the men," it was becoming a time to agree with whatever the most popular and beneficial idea out there was which would help catapult your career. Meat-eating knuckle-dragging men with strict obedience to The Master, was the new generation being groomed.

So great! Our fearless leader cuts us off in the middle of our little operation, didn't come out to the same operation either. I was amazed. It was as if this was fucking grade school. Fuck-head over here wants to be a spoiled kid and not allow us to play in his group. Forget that! We were in a fucking war and trying to not get killed, while doing our duties. The day goes on and communication with the fearless one was short and to the point. If not, there would be an uncomfortable pause. Our fearless one decided to go out with his bitch platoon and here they are on the radio. They decided to see how fast the new vehicle would go and were racing across the desert and making the cool guy club look way better than us on our field trip. Despite any intel we had of multiple IED belts getting planted out there, here they were on a joy ride. As they were off having such a good time, our platoon hits pay dirt. Sticking to the plan and getting out with the people started to give us a good picture of what was going on in this town, and the other surrounding ones. The intel that the locals were giving seemed to be pretty good. It looked like we might be able to stop some of the bullshit in the area and do some good as well. Of course, we were pending a huge mission and were all going to need to head back to the largest FOB in the area for a quick refit. While there, we would go and check on some stuff, get some stuff worked on, but everyone was thinking of the snacks that would be available for purchase. All the lickies and chewies always tasted better when you had time to build them up so much in your mind, and they were an awesome motivator when the sucky times came.

After getting all the new info I figured I would send up a request to switch rotations with another platoon. That way we could finish what we were doing there and still be able to make a re-supply run. Yes, it would suck, it meant we would be out longer, but we would be able to find the IED belt that had been recently placed. This would also prove that our intel was good. There was a possibility of catching them in the act. Getting them alive would lead to more information as well. There were people willing to help us to find these obstacles as well as being able to further develop a good source. Again, if correct, this would also confirm that our source was legit and knew about the area. Despite all our efforts and even being willing to stay out there and get the stuff, we were pulled off the mission. I think it was actually the lieutenant that was told that if we didn't get back the next day, we were not going to go at all. It didn't matter what we had or if we were able to reduce a big fucking threat in our area. We were not going to be allowed to change our day to do a re-supply. There was no talking, no switching, no leeway at all. I sat there in amazement. How did this make sense? We were able to actually get the bombs, find the factory, and get some bad people, all reducing the threat in the area, and probably save some lives. We were on to operations in the area, and just like that we were told to cease and desist. How could you turn something like that down?

To this day, I think about it, and it fucking pisses me off and kills me. All because it would fuck up the rotation. All that had to be done was to have a different platoon go early to a FOB. Shit, that would be something that no one would argue about. It would be getting pushed back a day that would be the hard part for us. We knew that and yes it sucked, but how often do you get to take out a large threat, and the people operating against you? I felt as if it didn't matter what we had found or did. We were allowed to do a mission we wanted and it was busy work. If we did or didn't find anything, so what? The lieutenant tried to communicate the situation and what we were trying to accomplish. Despite his best efforts, we were given our orders, and so be it. Guess we had to put the war off for Funyuns? Madder than hell, we did what we were told and headed out. Again, to this day, I hold hate in my heart for that shit. Never will I forget this crap.

We were constantly building houses of cards. We were told that we were there to fight for the people of Afghanistan. We were to care and give away free shit. We were sent out on missions every day to improve the safety of the area. We told the people we were there to help and that they should trust us, and they did. We were doing the right thing, and if what we were told was true, we should have finished the job. We let those people down and we were just playing a game. We didn't want to win. We left that day, and I knew shit was fucked up.

I was in the trail and the last vehicle. We were in a *wadi*, or dry river bed. I remember one vehicle going up the bank, then the second. We were snaking around and trying to be unpredictable. The vehicles made their way out from my ten o'clock position as we were following suit, headed out from the low ground. The third vehicle goes up and here we come, here comes the fucked up part of this bullshit ride. The nose shot up to the sky and we were all holding on. As the nose began to come down an explosion goes off and grabs your heart, throat, and lungs. As we were coming down to level off, a mushroom cloud appears. The first vehicle is hit. It is the lieutenant and first squad. The vehicle is in smoke, shit, piss and ass, and so begins the chaos. The second vehicle stopped and I told my driver to fucking hit it. We floored it and stayed on the same tracks that were made by the lieutenant's vehicle. I passed the other vehicles and told the driver to hug the side of their vehicle. As we are rolling up two soldiers from the second vehicle are sprinting up. We are close behind and the rear door is blown open. The troop door is open and men are falling out like bees. Not just any bee, but like a whole nest that has been sprayed and these bees are falling on the ground in a weird confusion close to death. The outline of the ramp is pretty clear due to smoke, dust and everything else coming out of it. As the men are coming out, so is smoke and you hope another one will come out. Guys are covered in shit and falling one next to the other. I jump on the net and call it up. At this point I don't know shit, just that the vehicle was taken out and the guys are not in good shape. I am trying to get numbers and assess the casualties, but at this point, the best thing that I could do was hold on to the mic, and get help out there as quick as I could. The actual money makers right then were the soldiers. You can look at a book, and think, *hah! I'll pass.* Maybe it just doesn't seem like a good read. Maybe you don't like the cover. These men, they are not what they seem. You could go ahead and pass them up but, it would be your loss. Buck sergeants, specialists, and staff sergeants didn't matter. Their fucking brothers were in that shit, we were pending who knows what. Just like that, this old book became a million dollar bill. I sat there and did the talking on the radio. Fuck sakes, we were hopping and popping and making money. Men had the medical equipment out. Doc was a smaller guy, but turned into Billy Bad-ass on the spot. Teams were separating the men, while security was getting sorted. After I sent in the initial message, I got outside and watched controlled mayhem in double time. Lenny was the driver and the blast hit right behind him. Roesch, was the Vehicle Commander (VC) and was trapped in behind the system. The blast pushed the systems to the back and he was not able to get free. Colunga and Swain were on the vehicle and got to Roesch and pulled him out somehow. Doc was directing the CLS's (Combat Lifesavers) on injuries and patients. McDowell was one of the squad leaders and was out setting up the HLZ (Helicopter Landing Zone) Brinkley was on security and coordinating the perimeter. Briola was on the ground and helping with equipment and personnel. Men were everywhere. Leaders, well they lead from the front. They set the example and are easy to follow. Every one of these men were that. Yes, the shit just hit the fan and without ever stopping, they went from moving, to full-out sprint. I do believe that there is nothing in this world greater than one man doing everything in his power to save another. Somewhere you have never been, in the worst place that you could imagine, a group of men that were rejected by their own kind, were doing all they could for another. All we were seen as were fucking pieces of shit, and at that moment, we were *the* shit! The most glorious and beautiful thing that a unit could do, was performed as if by masters. Without thought, or expected reward, these fucking heroes were the best example of greatness that went without knowing. Training and knowledge are taught and shared. This is different: it is your will to protect another. At this moment, they are hoping to save the life of the brothers that they have grown to know. It is fucking love motherfucker, and it is beautiful. I make my way to the lieutenant. He is getting pulled out of the vehicle and they are telling him to get his legs free. He said he couldn't, nor could he put pressure on them. He is pulled out of the troop door and laid behind the vehicle. At this time we have choppers in the air and en route. I ask him some questions to see how he would react and Doc sees blood seeping from his legs. As we are talking to him he starts in.

"Watch for secondary devices? What about security?" We were like, "Fuck that! We got that shit, let's worry about you!"

I talk to him for a bit and move on to help in the triage. Roesch was stuck in there and Doc told them to move him back from the other injured. Baron helps to pull him back and I remember them dragging him. Roesch was holding his arm at the time. As he was getting dragged there was a pistol being dragged on his lanyard. When he let go to reach out for it, blood just started to squirt out and land in the dry sand. It stayed there for a bit and then seemed to get pulled into the ground. He made his way to a stretcher and was prepped to get picked up.

I ran over to see Fairchild who was in the rear of the vehicle and he told me he was good. I looked at him and he was dazed and in shock. He was there and got shit all covered on his face. Lenny the driver was okay, but he was hurt and out on his feet. Woods, on one of his last missions, was dazed with eyes bigger than plates. Him and Rosario were together and pulling security between two vehicles, dazed and fucked up. I talked to them and they were gone. They didn't know what happened and were bleeding from the ears, eyes dilated and they were emotionally unstable. We got them to settle down, got them away from the vehicle and ready to move. I went back to finish the medivac request and give the best situation report that I could. At this time birds were minutes out and there was only one Blackhawk available. They were in communication and we were ready to get these men out of here. There was not enough room to fit all nine men, so the driver, Lenny and the squad leader, Fairchild, gave up their need for attention, and stayed. What sucked about the whole thing, was we could see the FOB. We were only 3,000 meters from the front gates. It was in one of those little low points that this IED was set up in. Since we were really close, we figured we would be able to get them checked out asap. We didn't see or think that they were having any internal problems, but what the fuck? We are 11 Bravos, supposed to be hard as woodpecker lips. Then again, it was a decision that was made and we would get them seen as soon as we could. That being said, there was a change, and I had to let the company know. Before that, the bird landed and we saw the wounded get loaded on. I went to call it in. As I was on the radio, the escort bird decided to land and they helped to get the most seriously wounded guys out of there. Again, those were some great fucking people. I found out later that the men were impressed and the impression lasted.

Okay, so here it is. Get ready for this and try not to do as I did. I called up to make an adjustment to the number of wounded actually being flown out and was given the response, "Yeah, okay. We'll talk about awards later." I fucking flipped. The things that were said were not for civilian ears, nor military. I do know that I will answer for that shit one day, but I will have to tell old St. Peter, "The guy was a dick!" My fucking leader just responds like nothing and thinks that I am a fucking punching bag in the middle of this shit. I was so fucking hot that the sand under the vehicle I was in turned to fucking glass.

"Is this a fucking pissing contest? Is this the fucking time that you want to take a fucking stab at the platoon you were done with again? Showing the fucking price for not kissing your ass and fucking sucking your dick?" This turd is now on my hate list. I want to be there the day he gets his, and fuck sympathy. Fuck doing the right thing, fuck this guy!!!

To add to the misery, here are some apples. You like apples, well here are some fucking apples. Parts of the vehicle were some 200 meters away. We were left there in the IED belt (the belt we were told about by the locals). One of the reasons we wanted to stay out there was to find shit like this, to find it and make sure what just happened to us, would not happen to anyone else. We found it all right. I called for support to come and help get us out and I was told that it was too dangerous. We were going to have to wait till things were done and a group was assembled to go recover that damaged vehicle. No QRF (Quick Reaction Force). No one from our company. No one was going to come out for a couple of hours. Well, it turned out to be seven. We were 3,000 meters from the front gate we could see. No one was coming to get us, and we were left out there alone. Our unit, our post, the command, the Army left us out there on our own. We stayed out there and were fucking pissed. We didn't get any other information or reason. Everyone questioned why would we be left out there?

Correct me if I'm wrong here, but this is the Army, right? Did we not join the Army of the USA? The best military in the world, deployed to Afghanistan–not Disneyland–Afghanistan. We have been at war for ten years. We have been deployed, trained, and heard all the war stories, and we are not getting help because someone thinks "It is too dangerous to get help?" Well fuck me! Guess there is a bigger difference in our versions of not leaving your soldiers behind, and it gets even better.

Good news though, the helicopters we had now, were gunships, "Seamus as well as Corsair." Those were their call sign. They were our aviation units on site. They were the only ones who actually helped us more than anyone else. Not only did help, but they stayed with us as long as they could. Till they were out of fuel. Now, they did have some fucking news to give us. They said that they were picking up chatter from radios that were talking about us getting hit. The enemy had fixed our position and were talking about attacking us. The same stuff came from the battalion. I then got told that we were to be ready for an attack. In a conversation with a pilot I told him that this was a good thing. Those motherfuckers could bring it because I had a fuckin' can of whoop-ass waiting for those fucks. Traffic was coming and going and we sat there. We fixed the position and security as best as we could and waited. I didn't know about no virgins, but these fuckers were going to find out. I was fixing to send as many of these fucks up there to find out, and the pleasure was all mine. Once the aircraft took off, then we were really left out there alone. My command was at home, and I did not want to talk to them. Here we were in Afghanistan and they could not recover the men from their company because it was too dangerous. For fuck sakes, where did these morons think we were going to go? Bermuda? We were out on a mission and knew about this very thing. We were willing to pass on our day of resupplying at the FOB to get the kind of information that would save lives, and we were called off. We were told specifically about the very IED belt that we had hit. Oh, and my dick-head first sergeant was just racing through the area hours ago, then it was okay. Now he probably went back to the tent to do his college courses. He didn't fight for us when we were almost blown up, so why would he worry about us when we did get blown up?

So here we are, waiting for the whites of the enemy's eyes in my fucking sight that is. Security was green and chatter was a must. I am getting reports from the battalion and they are hearing that we are in for an attack. At this point, the only other friendlies we had encountered were the medivac and they left. We did not know the status of the wounded, and at this time were only hoping that we would not hear of the flight becoming an Angel Flight. We are going over all equipment and making sure that we had recovered everything, so as to not give the enemy anything to use against us. We are looking at debris that flew over 200 meters from the center of the explosion. A blown up vehicle is sitting there, and we are trying to remember how everyone actually looked. Lenny was right in front of the blast, and was lucky as fuck to miss the blast. The lieutenant was not so lucky though. We are pulling security and I am sitting on the left side of the blown up vehicle. The other two are making the two other points of a triangle and pulling security on their sectors. As the time passes, there is a comment here and there. Talking about the brothers that flew off and what each one of us had seen. There wasn't time to think right then and there. You have done the drill and you are focused on that. It is training, and when everything goes to shit, you perform. Now though, it is after the fact. The quiet goes away, you start to settle down, and remember what you saw. You may have done something that you cannot remember, but if you saw it, it comes back. Sometimes in pieces. Others block it all out. Some remember another thing completely and do not believe what others witnessed them do. Now was the time that others put their memories of a person to the thing they saw. Then they remember their buddy's face, some sound or words, the pistol being dragged and the pool of blood in the sand. It then becomes talk about how this could have happened? Right in view of the front gate? We had a large tower in the middle that was used to scan and look into the lower spots for stuff being planted. It was the same one that Briola used to find a group that was digging around one night and ended getting their asses blown up. What about this question. Did anyone ever actually try to go out into the population and get with the people? Here we were on a 48-hour mission and found out this much. What was the fucking deal? It is kind of hard to make an effective plan when you are sitting in your HQ. How about when your soldiers are reporting their findings and letting you know valuable stuff, and you just don't fucking care? You make your decisions on what you think your boss wants to hear. Forget the intel and the ideas from the men on the ground. I looked back and remembered talking to the CO the first time we met and asked, "Why didn't we just break up the company's area into three?" That way we would get to see the same faces, and they could see us build trust and confidence in the population. Then again, who the fuck am I? Well I didn't pay for an education, but these guys needed a refund. Dumb as a box of rocks.

Now I'm just a regular guy but these educated fuckers were stupid as shit. I was answered and it seemed like poor me. I am not smart enough to know. I then remembered that the lieutenant was talking about the same thing after a patrol. I know it was mentioned several times and it fell on deaf ears. One of the elders said he had met different people and he didn't know who to trust, particularly because they say one thing and then just leave, then they have to deal with new soldiers on the next visit. It was only after the lieutenant told him that we were not going anywhere and were planning on continuing to come out that he gave out all the information that he had. He then also made the lieutenant a part of the tribe, a big deal. As far as the lieutenant was concerned, he was gone now, and there was no real chance that he was going to make it back to the war. I just hoped that he was going to be ok.

Now sitting in the duck blind the platoon was worried, shaken up, pending doom and looking forward to fucking something up. Five hours later, we hear that the recovery team is ready. It would, of course, take time. Why? Because we are in Afghanistan; it's dangerous. Plus we are stuck in the fucking IED belt that we were hoping to find, except we could not fuck up the rotation. So, they had to get an engineer asset that had a fucking grader/ bulldozer in front to clear their way out to us.

Good thing no one had to take a shit—they might have set an IED off. Are you fucking kidding me? We roll out the fucking gates and drive all over the place. Is the danger any higher, or the possible outcome any different? Nope. But we are expendable, and just like that, you know the difference between trigger pullers and support. Remember the fearless one, drag racing across the desert to see the maneuverability of his new precious vehicle with his bitch platoon? Now here we are, and despite everyone else risking it every day, today that changes. Instead of testing out that vehicle on how fast it went, why didn't he test it out on his way to us? He could have picked up the remaining injured and taken them to get medical attention. Nope! Not our guy.

Anyway, finally, these turds make it out to us, and we are like, "Hook this fucker up and lets Yallah!" Let's get this shit going, right? Oh no, not so fast. There is debris all over the place and it has to be collected. However, the fucking recovery team says no way are they going to do it, despite having the assets to do it. So, either we go out and collect it ourselves, or they are just going to sit there and wait. That, or they leave with the blown up vehicle. You know, the one we saw our brothers come crawling out of, bleeding on the ground. They would leave and we would have to stay and secure the area. Maybe someone would come back to collect all the debris? Like this recovery team. No, they don't want to do it. All because it is so fucking dangerous. How fucking stupid do these fuckers get?

If they were not going to do their job, then why hadn't we just got the fuck out of there hours ago? So, just to tempt fate again, we all dismount and begin to walk and comb the fucking desert. Yeah, just like that. Like the fucking dumb asses on fucking *Spaceballs*. I'm thinking just like the one guy when asked, did you find anything yet? Response, "Man, we ain't found shit!" And there is the sense of humor that we in the Combat Arms have used to get over the dumbest shit you never hear about. It is now so fucking dangerous that these fucks build a road out to us. It is *their job* to "recover" us. That's what a *recovery team* does. We know it is dangerous, however it's okay for *us* to walk around dragging our—might as well say *balls*—and knuckles to do another job that isn't even ours. So, we did it, all just to get back to a fucking tent, in the mother-fucking desert, to relax. Ha! More like for some blueberry Pop Tarts. Now here we are combing the desert as if mother-fucking leaf-eating environmentalists are fixing to protest, and we are really screwed. Like the police call rules say, if it didn't grow there, Pick That Shit up! However, how much could you take? I mean, one heaping scoop of bullshit after another. "You do not matter." You have got that by now. Really, someone just fucking shoot me already. I want to fly on the helicopter. I want to fly far, far, away. How much? You don't know. You think we are lucky? You have no fucking idea. Before we leave, we have to move our vehicles back, way back. Why? Because while hauling ass to get to the fucking men that were blown up, our vehicle stopped just in time. In front of our fucking vehicle, is another damn IED. Yeah, we could have hit it. We could also have blown it up while doing another person's job. We could have lost more men while combing the desert. So we pull back as they blow three more IEDs. One more could have been enough, but nope, we sat there and watched as each mushroom cloud is formed from the place we risked everything, over and over again. We did more than our share. We did more than our jobs. Despite all the "support," we had to do all of it, just to go to a tent we call home. We have to return to the company that finds you subpar, to a place where we are treated like we're not good enough. So we can sit and think about what the fuck are we really doing here?

We are alone. We will never be good enough. We will never have what we are supposed to. What we do have, is knowing. We know, and I know, if we don't take care of each other, we will die here, alone. The lieutenant is gone, and now, it is all on me. Looking back, it fucking hurts my soul, and I find it hard to fucking keep it straight. Like I told my guys back when I was in the 173rd. "Be careful what you wish for motherfucker, you just might get it." Here it is, and now I'm a motherfucker too. I needed to see the silver lining in things. Thinking about it and writing this story after the fact I can say this. When you have the greatest things to lose, you have the chance of being great yourself. It isn't till you decide that you are actually willing to die, that you let go and truly become free. Don't ask me how to get to that point. However, seeing the beautiful mayhem and those heroes' acts that day, I realized these men were already there. They had been there all along. There, they have been for a long time, all alone and waiting for their time, or that magic number. What other bullshit and events did they experience that made them that way? I don't know, but I can say this. It was not just war. No, it was the culmination of everything that turned what should have been a regular platoon, into dead men walking. So fuck it, if they go, I'm going too. Maybe we can take as many motherfuckers with us as possible? *Black Sheep!*

BAD INFIDEL

Previous page: A picture is worth a thousand words they say. This picture melts the ice and takes away the cold. Anger and frustration get you warmer than a bottle of Jameson. This vehicle is what Lt Osborne and Sgt Roesch were in. Here is where their careers ended in the military.

The results of a home-made bomb on a regular vehicle. This one was blown up right outside the entrance to our base at the time.

I was having problems before I got here, after I got to the platoon, and that was with a good officer. Now, not only was I going to have to pull my own weight, but do OJT again. How fucking hard can it be? Some probably think that they could do this better. If they were in charge they would know exactly what to do. Usually they are in the middle of the group and it's easy to be an armchair quarterback. I didn't really care and knew it was something else getting piled on my plate. It was going to be difficult and probably a pain in the ass, but I was up for the challenge. I didn't expect to fail, but coming out on the other side beat up and bruised. What's the worst thing that can happen?

The Men From the Mountain

We rolled into the FOB and led the vehicle back onto the small base. Both Lenny and Fairchild were taken to the aid station and looked after. At this time, I was tired, beat, and probably in shock from the whole thing. Was it the IED? The mayhem, and the wounded on the ground? How about the marvelous response from our fellow soldiers who thought it was *too dangerous* to come and get us? Maybe the part where we had to pick up our pieces in this IED belt we were in, just get back home?

Whatever it was, I was tired and didn't even have the ability to get mad. Then I heard a conversation from one of the bitches, laughing. They were talking and saying how dumb we were for going into an IED belt that we knew about. As if there was a freaking sign warning us to stay out and we chose to go in there anyway. No motherfucker, it was what we were told. We wanted to find it and warn others until it could get moved, but no. We had to leave all intel and return to go get fucking chips and dip. What a fucking piece of work some of these hard guys were. It is one thing to be a hard-ass, but some try to fake the funk and just come out as assholes. Then, I was given a fucking option to go to the FOB and get lickies and chewies, or not go at all. I was beat, and the rest of the men were way more experienced at taking this shit than me. Since the injured members of the platoon were there in the ICU, we had a chance to go see them before they were to take off. We could find out how they were and see them before they left. We planned on getting on the road and hauling ass.

The night passed and I can't even remember if there was a freaking fire mission that night. Usually the guns would go off right down from us and let you know someone needed light, or someone was having a bad day. I do not remember anything. What I do remember, was trying to get the platoon to Kandahar to see our brothers who were injured. We woke and with the three vehicles left, we began another day with one hell of a long way through some badlands. We had to travel miles to get to the largest camp in the area. We knew the scheduled time that they were going to get loaded on a plane and off to the States. We had to make it before they left, just to get some closure and know they were okay. Having no officer, that left me to fill in his gaps and start doing OJT, again. I tried to think what the hell the lieutenant really did? I know he rode up front in the lead, but what did he coordinate and get done for us to travel? Who the fuck knew? I was going to do it my way until I was told different. As for all the other stuff, I figured I would rely on the soldiers to keep me straight. To add to all the other stuff, not all of us could go. We were responsible for security on an area of the FOB's walls, and some had to stay and man positions. Either way, whoever was left, we loaded up and on our way, hoping to get there before our fellow *Black Sheep* were gone. We hit the fucking road, and there I was in the front.

Then I started thinking how fucking crazy it was up here in the lead: looking around and noticing every hill, crack, mound, piece of trash, or damn culverts. Everything seemed to give you the creeps and could have been the last thing you would see. At that time, fucktards were taking anything they could find to disguise a bomb and putting it out there to get you. At times they would use markers to let them know when to pull the trigger. If not, just bury it and hope you would hit it. In Iraq, these fucks were taking out the cement from the curbs and replacing them with another curb. This one of course had a 155 in it or whatever they could get to go boom. They would use natural markers like buildings and trees to be used like a front aiming point and a rear, maybe time your speed and get you that way. I started having all these flashbacks of how some of these things looked and some of the close calls that I had had. I was on a team for the training of the first Iraqi units. We were going down Mobile and came to a stop on the road in Iraq. I don't know what we were stopping for, but we had about 600 Iraqi commandoes behind us and we were leading the pack. Most times, I just got up on the gun and did those duties. This time was no different. So here we are on the hardball and it's about a hundred and hell degrees and the commandos get out. We were doing the 5's and 25's when we stopped. That was the new way to do things, so people would dismount and look around. We were bullshitting and talking shit about whatever was the topic of discussion and one of the commandoes walks up, and with his hand goes "Boom!" We can't speak too much Arabic, but there's a fucking international sign in the book that means "boom!" Right by our truck was a fucking 155 artillery round that had been fucked with and had wires going into the cone. Looking at it, I remembered the 155 round that got a private named Kershner in 2003. He took shrapnel to his side. The fucking thing didn't go off right and it looked like a peeled banana. We had it back in the Company area. A Co.(Alpha Company) 1-508th "RED DEVILS." Then, at that time the Red Devils were in the 173rd. IEDs were getting better the second time, and in Afghanistan they were killing soldiers left and right. I wondered if you had the time to think or have anything to say. So, as we were rolling down the road, I took time to give God a thank you. As we made our way down the road, I had Colunga in the back and he starts to get jumpy.

"Hey, this is not a good place, sergeant," he said.

I'm like, "No shit! I'm in the front, and these fuckers are aiming for me." He was like, "No, this is route Red Dog, and a lot of people get blown up here."

I saw the turn and knew all about it. In the Death Star, or my last company, the evil emperor had us drive down that thing. It was the place that you were going to get blown the fuck up, and then swarmed. Despite having the road on "Red" status, we went on it anyway. We went all the way through the villages, to a firing point that was occupied by the Canadians. When we rolled in, they asked us why or how did we get there, and we told them on route "Red Dog" and they were like, "Are you fucking nuts?" I looked and wondered why. Then they began to cover the history and all the bad things that had happened there. They said they never left their area, and if they did, they did not go past the first turn. They lost vehicles and men every time they did, and *No Mas*. I had a fucked up feeling just being this close to "Red Dog" again, but the men knew it way better than me. We rolled by and just ahead, came to a complete stop. Up ahead the road had been closed off and EOD, (Explosive Ordnance Disposal) were out. Usually, they don't just stop in the road and close off traffic. When they did, it was because they found something, so we pulled up and waited. We found the frequency that the engineers were on and we tried to talk to them. There was a buggy doing the sides and a larger transport blocking up the road with a larger antenna.

After a while I radioed back to McDowell and asked if we could find a short cut. The lead vehicle moved up far enough so that I was able to walk from on top of mine on to the engineer vehicle where we talked. He said that they had found a big one and that it was going to be a while. Assets were en route to the location and going to detonate it in place. I thought about it a while. If we didn't get to see our wounded brothers, we risked the whole trip for nothing (not Swain, he had a request for Newports and was stuck on gate duty). Not able to make the trip, he had a list. Whatever the outcome, that was going to have a funny ending. I talked to McDowell and the actual road we were on went around. We were at the fork in the road where the road could go straight and eventually come back onto the same road. After waiting for a while, I told the men we were headed on the straight part which would meet up to where the hardball comes back around. It was like 15-18 klicks (one klick equals one kilometer or a thousand meters). Not a problem, and we better get going. The last Stryker went first and waited, then we passed them in my Stryker and took the lead. All of the sudden about half a klick in I get Briola over the radio." Uh, sergeant? This is not where we want to be."

Colunga comes back and says, "I remember that building, and that's the field that they carried me out of."

No one had actually driven through the area before, but they had some fucking fights out there. The longer we drove, the more obvious it became evident that this was a mistake. So here we were in like the Beverly Hills area of the Taliban. We are working our way down the road and Colunga is tripping out. Briola is talking.

"We need to get out of here. This is no fucking sightseeing tour bullshit. This is where people die." The roads were tight. To make things worse, there are burned up trucks staggered every so often. It is as if they were trying to keep us out, slow us down, or trap us there. On the edge of the road were ditches that were like eight feet deep. Our vehicle had a bad-ass driver and everyone called him Iggy. He was calm and cool. He never said too much, but man he could drive that thing. At one point we were out of the vehicle guiding him as he drove, squeezing through the last burned truck cab.

I watched the second vehicle come through and then started to get messages over the radio. I heard McDowell shouting "Stop!" I didn't know what the hell was going on and didn't care. At that point I wanted it to be anything else than being stuck. I am on top sticking out of the hatch. I turn around and see the last vehicle's antennas. My antennas, well they are straight, the one behind, they're straight, the last one, they're at forty-five degrees to vertical. It's in the fucking ditch. At the same time, I am made aware of the fact that our road–the first road I took to get to see our injured–the first time I'm in charge–this very road we are on–is not even "Red." It's beyond red, it's completely "Black." It's fucking closed!

Of course, we hadn't heard that and now here we were. Guys are remembering the last encounters out here. Everyone is on high alert. I'm out and wondering what the fuck to do, so I get the leaders and we close it up for a huddle.

"Can we recover this vehicle?" Someone had an idea. "Okay, walk me through the plan."

"One vehicle hooks on the front and pulls to the eleven o'clock position. The second, clamps on to the high side and pulls to the nine o'clock position."

"Okay, who is going to lead this shit?"

The vehicle crews get together and I talk to the RTO (Radio Telephone Operator), and he says that we are being advised to leave immediately. The area is completely black and there are no friendlies out there. I'm like, fuck that! We are fixing to get rolling and they can talk to us later. Then, here comes the terp.

We are like rock stars: no one has seen Americans in six months. The bad guys have a stronghold on the area, and Americans just seem to be getting kicked out, or killed. The terp said the people here are friendly. "They do say, sergeant, that you need to leave before the people from the mountain return."Six klicks away is the fucking mountain and the fortress for the Taliban in the area. He said they will kill all of you and they are sure it is going to happen. Well, great! Tell the people in the mountain to stay the fuck home. As if anything else could add to the great Spring trip of 2010. We get the vehicles hooked up. I'm like, "How the fuck did you fall into the fucking ditch that we all went around?" I was busy trying to calm the masses (and myself) down by doing this and that, and they gave the vehicles a good tug, but nothing. So, here we go again and they told the drivers to put them bitches in reverse and keep going till we are out. Here they go at it again and even I'm shitting my pants. All three vehicles pull and *presto bitches!* That shit worked like a charm. Everyone was talking and saying, "Wow, didn't think that was going to work."

I'm there saying, "Hey motherfuckers, 'People From The Mountains?' Load up and lets Yallah!" Just then the local police pulled up to watch the show. I told the terp to tell them to get us to the nearest hardball so we can do like trees and fuck this shit outta here. They took off like a bullet. We were on soft terrain and I was hoping these were not the fucks from the mountain, or some other asshole who wanted to fuck us up. Then, they stopped and showed us the hardball we were looking for. We recognized a bridge and some blown up silos. Happy as fuck, we tossed some MREs (Meals Ready to Eat) to the police and hit the road. At this point I told the RTOs to report that we were gone and that they can turn that shit to green, let them know that the road was good and "We're Out!" The rest of the way was pretty easy. We came into post and had to find the ICU. They had the lieutenant front and center of the nurses station. Both legs were wrapped up and he was in a gown. After finding him and Roesch, not to mention Woods and Rosario, I went outside and told the guys to be quiet. We would have to go in groups, but then again, fuck that!

We stormed the place. We sat there and talked about what happened the day before. The lieutenant said that he was going to have a lot of surgeries. I told him he was a good man for being an officer. I was glad he was okay and it bothered me. He said, "I found out that I was allergic to morphine." I didn't know where this was going and could only respond with "What?"

He said, "It was either that or he had pushed the button too much." All he knew was that he died. I didn't know what to say or do. Is there a normal response for something like this? He said he flat-lined and they brought him back. Like normal, this was the perfect place for infantry humor. "Wow, sir, your sense of humor is awesome on drugs. You did say that you died right?" He kind of chuckled and laughed like no one else I have ever heard do before. Despite all the bullshit and the fucked up situation we talked and enjoyed the short amount of time we had left. We took pics with the lieutenant, and Roesch. While this was going on, the stories hit the fan. Colunga, Briola, and others were talking. "Do you know how we got here, sir? You're not going to believe it. We went through Jeloram!" He was like, "What?"

"Yeah, and them stupid fuckers in the third vehicle got stuck."

Lieutenant's like, "No!"

"Yeah, and the people said that we were safe, but we had to leave before the people from the mountain returned. Plus the 82nd had not been over there, and we were called and told we were not supposed to be there, and the area and road was black."

It was funny to see these fuckers tell on me.

"We got out, left, and made it here." The guys were happy to be alive. We were happy that our fellow members were gonna make it. I felt warmth in my chest. Here we were in the ICU talking to the men that were blown up one day ago. We had one hell of an experience getting there, one that will go into the history books. Outside there was a war going on, and who knows how many will not live to see it through the next "Red Dog" or "Jeloram" or an explosion? Despite all of that, I felt warm and for some reason it felt like a Christmas party. I took some time to look at the soldiers talking to their brothers. The difference between the combat troops and the hospital staff that only sees the death and injury is enormous. The moment was not long or planned. There were no parts being played or anyone acting hard. If anything, everyone was exactly who they were. It didn't matter the location or the circumstances. These soldiers were not being anything but who they were. Through everything they had experienced fighting, and in the company there was one truth that everyone shared. Together in the platoon, no one had to hide or be something they weren't. They had been through more than most and less than others. Here, everyone was accepted for who they were and this was their sanctuary. The last twenty-four hours were gone; here soldiers were gathered in celebration of life. I thought about the racket we were making. I was sure that we were in trouble and probably going to get kicked out, but I wasn't alone in feeling how much they loved each other. I watched the ICU staff members' eyes fill with tears. They were watching the men and listening to them talk. They were listening and hanging on to the words as they came out, focusing on their stories and what all they had been through to get to see their brothers.

Soldiers standing around several beds and talking is not what they got to see every day. As we said our last goodbyes there were tears in the nurses' eyes. Not particularly for the wounded who were going home, or for the turds that broke all the rules and visited the injured. I like to believe it was for the amount of love that they witnessed there. It was odd and loud, but genuine and true without any filters or bullshit. I spent some time with the lieutenant. It was a hard thing to do; I knew he was going to go home and get taken care of by a real nice girl that cared about him. The war was over for him. Now we had to get ready for a huge combined mission in the Helmand province.

Being scared for your life, that's daily. Here, its all smiles and we are happy to see our family for just a little while. We are in the hospital visiting the injured from the day before. Lt Osborne is on the bed. To his left, from back to front: Spc Gutierrez, SSg McDowell, Sgt Burk, myself, Pfc McKeen and Pfc Williams. In front of us are SSg Woods, Sgt Bae, and Pfc Spence. Sgt Fabish and Spc Barron are at the foot of the bed. On the right, from back to front: Pfc Iglesias, Sgt Colunga, Spc Rosario and SSg Briola. Far right is Sgt Nichols.

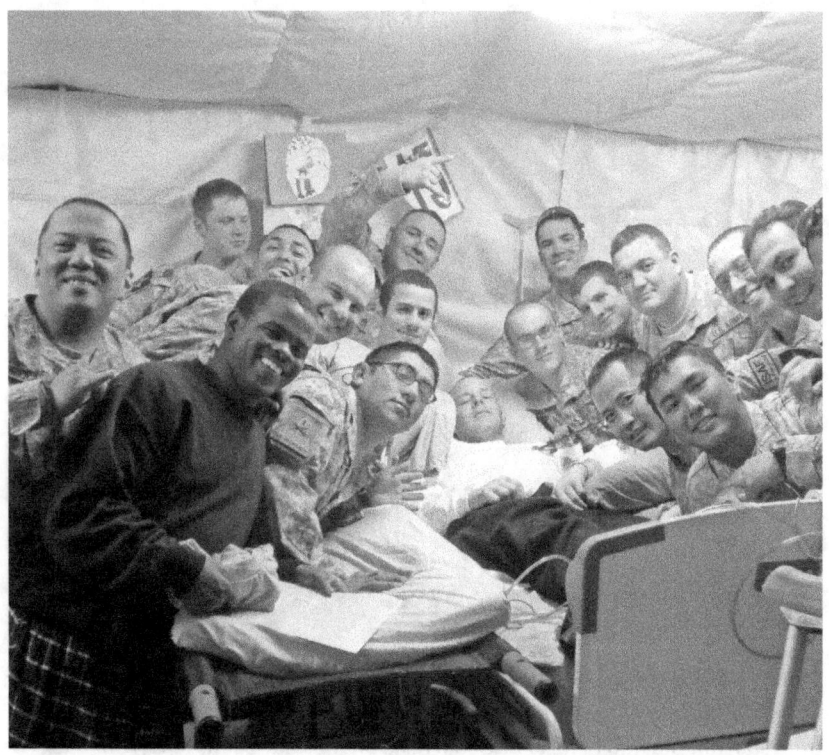

Here we are invading Sgt Roesch's sponge bath, and he doesn't look too happy about it. I did see the nurse and she had some fat fingers with bigger knuckles. On the right from back to front, Pfc Williams, Sgt Bae and Pfc Iglesias. Behind them, from back to front: SSg McDowell, Pfc Spence, Sgt Fabish, Pfc McKeen, Spc Barron and terp 1. On the left, from back to front: me, Spc Rosario, Sgt Colunga, Spc Gutierrez, Sgt Nichols and SSg Woods. In the far back is Sgt Burke. SSg Briola is on the far left in the front.

The Platoon Status

So here we were. Right before the mission and we were getting ready to go. The lieutenant and Roesch were gone, they flew away and it was not the same after that. Brinkley, who was the "Acting" platoon sergeant... hold up, I need to set the record straight.

He was the platoon sergeant. He was the senior NCO for the platoon, as was Montez. The military had the idea that the position belonged to a certain rank, but it could also be filled with good men. Were they capable? Yes. Did they need the rank to do the job? No. The military believes that they are there and it is expected of them to step up and, "It's their job." What the military does not take into consideration, is that no one wanted the job. Not in the battalion, and not even in the company.

Brinkley had come down from drill sergeant school and was waiting for orders. He was also sucking up an injury and needed to get fixed up. Both him and Woods, our FO (Forward Observer) were across from me and some of the first guys I had met. Now Woods was replaced and Brinkley had to face the hard decision of taking care of himself and leaving the men, or staying. Brinkley wanted to be successful in the future and wanted to get his knee looked at. I needed him there, but it was not about me. I needed to take care of the men and he was one of them. If that meant letting him go, that was what I had to do. I told him to get better. He had way over the amount of squad leader time necessary for a chance at promotion, and this shit is not fucking easy on the mind and body. One more thing, since the time the lieutenant got hit, things had changed. Brinkley had lived with the lieutenant since forever. They grew together and had been through other fights before my time. You get used to the odds and ends of another person and it becomes part of you. You know so much about the guy, you can look at shapes moving in the dark and tell who someone is without seeing anything recognizable. Brinkley had seen injuries and the mortality of men, good men that were gone. Living with that weighs on your mind and makes you ask some of the oldest questions there are and it distracts you from doing your best. Like everyone who ever served, each one of us carries that part, day, decision, for the rest of our lives. In turn, we have lost a bigger part of our selves doubling the amount of change. So Brinkley, the lieutenant and Woods were gone. Another one that changed was Fairchild. He was the First Squad Leader, but after climbing out of that Stryker, there was a dullness in his eye and spirit. No one can pinpoint this event or that one, but something has changed. Fairchild, well he was shaken up, and he was good to go. Since the lieutenant left, I told him he was going to be my platoon sergeant. Take care of all the shit he usually did, plus the other squads as well. When we would walk into a meeting, they would often ask what the hell he was doing there, and I said he was the platoon sergeant.

 Again with the jokes and bullshit. I was told that a good NCO didn't need to have a platoon sergeant, he could do it all on his own. I on the other hand knew that I forget shit, and I need a backup. This wasn't some fucking board game; it was real and we were dealing with lives here. I was told that "others," specifically the first sergeant, were able to do it all when it happened to him. Fuck that! I'm not playing a game. Perhaps I could step it up like everyone did before me. Then again, I didn't want to make a mistake that would have a heavy price. If one man could do it all, then why do we have an officer and NCO? I mean that is the breakdown right? Two people for two jobs? Fairchild, would have had to do it anyway if I wasn't there. He would have been the platoon sergeant. Besides the losses, we were given a couple of guys. As always, they were the ones that were trouble for other platoons. They were sent to my platoon and fuck it, they were going to do their job, and I didn't want anything else. So, in the trade-off for Woods, I got a young Pfc Weinel, Mr. "Go Wolfpack."

It looked like the Longhorn sign, so fuck it. It was close enough. From the head shed we were given Vinyard. I ran into him when checking out a weapon and it seemed he was one of the first sergeant minions. To make the trade go better, the first sergeant talked to me and told me how good a trainer and leader I was. He knew I would give Vinyard the best opportunity to be successful and most of all a good shot. This must be something that they teach in school: how to get rid of your turds with a smile on your face. With the "good ol' boy" speech he was the third person that has tried it on me. I guess flattery worked, because I said okay. No one else wanted to take him, and if anything else, we never rejected anyone on the island of misfit toys. The next sergeant we got was Taylor. He was a cool guy from Chi-town and somewhat headstrong. He had been here and there and he was sent to me. We don't look at color; hell I'm a white Mexican and was given so much shit when I came in, I didn't want to do the same thing. Vinyard was from Texas, and he was white. Taylor was from Chicago, he was black. From where we were, we were so deep in the pits of the fucking dungeon, we were all black, Black Sheep, that is. Taylor was cool, but my concerns were with Vinyard. I remember saying before that the enemy isn't the top of the list of dangers in war. It was people in the same uniform, other branches, coalition forces and then the enemy. I was thinking that Vinyard was sent to the platoon to report to the first sergeant. So, I plain out asked him. If he was such a good buddy with the first sergeant, why did he not get to go to third, first, or fourth platoons? He just said he liked the platoon, and he was not friends with the first sergeant. As a matter of fact, he said he hated that motherfucker with a passion. He was treated like shit, expected to do everything, and supposed to read his fucking mind every fucking day. The amount of hoops that he was supposed to jump through were retarded. I do not know if it was the years, amount of shit I had heard, or the faces of people that I had seen. Whatever it was, I felt like this man had been through his own hell and I did not have all the story. After he came over to the platoon, I noticed that he was still up there in no-man's land at the company CP. It was a known fact that no one was allowed to be there and no one was ever caught there because we would get a call on our little radios. So, I talked to Vinyard and asked what was going on. He let me know that besides being moved to my platoon, Dicks wanted him to maintain all the companies gear to include weapons and tons of other shit he was signed for. To me, that was double dipping and I brought it up to the first sergeant. Blah, blah, blah. Yakety-yak yak yak. All I heard was bullshit after bullshit. He took one of my guys, from my platoon, and didn't really replace him. He fucked me over again and I am sitting with the smallest platoon, not only doing the same work load, but also doing company shit with "my men." So, I said, "Okay, Vinyard, what are you responsible for?"

Hell, turns out he had access to big screen TVs that were in the Connex, sitting there in boxes. Third Platoon had not one of them but two. We had so much shit that we were not even told about, stuff for our morale and welfare, packed away and not given out. Hell, just when you think you know it all: wrong. What we did have was because of our lieutenant. He left his TV and X-Box and we would play on his shit. We were using our own stuff: that's fine. But hoarding shit was another deal. When we say we were hated, we were hated. Giving stuff to the people that kiss your ass was fucked up. Vinyard soon signed over control of some of the stuff he had, and he was happier for it. Going into a mission like the one we were facing, these things were not that important. It could keep you up at night, but not that fucking important. Taylor was from the head shed as well. He talked about the stupid stuff he was having to do. What fucking made me crazy, what made me want to skin a fucker alive, was that I came to find out that Dicks and the third platoon sergeant were in the CP laughing when they found out we were hit, the day they made us come back and not finish what we started. Where we lost one vehicle to include the lieutenant and Roesch. Taylor was there in the CP when the call came in, and witnessed them laughing and asking how stupid could we be? We sat there and did more than most. It was "too dangerous" to go out and get us. We had to comb the remains in the IED belt and these two motherfuckers were in there laughing at what happened to men in their company. Taylor also mentioned that he said, "We would talk about awards later."

Only if you were on the radio, and or heard it on the speaker box could you have known what he said to me. This was more than serious, it was deadly. Knowing that someone laughed at an event that could have taken the lives of soldiers that served their country, under their leadership and responsibility, made me sick. It didn't matter what fucking badge, bell or whistle you'd earned. If you were not able to fulfill your basic responsibilities as a person or an NCO, you were in a whole pile of shit. This changed the game. Before it was all rumors or speculation. We often liked to discount stuff as bad luck or *Yeah, we're the Black Sheep, no one likes us.* This was different, we had almost been blown up by our own fucking guns, nothing. Lost a vehicle, lieutenant, and injuries to others, and nothing. Nothing but laughter and shit. We were headed back to our FOB, and going to do a turn around and step into this huge mission. So we were ready to do whatever we were tasked with. If you ask me, that's why it's so much better being in the dangerous positions. You don't have to worry about your command and get fucked with as if you were a toy. No one wants to come out there and face that danger with you, so you are left alone. That is fucking sad. It is true, but a sad fucking fact of the matter. So, when people say that everyone is a hero just because of a deployment, save it. If anything, maybe a few others lived like this, but it is rare and a fucking heartache.

Left to right: Spc Mulch, Spc Gutierrez, Sgt Owen and Spc Weinell.

From the top, left to right: Pfc Barrow and Pfc Pylant. Spc Mckeen and Sgt Taylor are standing up on the back of the ramp. Front row: Spc Barron, Spc Pate, Sgt Nichols, SSg Briola, Sgt Owens and Spc Gutierrez.

Spc Gutierrez, Spc Swain, Pfc Spence, Pfc Pate and Pfc Iglesias

In the back from left to right are Spc Hatfield, Spc Rosario and Spc McDougal. Kneeling in front are Pvt Lazaro and Pvt Jackson.

Standing around with members of the Plt. This is possibly a ramp side brief. Yes, my hands are warm in my pockets.

"Mad, I Tell You!"

After we said our last goodbyes we headed to go and jumped in the vehicles. It was a "turn and burn" so we wanted to make the rounds on the FOB. We were all eager and ready to go back to our home. After all it had already been a long day. What I didn't realize were the effects on Woods and Rosario. Both were happy to see us and we all had our celebration there in the hospital. It wasn't till we were ready to leave and go to the "Boardwalk" on that post that the expressions changed on their faces. It indeed was hard for Woods and Rosario to get back in the Stryker. We all knew that there were going to be things that were going to stay with us or change us forever. These were things that we expected and accepted. However, to actually see the hesitations and emotions come upon them visibly was scary to say the least. Something that we had done a hundred times, maybe more. It was actually simple and required little effort. I don't know if you want to call it shell-shock or nerves but there it was. It was one little link on a chain that was connected to a weight. Holding one link isn't hard. It isn't something that really looks like anything, but pulling on it, or having the other end pulling you? Well that's an eye opener. I guess being with the group had given them strength from us all. Being all together allowed us to go through the reintegration with them. Twenty-four hours ago, they were in the same type of vehicle when it blew up. Whatever was in their brains and their thoughts, those memories were rejoined to the aches and pains of the incident. I didn't think they were expecting to be back this soon. What they did have going for them was that they were on one of the largest FOBs in country. Their brothers were there to link up with them and we were fixing to have a good time. They had a couple more days to get evaluated and make sure things were okay. I wanted them to take care of themselves and not rush back. I was never too concerned with next week or next month. I just stayed focused on what was here and now, focused on the things I could do to help out and keep the lieutenant happy. We had been to a couple of meetings to plan for something that would probably get cancelled. We were told that we were selected to go, but some things are hard to plan for so far out. Most of the time all these big missions were for nothing. Everything was ramped up with all the bells and whistles. Then you start wondering where was that letter I wanted my wife to have if these things were as bad as we are told. This specific mission required us to go past our area and out further west into Helmand province. Once there, we were going to do something joint: "the largest (whatever) since Vietnam." For me, I had to wait and see it, to believe. All I cared about was my part of the pie. Anyway, it was hard to swallow that this operation was that important. How could it be, if we started to read about what we were going to do in the papers? If it was so important, why was this shit all over the damn news? Surprise, boys: the secret is out! Just like that we started to read about the bad guys. The enemy had begun to fortify its positions and prepare for war. They were able to set the battlefield how they wanted it, in their backyard. So, after getting the good stuff, we returned back to our little FOB. Straight on the road and no fucking detours. Swain was at the gate when we came in. He greeted us like a regular Joe would:"Did you get my smokes?" "No. They were out!"

"You'd better not be lying, or I'll shoot you in the ass!"

We were home, back to a fucking tent, but it was ours. We

were going to get started on maintenance and get all equipment ready for the largest "something" since whenever or whatever. I didn't really put too much into it. But the word got out that this was really going to happen. It was on and we were definitely going and our company was leading the charge. It was such a fucked up situation it had to be so.

I know it was a huge fucking deal. Before the lieutenant got hurt we, Second Platoon, were tagged to be breach security. In plain *Spanglish*, there are 3 basic parts. The first is security. This group goes to the desired location and pulls left and right security. They make sure that others can do their job, and keep the door open for business. Just like the door man at a club.

The second group are usually a little bit of fanatics. They love their job and that comprises of blowing shit up. They talk REALLY LOUD sometimes, and consider every recipe to need a little more. They also have sayings like, "P" for plenty. They are engineers when you have a mission this big. Infantry and engineers get along too. After all they are grunts with shovels.

The third are the trigger pullers and masters of their own fate. This is where infantry can do exactly what they are supposed to do. This is known as the assault. Mexicans, Asians, people from the islands, country folk, city boys, brown, black, white, rich, poor, ugly, tall, skinny, or chunks. You can't really tell anyone apart, but there are some qualities we all share.

Here, no one gets a trophy unless he wins. We are God fearing, country folk. City slickers, wave riders, pagans or heathens. Some are educated, others need nothing but a job. We come from the hills in Virginia, big sky country up north, or from the plains of Texas. Above all, we like to win. We love to know that all I have to do is look from 10-2. Scotty is on my left and Pablo is on my right. As we move we are followed, not by the helpless. Not by the sick or the weak. Not a crusader, missionary, or leaf eating tenderfoot. We are not targets, or the weak *infidels* from stories of old. No, it's the total opposite. With me, come the *Bad Infidels*.

Men with a desire to get this done and over with. Let's quit politicking and win. We party like rock stars on Thursday and run till we puke on Friday. Then run to Class 6 (Liquor Store found on post) to get a beer. We were the homecoming king and the guy smoking Marlboro reds under the bleachers with the prom queen. Beer drinking, shit talking, booze smelling, dip chewing, motorcycle riding, church going, suit wearing, red blooded American that you want fighting for your privileges. Weak snowflakes can't make it or die. We are loud, but respectful. We carry a big stick that says "Momma's boy," but usually has a bayonet attached. It also comes with the option of grenade launcher or flame thrower.

We had sat in the company command and gone over the details over and over again. The lieutenant and I were not surprised that we were the "Security" since our platoon was not in good graces. It also made tactical and common sense though. We were the smallest platoon. We had not been together for a while and were going through changes. An assault, ambush, or a big mission like this has a lot of moving parts. However, if you have done this as a platoon, on the ground it is pretty much the same damn thing. Instead of squads or teams, you are using larger pieces. Our company was doing the same thing I had done over and over. The break down was like this. Second platoon would go up to the breach site and pull security.

Engineers would come up, clear the obstacle and open up a lane.

Third platoon would begin the assault. First and fourth would follow the main force and pick up positions to maintain movement on the main road.

You want your assault to be strong, consistent, experienced, and over all, the strongest team, squad, platoon, company, battalion you've got. Now on the eve of this massive thing, I was pretty confident. We were security, and that was all that mattered to me.

All I had to do was guard the door. That was our piece of the pie, and basically support. I could do that easily and I felt comfortable even though I didn't have my lieutenant. So, at that point I did not care. I was down one vehicle and only had twenty-six guys total. Getting left at the breach was basically a vacation, it should be an easy fucking thing. At this point, which was around month seven, we continued sending people home for leave. Units would rotate a soldier home and do so all the way up to a certain point in the deployment. Usually people tried to do the math, and figured it was better to go home early. Maybe some were thinking it was better to go late. Well these are luxuries that you have the higher you are.

I for one, thought like the old sergeants from the past. As the platoon sergeant, well, I stayed back with the medic. I counted out the packs on patrol and I counted them coming back in. I was also the last guy out and that meant everyone ate before me and went on leave before me too. Now, Swain, well he had picked his date. By coincidence, it was right before the mission.

In order to celebrate the event, he was carrying a cigar in the band on his helmet. He was counting down the days and Colunga was giving him shit. He would say, "Swainey-poo! You're going nowhere." Swain had a lot of experience and he was not a stranger to any gunfight. When the war first started and as enemy's tactics changed, we made it up as we went along. Swain was in at that time and did main missions on the gun. Not by choice, but if they were going to put him out there, he was going to do the damn job. That takes a different type right there. You are out and alone in the back of a flatbed truck and all you've got for shelter is a pipe coming up from the bed to put your gun on.

This was the kind of stuff he did for two years, back to back. Sure he was a little rough around the edges, but we all were. Swain seemed like 140 years old and that's how he sounded. Briola, was like 160 and looked like Yoda. We would start by saying they fought against each other in Vietnam, and that would start a whole night's comedy. It was how we would kill time sitting and talking. The day before the mission, we formed a smoking circle and broke out the *Romeo y Juliettas* that we purchased on the main FOB. Perhaps it was because of the coming mission. Probably the event that happened a week ago. Maybe it was the realization of all that we'd experienced before, looking back and knowing it was now time to go again? We talked about the lieutenant and the others, the injured getting checked out, even some of the guys coming back from leave. Swain was waiting for someone to come back and tag him. He was next to go, and maybe he would miss the next *Hooah!*

We spent time at a burn-barrel getting rid of stuff. Everyone was moving slow and the mood was quiet. As two or three of us stood around the flames you could see a look on each face. As one person was talking the others listened and watched the flames dance as if we were hypnotized. Someone would then come out with some noodles and cheese. As we listened to the Sgt's give us a thumbs up on the tasks that needed to get accomplished I listened to the squad leaders make decisions and corrections without making a sound.

I thought about all the stuff that had transpired in other places and recently. Their voices were as if they were off away in the background somewhere. The nights were no longer sweaty and sticky but required a light jacket. We looked at the stars and felt the nights were getting cold. It was our last relax time before we would return to the fighting. I laid down and said a prayer that night. I am a role model for no one. I wasn't good enough to be treated like others, and far from being any poster child. Nor was I the timid boy that I used to be. I did remember the place I came from and the values of my family. Even though I was not a choir boy, I did bend my knees at night, alone with my Creator asking Him for strength and ability. I also gave thought to my wife and kids, and hoped they would never have to know a life like mine. Those of us there, we were not special, we were not taken care of, and we were not a puppet platoon. We were Black Sheep, and it came to mean something. There seemed to be a pride in knowing you were going to get crap. You knew shit was going to be coming your way and you just had to deal with it. It was like swimming with a brick, while everyone else isn't. You get used to it, and after a while, it seems to make you stronger and better. With time to refit and seeing our friends off we were in preparation mode for a great big mission. We had ended a chapter in our lives and did it in a good way, forgetting about all that had happened before, and able to get a fresh start. I had been in other operations that had various different units, all moving and conducting their own missions. This time, with all that I had seen and what we had been through, I had mixed feelings. Maybe it was the question, or not knowing if we were going to have anyone out there to help us out. The danger that I was worried about, was getting fucked over by our own side. There was no one to go to and no one that was going to get involved. Knowing that we were actually at the mercy of grand old fuck face—that worried me.

    The unit was still relatively new to me and there were a lot of hurdles and obstacles to overcome. Now with the lieutenant gone, I had to get into the realm of the officers and whatever crap they did, which was not too different. It was pretty much "Do this!" There was no room for discussion, the information was direct, and all that was needed was to simply execute. No brainstorming or planning. If there were any questions that I might have, I went ahead and asked. Instead of an answer or clarification, it was played off as a joke, something funny. It made you feel like a dumb-ass, and you stood there and fucking took it. The others laughed not because it was funny, but because you were being made fun of. Laughed at, ganged up on, and treated like a shit bag. I remember during one of the first briefs for the mission coming up, we were designated as the security element. The info went on and the intel was normal. The enemy was aware of the pending mission and it was believed that they were preparing for our arrival. We, however continued to plan and adjust everything up to the timeline as well. I specifically remember the end of this brief. After this specific brief and after all the questions had been asked, I remember getting up and the first sergeant and his favorite platoon sergeant were bantering. Yak yak yak, blah blah blah. The third platoon was assigned the assault portion. We would move up, pull security, and allow the assault platoon to pass through and then they would move onto whatever objective. This was prior planning that was done before we lost the men and Stryker. Our piece of the pie was simple, plus expected. The way I was looking at is we were hurting on man power. The lieutenant was still there, but we were not as full as the other platoon. This is the way things usually go and that was okay. Their platoon was almost full, and they were the bad-asses. They were the ones that were the favorites and in good standing with the company. What was fucked up, was as we were collecting our shit to get back to the hooch, the platoon sergeant turned to the first sergeant. "We ought to let second platoon take the assault. That way Ruiz here could earn his Bronze Star."

"Sure, we'd do it," I said. Fuck it, we were not scared and I was not going to back down. It was fucked up that he would say something like that. Sometimes you get all this stuff and information that makes things seem impossible and dangerous. Then you go out and do the job and it was really not that bad. However, if the enemy was expecting us and doing what they said, it was looking like it was going to be a mess. So when he said that, I, for the most part, thought it was because of fear. If people are making jokes about something that has to do with something serious, It usually isn't a joke. Then again, the chances of changing up the entire company mission was not something logical. My experience told me that there were going to be meetings after meetings. Of course we would get told exactly what to do. Then, re-checked and double checked. After all, nothing really came too easy with this plt and would be drilled into the Lt. Therefore, the third would do it, because that was their mission, but if he could get out of it, he would prefer to do that instead. If pulling strings were able to make that happen, he did it right there in front of me and the first sergeant.

This was coming from the same guy that walked up to the medivac helicopter and got on it. During a movement to contact and as the entire company was walking into the Argendab. Everyone knew that he was way in the back of the company formation, but somehow walked up and just jumped on the fucking helicopter. There he was right next to another soldier in the company who had his shit blown off from an IED. The soldier told the "sick" SFC that he was a shit bag.

My understanding is he got a Purple Heart for that. However, who said anything was fair? There ain't shit fair in this world. We come in, and we go out. What happens in the middle is a competition, and up to you. The only thing that you could hope for is to fucking have a say on how you are going to go out.

Being a soldier, you get to have your say, and either fight for your life, or not. Maybe you made a mistake and thought about not being Combat Arms? Fine, re-enlist and change to housekeeping or whatever. He was just choosing to pass. Skip his turn, don't pass go, don't collect $200, and keep his ass in jail. To me, that is not living free. It makes another take your place, and that is not honorable, it's fear. Fear is not freedom, it is the opposite. Anyway, the shit-talking is all ways a good stress relief. We talk shit and we do it a little different than others. So, no harm, no foul. He was a turd-bag and that was not going to change in my book. But he looked like a soldier. He looked like what you would expect a soldier to look like. Things here were weird and you could not trust the look of a book, the words from a mouth, nor the plans from the company. Finally, after losing the vehicle, the Lieutenant, Roesch, we are fast forward to mission time. It was now time for hands on rehearsals and what not. First, we went out to Leatherneck and I guess we were early or something. We didn't take everyone and all we did, was sit around. The next time we mounted up and we went to conduct a link up on Leatherneck. I don't remember too much, except the weird ass aircraft and how the post looked as we approached from the hardball. They did have a good PX/BX and we had chow there. For the most part we were separate and kept away from the home units. I don't know why we were there again. There were briefings but only for the company command. Information was kept simple. Let's go here. Sit and wait. Let's go back. Sit and wait.

Once on our way back, out of nowhere, a storm hits us and it begins to pour. It seemed to be a great break from the open sky we were used to seeing. The days were now getting cooler and then, it was not so good to be out in the elements. Before too long we were hit with buckets of rain and hail. There is nothing better than being on a fucking vehicle and it begins to hit you as you're hanging out the top. The last time this shit happened to me this bad, I was a lone gunner. This time, I was in the squad leader's hatch and I had periscopes. That meant I could close the hatch and just watch from inside. It sounds good, but the only problem was my driver could not see shit. The camera he used to drive while buttoned up became caked with mud. That meant driving while inside was not possible. We had to find a way to stay in the convoy and not get left behind. It was either do something, or call up and ask for everyone to stop. That would lead to more and more crap. Why would the camera have mud if it was raining? It was all because since I was the lead vehicle now, for the platoon, I had the rollers put out in front of my vehicle. This incident, I was thrown in the back of the company and had to go through their muddy mist. That made for a face full of sheep, camel, and human crap that looked like chocolate milk. Not to mention the extra wheels on the rollers in front of the vehicle.

The VC, who is also the gunner, was talking shit to Iggy my driver. Yeah he meant well, but Iggy was driving a seventy ton vehicle loaded with shit all over the place and us inside. Finally, I got in on the conversation and I told him to knock it off. I was talking to Iggy and we had to figure this shit out quick. I ended up, getting out of the damn Striker and being his eyes. So here we are rolling in the fucking storm and I'm directing Iggy where the fuck not to go. At first it was a little left and right. Once we were able to see how well the reactions were to the directions, we were fucking golden.

Iggy can't see shit, I'm getting soaked and then here is a fucking gas station coming up on the side of the road. Just a little building and some pumps like you would see in an older movie here in the US. The only problem is we are winging this and going around 45-50 mph. Now Iggy is doing good and I don't want to worry him into over-correcting. We would then end up doing a side to side, turning into an up and over. So, I say, "left" and he does, then I go, "a little more," and we are set. Here is a damn fuel station and we are going too much to the right. Like straight for the thing and I'm saying. "Left, Iggy, left, a little more, more," and then, "Ding, ding, ding ding." We missed the pumps, the building, and everything else, but we were so close that we rolled over the fucking hose that lets people know you were pulling up to get gas. To this fucking day, and forever more, if I hear a fucking bell it reminds me of blind Iggy and the time he 'buzzed the tower'. In this case it was fuel pumps, and it was awesome! I can say that now, but pretty sure Burk who was the VC was just as fucking nervous and somewhat relieved. Burk was relatively quiet and he knew his shit. Roesch was one of the top men in the platoon for the vehicles, and he was in charge of running the crews and getting it done. After he left, it was Burk that I relied on to keep us up and rolling. Barron was another good man who helped the vehicles run smoothly. Often they did their shit way after we would get in off from a mission. They would down load and head straight to maintenance and get right to work. There was no fucking micro management and as far as I knew, they were way ahead of their jobs and letting me know. Just look at it this way. There we were stuck in the middle of the fucking "Men From the Mountain" area and they recover this other vehicle from the ditch and just like that, we are off. We didn't have any breakdowns and the weapons systems were locked, cocked, and ready to rock the whole time.

I had seen others that were not as careful for their vehicles. Not these guys. They were not only a part of the team, they were the team. They busted their asses and they worked hard to make sure we could get to where we were going, able to get there and ready to pop a top on the can of whoop-ass they had been working on, and come back. We were all grunts. There were no differences between the men. Sure, there were some that would have loved to get on the ground and feel the sand, just as well as there were some that would like to get their asses in a seat. It is ideal to make sure everyone is interchangeable. Simple units like this made it necessary to cross-train everyone. That was our back up plan. People get hurt, get ill, go back to main land. We don't get fillers and we have to cut some other team short to just be mission capable.

Way before I got there, the men found their spot. They found the place that they were comfortable and that is where they excelled. At times, there would be a rotation and people would change it up a little, it did seem to work well. I learned something from the old crusty sergeants, back in the day. Basically, it does not have to look good, nor does it have to make sense. If it works, it fucking works and do not try to reinvent the fucking wheel. Because if you fuck this shit up, I Will Personally Smoke The Living Shit Out Of You And Make Sure You Never Grow Hair On The Top Of Your Head. *If it ain't broke, don't break it. If you do, I break you.* How awesome is that? I didn't take it as rude, or vulgar, but I took in the information that they were trying to relay. It was made colorful, funny and maybe serious to a point. That is how I learned to do things and how I helped the other young ones to remember as well. Plus, no one wants to get smoked to the point where they cannot grow hair. I don't know what that would be like, but I'm pretty sure it begins with "Front leaning rest position, MOVE!"

We made it back to the FOB and through the rain, hail, piss and ass. We watched as flash floods formed in minutes, from nothing to a fucking river in the middle of the desert. When we made it home to the tent, we crammed into the lieutenant's palace and sat down to watch his TV. Most of his stuff was gone, but he had left his small TV and X-Box. Everything else that was there, we left it all in place. Maps, pictures from a magazine, just little odds and ends stuff. It just seemed that he was still around and fixing to come in at any minute. It was where we gathered and all watched shows and hung out. So we were there warming up and the call comes over the radio that the company was ready to go. Hell, that was everyone except us. So, we rushed out and got in, and off on the road again. Now our platoon was in the back because I wanted to take the fucking mine rollers. It was a pain in the ass, and it slowed us down, but fuck it. Why have it and not use it? At some time, who knew but we might have a need for the damn thing. For years, we would go through the packing list and all ways end up taking shit we never needed, or ever used. When we were freezing our asses out in the fucking woods, we would have a rucksack full of snivel gear and never be allowed to have it on. If you were cold, stay busy! We would get up and have to move and they didn't want you to have it on because you would overheat. It's fucking eighteen degrees! I could use some heat!

So it just became part of the task to take stuff that you might need "just in case." As you grew up in the military, you became the guy that was telling people to get up and get it on. We are going to move and it was because we were getting cold. I came to find out that all that warm stuff we had for cold weather did keep us warm—only because we had to drag that shit everywhere we went and didn't get to use it. This time, I have a fucking mine roller and we are in the rear with the gear. At this point it is First Platoon, Third Platoon, Fourth Platoon, and HQ. For the first time ever, our company is complete and moving. We are headed back to Leatherneck and into our staging area once we arrive. It has been over a month and it is known that the enemy has continued to prepare for our little mission. It is supposed to be bad and a real good fight. Our group, which is made up of different companies out of the Brigade, were formed into a task force and given to the marines in order to do this major offensive. Again, I must say that I'm thinking it's still a fifty-fifty chance of it being what they say it is. Everyone is talking about seeing this, or hearing that. The platoons are all together, but I grew up being told not to worry about the things you have no control over. For the things you can control, you do everything you have to in order to be ready. What I knew was that being security, you might get shot. It was reported that there was an anti-aircraft gun on the ground or something big, maybe some IEDs, machine gun teams, as well as snipers too. As the security, who gives a shit? I go to the breach. It's like having the range to yourself. Bad guy over there, bam, bam, bam. Target over there, bam, bam, bam. Oh, here is the assault, they go by and, "Have fun storming the Castle." Our job is done, and all we have to do is sit and wait. We will get tasked to do some prisoner escorts. Maybe some extra security. We might even get important people and escort them to the officers in charge. You are extra, and will be used.

It's time to shit or get off the pot. Prior to executing the assault into Marja, we stop and pass on tools of the trade. We scrounge what we can, and make the things we will need. Pfc Williams takes a look at one of the charges and tries to overthink it.

Doc Pilgrim, our medic. Never missing out on a learning chance, Doc looks at the items necessary to build our charges. Pfc McKeen is in the back as Pfc Spence and Fabish look at the assembly of our tools.

Reality hits, and when it hits, it's hard as fuck! It's one thing to get treated one way. Maybe it isn't only you, and others have it just as bad, if not worse. Well I didn't think that at all. At first it was a rumor and then a whisper. Then it grew into almost getting blown up, and no one gave a shit. Then actually getting blown up, and no one gave a shit. It was funny to them and we were laughed at. I guess I was still a sucker? It was becoming normal but now, it wasn't perception or the imagination. It is 100% real. This time it was no accident or mistake. Here, you get nothing but hate, bullshit, and fucked. It's wide open for everyone to see.

Do Not Go Gentle...

We get to the Leatherface, eyes, nose, or neck, and make our way to the main staging area. This is where we were going to set up for the night. We refueled and started to go over our equipment and vehicles. Radios, maps, land warrior, and shitloads of stuff. I didn't know how much of a part we were going to play, but we needed to check it out. We had time, and let's use it to check all of it out and recheck. I was wanting to make sure the vehicles were good to go. Crews would oil, grease, run system checks, calibrate and have a nine line, (A MEDIVAC request format that contains required information in reporting injuries by type, numbers, location, and other information) taped next to the radios. Medical equipment was good, with no cracked I.V. lines, no expired bags. Doc would identify every CLS and EMT-certified pack and go over the actual ABCs and what to slap on for what injury.

We were hours out at the time, but most of this stuff was checked at least once a month. I asked the squad leaders if I had left anything out, and I'm sure I did, but I knew the platoon was ready. I had seen them work, as well as react to the incident when the lieutenant was hit. I gave them a timeline and we went to work. As we began to prepare and make our final checks, I was called into a final meeting. The next time we would get together would be for the back brief and any questions asked would be given an answer then. So, here Fairchild and I go and it is on. We start to go over the company's plan and—what the fuck? It goes like this. "Engineers get on the road and mark the breach. Okay? Third platoon goes and sets up security for the breach, then signals via whatever."

"What?"

"Next the assault element, Second Platoon, will go into the breach, dismount and assault. You are to occupy and begin clearing here and work your way that away. The Afghan army will be with you with their Canadian advisors. They will take the lead. You are there in case shit goes wrong."

"Uh, I know we are to hold all questions to the end, but a month ago when the lieutenant was here we were told we would hold the breach and Third was going to assault. When did that change?"

I did the one thing that you were not supposed to do. I had dealt with a lot of crap, but this was something that I didn't expect. Nor would I have ever believed it would happen. So, in front of everyone, I stopped the CO and wanted to know. This was not ordinary, and it was big. Was I right for doing it or was I wrong? I would like to think I was both. I also did it so everyone would at least know I did something. The first sergeant turns and looks at me and says,

"Remember, I told you that you were going to be the assault?"

"No, I'm pretty sure you didn't and if so, I would have known and remembered that. Not to mention we are down the lieutenant, a vehicle, have half the men we are supposed to, and who the fuck is planning this?"

"Well, I must have told your platoon sergeant."

Then, to the CO, "Go ahead sir!"

I looked to check with Fairchild and as the brief continues he looks at me and says, "No fucking way sergeant! He didn't tell me shit."

So here I stand, and start to think that we had to change

everything that we were planning on and we had no time. Everything was going to have to be changed. I quickly had to brainstorm and figure what were the most important things we needed to do? As security, we didn't have to pack or do shit. We were going to sustain off of the vehicles. Now, we were going to get left off and have to walk in. That usually required at least 72-hours of rations, ammo, and gear. The whole task force was going to start rolling in hours. Then, we were simply going to be left off, special delivery like a pizza. It stunk like shit. The changes didn't come from the CO; he didn't say shit to me. However, he obviously had taken the word of First Sergeant Dicks that the changes were good and we were briefed. I couldn't think of anything ever happening that sounded or worked like this ball of shit. I had never experienced such a big change like this.

This is not how the Army works. I've been in it for years and there are way too many meetings to coordinate something simple. We never were briefed any changes. Third turd had tried to cower out that one time. He wanted to act like Billy Badass and talk shit, so yeah, *if you're scared, I will do it*.

Believe me, formality is not my thing, but it is a constant. Op Orders, Warning Orders, and even Fragos (Fragmentary Orders) have to go a certain way. Second, fuck the 3rd platoon Sgt for being weak. So I talk shit to him, he tells the company 1Sg, and they tell the company commander, and he changes the whole order and just doesn't decide to tell me? Uuhhh, there are literally only hours before the attack. Nahh, even your simple nutless, window licking, tree hugger knows that *Rulez is Rulez*. Afterwards I talked to Dicks and confronted him. I told him he didn't tell us shit. How did it make sense to send the shortest platoon, without an officer, into a fight as the main effort? He started to poke around and hint that I was scared and what not. Arguing with this dick was getting old. He didn't give a shit about anyone. Okay, well that isn't true. He gave a shit about others. He didn't give a shit about me or the platoon. He had chosen to change the specifics to the mission.

Somehow this was okay? Now, we were leading the charge for the entire task force. It just didn't make sense. The strongest unit was staying back and we were getting sent into the grinder. Our odds were slim to none if half of what we were told was actually true.

The lieutenant was gone, Third was getting over and again, we were getting fucked! Again, who do you talk to? What do you say? So I said, "Fuck it! You think we are scared, you are wrong. We will take the fucking mission and we will do the fucking job. If anything does fucking happen, you better hope it happens to me." Pissed off and shocked at what had just happened, I made my way back to Fairchild who was already talking to the other squad leaders. We gave them the change to the mission and were getting the same questions that we asked ourselves. *What? What is up with Third Platoon? Why did it change?* All I could think of was me. Yeah, it was a cold hard fact that I had the health and welfare of the Black Sheep on my shoulders. Mission first and soldiers always, but as their leader, there was a price that had to be paid. Yes their lives had improved, but now they were going to have to be put in danger, for no reason whatsoever; we had been put in the hot seat. I now did something that I am very good at. I told the guys to gather up. I was not going to sugar coat shit. I had never received any change to the mission. I was aware that Dicks and Third Turd were talking shit because of fear. Not one thing that had happened back in the States or since we got here meant anything. From now on this was our life and we will fight, out front for everyone to see. We were not liked and we were not friends to many. Most of our friends were in this very group.

I often felt like the most important thing on my uniform, to me, was my name. We all have a date and time. We will all go through the same thing. Before, I told them that if anyone was to ever try to take our lives, that we would do everything in our power to remove them from the face of the earth. Now we were going to do so to protect our brothers to the left and the right. This time, it was put up or shut up. We would be the ones pulling the strings and if there was going to be a fight for our lives, we were going to have some say about the way it was going to go. I said that it is in my name and the ones back home that I do this. I am from Texas, and we ain't taking shit from nobody. So, here is the plan.

We would go and try to get some mine detectors, not the ones we had, but the good ones. Ours were the shitty ones, and they bounced off all the iron in the ground. I wanted them to get a class in operating them and make it count. The point was for them to return, and to train others on the detectors so we would have some back up operators. Time was not on our side and we were within the final hours before stepping off. I wanted them to hit up the other units and see if we can get anything they do not need. We were going to do a platoon class on different things that we were going to use to clear paths for travel. We were going to use the detectors, and not just stomp around till something went boom. We were going to have to go over breaches to make our entrances. We were not going to risk doorways or paths, we would try to stay off the norm, and do our own shit.

Doc would look for medical supplies and check and make sure all vehicles were good to go. PCCs and PCIs were done, but we wanted to re-do everything, pack light and bring anything that you would want in a fight. Most of the larger stuff would be in the vehicles, so we were packing extra for our aid bags. I wanted to plan for the worst and didn't care if I was wrong.

Once dismounted we were going to have nothing except what we carried. Yes, I said dismounted. To go along with the assault, we were told we were going to leave our vehicles. Actually, they were to get used by the company. We were not going to be able to position them to have security or watch our movement. That was also a change from what Third was supposed to do. They were initially going in 100%. As for us, well it was just going to be a dozen or so. How 'bout them fucking apples?

All batteries were to be replaced and have a supply plus extra, and forget clothes. Most of this shit was common for the squad leaders and it just got done without saying. The men were as pissed as I, but had gone through this before. They mentioned several other times when they were the ones that were picked and had to do it before.

Once again, I was made aware that this was their usual experience. They had been here the whole time and suffered the same fate over and over again. They had been here, waiting for the next time they were called upon to do what others would not. I don't know if it was me feeling angry, again, or just the thought of what we were fixing to do. Twelve hours before all the parts and pieces were to start, we were given up to fate. I had been in places where changes were made on the fly, but this was something special. I guess changes and conversations were made telepathically here. Despite all that was said, I was never told. I would have said something due to our status. I would have requested other assets and equipment, and we would have trained and prepped. Right then and there, bitching and griping would have done nothing. Tag, it was our mission, and I preferred to spend my time getting ready. Fuck those motherfuckers! Still, something was not right.

Since we had arrived at the staging area, things were talked about being easy and nothing was really important. It was just another mission, and everyone acted as if we were not going to see or hear shit. It was as if everyone was considering it a waste of time. However, looking at someone in the eyes, sometimes, those eyes say something different. At the flip of a switch, when we scattered to try and get anything, the picture that we pieced together said something very different. Colunga and Briola made it back with metal detectors as well as a map. I don't know where it came from, but we were obviously way the fuck under-informed. There were fighting positions, IED Locations, minefields, suspected anti-aircraft guns, machine gun nests, sniper locations; you could not even see the fucking terrain because of so much shit on it. Again, we were not in the know, and poorly informed about the whole thing. For some reason, what we were briefed and told didn't have half of all the dangers we were looking at. Yes, we were given the company's mission, and yes we were each tasked with this and that. What good did that do, if everything was changed right before the kick-off? We were just not aware of the risk, or the percentages. At this point, we accepted the fact we were going into harms' way. Fine so be it. What our own command could have done was at least give us the full information about the hazards and/or the possible enemy capabilities. So, using my chain of command, I went to Dicks and asked to get a MICLIC. I don't even know if that is the right saying or spelling. I had however, seen it used and knew what it did. It was a trailer or whichever delivery system that it was on and would shoot out a web of explosive devices that would clear a small area. Since we were going to dismount and go in on foot over open terrain, I wanted to at least be able to make it through the first hundred meters without dying on the beach. Sure it is loud and says here we are, but fuck it! Third would support from the breach and we could limp our way to a strong hold and fight from there.

"No," Dicks said. There were only two there, and he did not think that we should use 50% of an asset for nothing. He said that nothing was going to happen, and that it was all bullshit. The reports that he had seen (which I hadn't), "were full of shit," he said. Wow, so he is admitting that he had seen reports that said something different. At least he acknowledged that there was a threat, but his opinion was that it was all a lie. Holy Fuck! Houston, we have a problem... and it's this fucked up piece of shit right here. I couldn't believe what he was doing. So he was lying through his teeth, but now he is trying to make it a good thing; as if he had a crystal ball and was seeing the future. In the military, we plan for the worst. This is how it goes and you are ready for it. But this motherfucker is doing the complete opposite and down-playing it even though he was told it was going to be bad. He just decided not to tell me, after he didn't tell me that he changed the mission. As he spouted all this crap to me, I reached down to my cargo pocket and pulled out the map.

"Well, this is what I have seen. If there is an asset that can help us do our mission, why don't you send up the request at least? I am requesting an asset we have and despite your opinion there is everything that says we are headed for a world of hurt."

He didn't even put forth the effort to squeeze a mic. He walked away and left me there, alone. In the middle of the fucking task force and our company doesn't do shit for us. We have to go beg, borrow and steal to get stuff that should be provided. Then again, we didn't know, and had planned on doing something else. So, by this point I can't help but to grin and laugh. I walk back to the platoon, and we begin to make our own breaches/charges. As an infantry man, you have to be a jack of all trades. You pick up skills and stuff that are passed along soldier to soldier. Some use it to make themselves useful, others for job security, and then again to be needed. If you are not, hell we can send you to the Black Sheep and you can be a mule. There you will get used as a tool for whatever comes up. There was a time when we harnessed the skills of the trade and taught them to younger soldiers moving up. However, lost to the ever changing technology of war, soldiers now expect to be given the tool for the job. Yeah, right!

Instead of being adaptable, they have become used to achieving something like a skills test. Not thinking outside the box and being unable to adapt makes operations difficult. You have to be able to think about the problem and solve it. Now we in the infantry have come to know this "Skills Test" as the EIB, otherwise known as the Expert Infantryman's Badge. Like it or not, you were going to take that shit like a champ. Want to or not, you were going to do it. It has become the fucking summer camp from hell. Mostly now it has to do with equipment and little computers. Most stations could be a test for the end of your AIT, to get your ass out of training and off to your first unit. Then again, who wants to fuck with Night Vision glasses (NODs), pluggers, and computer shit, just to get to graduate? "Not I," said the blind man.

Like I said before, you will train and test for it, and these are tasks supposedly done in any infantry operation. Here we were taking the time we had and putting it where it counted the most. We were busy at work, and I looked around and saw the others doing bullshit. We finished up our shit, and were fucking around with the last of what could be done. Then, I saw a face that I had not seen in some time. It was one of the battalion's CSMs. He was in the lead for the task force and I had met him once or twice before. Me and Sampson were known to go and ride a bike every now and then, and that is where I actually was able to get to know him a bit. I saw him getting milked by Dicks and the Third Platoon sergeant. I was passing by and all I said was, "hello." No big deal, and we began to bullshit.

I asked him if he was going to get to do any riding on his R&R, and how his wife was doing? He was from Texas as well, and from the same dirty, shitty area that I went to school at. The towns were around thirty to forty miles apart and we knew the area. He asked me what I was doing there and I told him I had moved to the line. We were talking and I started to feel the gleam from my first sergeant. Him and the Third Turd looked like idiots with jizz on their chins. Sorry boys, did I fuck up your feeding time? Good! They were just astounded how I was there having a conversation. The CSM went on about his bike and plans he had for riding when we all returned back. He was wanting to put together a ride down to California or something like that. He had been working on the specifics and it was interesting. Having someone high up that liked to ride was not a bad thing. I told him I had my Harley in and around Fort Lewis and was thinking about riding down to Texas. We were talking back and forth, and then my first sergeant stopped me and said, "Sergeant, if and when you are done, if you would take whatever information that the CSM has for me, when you are done talking to him? Let me know."

He and the Third Turd walked off. The CSM asked me what Dicks' problem was and I simply said I didn't know. By this time, I would have got into a fight with this ass, but I was now just numb to the fact that this fucker was useless. As for the CSM, I didn't expect to have a good conversation, nor someone to take the time or remember me and the wife. Most of the "events" that happened were for the "better" people, more respectable. The way most saw me was probably a no-one: not good enough, a stubborn ass that was nothing but trouble. The CSM was just making the rounds, and seeing the men. We were not a part of his battalion, but it was good to have a normal conversation with a person. There were only a hand full of leaders that ever did the same. The majority of leaders were doing you a favor just to acknowledge your presence, inspecting, questioning, or micromanaging. When it comes to leaders, very few have been said to be a soldier's soldier. Someone who is a soldier and remembers where he comes from and remembers being in your shoes. Where I was at currently, I didn't have to worry about impressing anyone. If anything, the men impressed the shit out of me. Yes, I was the acting Mother and Father to the platoon, but I think that they liked me and saw me as one of their own kind. After the CSM left, I *had* to walk over to the first sergeant and let him know that he left.

So once again let's recap what is going on. My first sergeant hates the platoon, and me. He has shrugged off the fact that we were almost killed and has laughed when we were hit. He refuses to give us any "real" information, he changed our mission, and I have to walk up to him and let him know that the CSM was just checking on the troops. Naturally, he begins with questions.

"How do you know the CSM?"

"You were sent over here to take my spot, weren't you?"

"What do you know?"

"How do you know the CSM?"

Then, he turns it around as if I was just out of line and kissing ass. I told him how I actually met him at the Harley dealership, and then I just stopped talking. "Kiss my ass motherfucker," is what I should have said. "Fuck you, and the little island you're living on." We are in a predicament that he has fucking put us in, and I am supposed to feel bad. Fuck that. I said "Roger that," and went back to the ghetto. The nights were getting damn cold and there was some need for the heaters. Some people just get downright sick moving in the vehicle. You are either freezing off your ass, or burning up. You at one time were clean, but you are a dirty grunt the minute you begin to move. There you go, you get in your seat, you can't see anything except the inside of the vehicle and you go up and down. When you go fast, you go back. The brakes come on, and you go forward. Add to the fact that you are hearing the radio and the traffic coming across. "Low area or wadi. Hold on guys, we are going up. Brace yourselves it's gonna get bumpy." Sometimes you don't see or hear shit and it's just a big fucking surprise. We strapped in and began our movement. We fell into formation and formed a line going to our next rodeo. There were engineers leading the way this time. They started before we did, so all we had to do was follow the route. Well, there were so many vehicles, imagine driving home in a traffic jam. There you are in the middle of not a number of cars, but of miles of cars. Sure, there is one lane. Tons of room to deviate, but nowhere else that was cleared by the engineers.

We would go fast, then slow. Stop and then go. It was worse than a fucking division run and the slinky effect was 100% in effect. I was watching the screen and would talk to Iggy. He, like the others, was in the driver's hole and had their little things hanging here and there. Most of all, they had fucking sugar and energy drinks. One of the drivers was Gutierrez from California. He was, no not white, but go figure, Mexican. It was widely known that he drank Monsters and would have a case hidden somewhere. Like the other drivers, Iggy had his shit. He didn't talk much, he was quiet. I would sit there and talk to him just to make sure he was okay. Every now and then we would stop and he would recline back and take a nap. He would get woken up by either me or Burk telling him to, "Wake the fuck up! We're moving." He would get back up and we would sit there and follow it with, "Are you good?" He would say, "Roger that," or just say, "Uh huh." Then again, I would have to rest my eyes and see Burk over there with his head leaning against the top of the turret and in front of the screen and tell *him* to, "Wake the fuck up! Damn son, we just fucking left and you are cutting Z's like you were getting paid for it!" We wandered through the desert and made it to daybreak. We finally came to the last point before we would all split up. We sat there watching the engineers clear the route on to the road and we were out of the vehicle waiting. So there we were, at the start line and we noticed some yellow jugs off to the left in an area that looked like a dry river bed. Hmm, do you think that is an IED? Someone got out a robot and sent it that way. Sure enough, it was uncovered in the rain, just sitting there in the low ground. Tag it and send it up. Then there was another one. We were watching the engineers clearing the start point and we are noticing IEDs just out in the open. I remember standing outside of the vehicle and smoking a cigarette. Yeah, right next to the fucking vehicle with a fucking dip in, because:

1. I was tired.

2. I wanted to take a look at what was about to happen.

3. We were going to link up with the Afghan Army and we had never met them before. We did talk to the Canadians and they were okay.

Last, who knows what the fuck was going to happen that day, but there were IEDs, that was for sure. Plus, someone was preparing for our arrival. How much more info did we not get that was right? So fuck yeah, I was smoking and dipping right next to the fucking vehicle.

The engineers made their way to the road. Once it was cleared it was time to move out and secure the breach. Once they took off, we knew we were next in the chute. The plan was for us to dismount and hold the position till the Canadians arrived with the Afghan unit. Despite the fact we were out in the fucking open, with a good 600 meters to the first cover, we were to dismount and stand fast. I do not know why we weren't allowed to take the vehicles, but from there on, it was just the 14 of us. The vehicles were to stay at the breach and then go to another unit and help with route security. I knew if we were going to get into it, it sure would be nice to have some support. So, we talked about it, and the crews knew if we were caught in it, that they were going to bounce the route, and come to help. It was not what the higher-ups had talked about, but it was what was going to happen if we were pinned down. As Third got set, we waited for the call. Time passed by and we get told that they are set up so, off we go. We made our way to the breach, pulled in enough to let others pass, and we dismounted. Command didn't want to let the vehicles off the road because well, they would blow up. We were okay to go, but not the vehicles. That was a no-no. We went out, did a quick link up and off we went. We pushed out away from everyone and laid in the prone and pulled security. We were in some kind of field and out in the open, so we spread it out and got low. The vehicles moved out and we waited for the unit to link up. After a bit, we were met by the Canadians and they were trying to get the Afghans to move. I had done their job before and I knew the hassle that they had. I didn't mind the mission we were doing, just the way it was given to us. As I looked at the Canadians one thing was certain. I sure as hell would rather be doing our task than having to do what they were doing. Finally, they were able to form up and begin to move. I kept thinking that the whole mission and the way things were going, might have not been too bad. Did we really expect that we were just going to get left out to get hurt? After all, didn't I remember hearing about anybody being the back up? We were there only to support the Afghans? Once they dismounted, we broke to the left to get into a wadi. There the units got set, got on the same piece of music, and began to clear compound to compound. As we worked and went from place to place, we started to notice that holes were dug out as firing ports for the enemy to fire at us. The walls to the compounds were cut up allowing the enemy to shoot from and have some cover. There were rectangles cut out, and they were perfect for watching and shooting. While I was in one of the compounds, I looked out of a hole and knew it was a firing position. My fucking heart started to race and I thanked God that no one was there. I looked out and was watching our Third platoon at the breach. They were pulling security as elements from the task force were driving by. I focused back on the compounds. Doors were cut through walls so you could go straight from one end to the other without having to go around corners. There were straight routes through the rooms of the buildings so the enemy could move fast.

There were signs of life, but some places were just abandoned. Some places had everyday items left behind, and others were cleared out completely. We were on the move and it went on and on and on. After about an hour or so, we found ourselves walking down a road in the village. Yes, down the fucking road and following our friends, the Afghans and Canadians. All of the sudden there was a crack and the zing of a bullet.

You knew the sound and knew the front element was getting welcomed to the 'hood. Then, like in Iraq, the death blossom happened. We were unable to figure out what the fuck was going on. It was going on in front of us, but what the situation really was, we didn't know. The unit to the front was in contact, so we began our march to the sounds of the guns. We picked up to move forward to check this shit out, and then I saw a soldier come back from the front. Then another, and finally the Head Canadian came back and said they were done. The Afghan Army was not interested in the fight, and were coming back to sit behind a wall. I didn't know what the fuck to think, maybe it was a fucking joke? As more and more Afghans came back, I watched them sit down, put down their rifles and start eating frosted flakes.

No fucking shit! Okay, let's move. We all have tickets to this gun show – so move is exactly what we did. We worked our way to the last covered area we could. Like team work the squad leaders put the men on line and began to return fire. I came up on the net and sent up the TIC (Troops In Contact), report and began to go to the front. We were being engaged by the enemy from buildings that were 100-300 meters away. These fuckers were good because they were in the houses and shooting from the shaded areas. They were not coming up to the windows and setting up a position, but sticking to the back walls and firing from covered and concealed positions. I made my way to the front and took a look at what was going on. We had set up in a small compound and were behind a wall. It was about chest high and the men started to focus on the muzzle flashes from the houses. We began to concentrate on an area where the fire was coming from, to identify individual spots. Soldiers were talking and shooting, giving descriptions and of course cussing up a storm. The squad leaders were making money and splitting up the targets. I didn't have to do shit. Colunga was at a break in the wall with the saw gunner. They had picked up a position on the ground and Colunga was directing his squad's most casualty producing weapon. Briola was telling the men to conserve the ammo and watch to the left flank. By this time, we were supposed to have friendlies out there somewhere and we didn't want to get smoked by our vehicles. Swain was doing his best to hit anything, but that's why he had extra mags.

I was across the break from where the saw gunner was suppressing the enemy and watching to see if we were okay. I got my ears blown out because the saw was lighting it up. It had a shorter barrel and till then, I didn't know how fucking loud it was. As the gunner turned to adjust fire, the concussion hit my ears. The only information that I had was what I could see.

I was back in a corner of the wall. The break in the wall was maybe three to four feet from the corner of the compound. I looked down the line and saw the results of training everywhere. Gunners on the 240 were doing the drill. Of course there weren't three-man teams, but there was improvisation. Positions had been taken, and then the leaders adjusted the men and weapons systems. Leaders were yelling and giving out information and at times right next to the guys and pointing out this or that. Everything was on cruise control and was on point. I could hear only echoes of the words and sounds. The hearing loss was temporary and I was trying to get a good look at what was developing in front of us. I then leaned back and figured I'd better give it a second or so. I could hear my heart beating and my breathing louder than anything. From where we were at and what was going on, we were in a good position. I realized once again, I had made it to where I wanted to be. I chose to take some time so I could remember where I was and with who. I was at the corner of the wall and saw the shit bags, on line, dealing out first class tickets to paradise. I had no control over anything and had to sit there for a few seconds just to remember what I could. The only way I could do that was as a painting. Swain is on his feet and taking his shots. Colunga is kneeling next to the saw gunner across from me yelling directions and pointing. Briola is on down the line and going from one spot to the other. The 240s are rocking and talking. One 240 goes for a belt change. Pait is the gunner and has a helmet cam. In the video it looks like a video game, you can hear the buzz of some of the rounds passing by. The saws pick up their rates to adjust for the 240 changing to a new belt. The other 240 slows down and an extra volley is picked up by an alternating saw. There are rounds impacting in our area, and one goes over the wall and above Swain and Fairchild. I see them duck and they are wondering if that was a round or not. Then Swain gets back up and returns fire and it happens again. He yells out and relays the info to the men around. I look back and see the Canadians waving at me. They are at the back end of where we were in the compound. I look and see them waving me down and calling me. I bounce back and they are asking me what the hell am I doing? I said fighting. He asked me if I was aware that there were bullets landing all around me and I said no. I didn't notice shit. He says that we were taking pretty accurate fire and I said I knew. Then we spot someone with eyes on us. During a fire fight, people are not just going to sit out there and watch the fight. I tell Wynell to see if he could get rounds over on that guy. He says we were not a priority and that the Navy ANGLCO were priority. Well fuck sakes, why didn't you say so? Maybe it's this big motherfucker right here in the weird uniform? I walk over and ask him if we could get some mortars to do anything. I tried to see if maybe, he could fire some rounds on the building to the front. He said no. We pointed out the people out there moving around and he said no. At this point it feels like my first date with Miss Rotten Crotch, but she is just being a bitch and saying no. Right now we are engaged with the enemy. We have every intention to send these turds to their place of their own choosing. It is said to be all awesome, so why are they fucking hiding? They claim it is awesome, we believe them and are willing to help, but I am sensing doubt on their part. As a matter of fact, now that I think about it, they are being difficult. I might go as far as to say that they do not look like they are willing to go yet. Well too late now. We have locations set, and positions located but cannot get any supporting fire. The deal is that there were helicopters that were on "Standby" to help cover the unit on the road, and they didn't want to fire because of that. So, there you have it. "We" are engaged with these fuckers over there. You can tell by the flashes there, there, and there. Those are the buildings they are in. Those guys out there are moving around and not just sightseeing, and we cannot get a simple fire mission. Why? Because someone has an asset that they "might" use "if" something "might" happen way over there. Therefore, "we" that are doing something, and needing the assets now know nothing is going to get approved because of something that might happen. To make it worse, we are at the edge of our boundary and not able to advance. We are locked right where we are, and going nowhere! Then someone takes a better look at where we were and sees a possible IED under the mat of the building. So, I am like, "Great. Well let's check it out." I head over carefully and poke, I mean see what's under the mat. Yes, there is something there. I pull out my paratrooper's knife and begin to probe. No assholes, I am not an idiot. If one of these things are found, all missions stop. You freeze and own that fucker till it is confirmed or denied and only then can we move on. Usually that was the best way to stop a patrol, and mission. As I probe, it turns out to be nothing but trash.

Again, this was a fucking EIB task back when I was a private. We would have to know how to emplace, camouflage, and set a mine. Then we were tested on deactivation, recovery, and you are either a go or no-go. For the old timers out there, remember on the task, you didn't have to use the wrench, but you did have to attempt to use it, and touch the two together. If you didn't, "See you next year motherfucker." Yeah politics, in the infantry! Fucking Hooah!!

So here we are exchanging bullets and it comes to me. These fuckers want us to come to them. We can't bomb the shit out of them, and we ain't going nowhere. Company is crying on the fucking net wanting this and that. People want to know blah, blah, blah. The Navy guy is stuck to the mic and can't do shit. So, we yell to slow down our fire. We are engaged but can't shoot through what these guys are hiding behind without expending a shit load of ammo. I sit down and reach into my cargo pocket and pull out the best fucking secret known to me. Blueberry Pop Tarts, crushed up, in pieces. So here I am, and I start to chat with the squad leaders about the situation. I know that you always have to keep the troops informed. So, here I am telling how no matter what is going on, we are not allowed to go further, nor are we able to get any help from anyone. I'm sitting there and one of the other men looks back and says, "What the fuck? We are in a gunfight and like nothing you just pull out blueberry Pop Tarts and eat 'em?"

"Yup! That's what they're for, and they're all crushed up nice like I like 'em." We are getting accurate fire from some clowns and they have the advantage. We settle in and look at it as a waiting game. People are using their sites and we are doing some damage, but we cannot get to the enemy and that lets them do whatever. At this time, what seems like fifteen minutes isn't, because it is really going on hours. We are locked down and these fuckers are taking their fucking time on us. Then, Williams yells that the vehicles were coming. I said, "What?" He said that the vehicles were on their way. Now, I know that there are plans, and things that people say. Sometimes it would be nice if people did what they said, and this was it. The crews broke off and were actually coming our way. It took them however long but now, they were on the way. I turned back and saw the cloud of dust coming. What an awesome thing to see. All I could describe it as, fucking buck sergeants! Those glorious loyal bastards. I told the men to continue to suppress and conserve ammo. I told Fairchild I was going to go to the vehicles. The men would hold what they had, and I was going to go to the vehicles and use them as the maneuver element. I would be in touch with him via the radio, and the crews were going to get a piece of this fight. I moved to the rear edge of the compound and told the guys to pull up to the forward edge. Once that they were in place, one of them was going to drop the ramp and we were going to try to get in. I was going to come into the back of the vehicle with Willie and we were gonna move. The vehicles pulled up and I said lets go. There was a zing and a zing.

Willie yells, "Are those bullets?"

"If they aren't, those are some bad-ass mosquitoes," I said. We got into the vehicle and I got the headset on, told the crew to stay off the road and we were going to alternate. We talked about how we were going to move, what to look for, and here we go. We began with the 50cal. and the MK-19. As one bounded forward, we suppressed, allowed him to get set up. Then he fired and we moved up. Pretty soon we were just shooting, moving, and communicating. How cool and how fucking simple. How about this motherfuckers?

I told them the enemy was spotted in the houses and shooting from inside. Boom, boom, boom! The MK-19 makes that little sound, and it's like taking a shit. Ah. Followed by the boom, boom, boom. Right after that the .50 goes off. PPPPPPPPPPPPPup. PPPPPPPup! I felt happy inside and that takes a lot. However, everyone has their part, the guys on the ground, the guys in the vehicles, and each one does so without a second thought. Everyone knows what is expected and they simply do it. For the first time, this bucket of old bolts and parts is working despite being held down and thrown into the breach. I realize, that despite everything standing in the way of the men, our platoon is working. We are cooking with Crisco now, baby!

I don't know what it was like to get to us, nor if they were worried, but it must have been hard work because those men unleashed some fury and waxed that ass. Goot somehow had a saw with him, odd because he was a driver, and he said, "Sergeant, can I shoot? I just want to shoot!" At this point, we were shooting and moving and I said why not. Goot cranked open the driver's hatch and said, "Say hello to my little friend!" He laid in on the houses and went cyclic on the saw. I'm on top in the gunner's hatch and see our fucking antenna shot off the vehicle. Rounds are hitting the vehicle, but it does not matter. These fuckers wanted to play. They had their fun, till the fucking crazy crew shows up, and now it's time to "Puff, puff, give, bitches." The crew begins to lay waste to the buildings. It looked like a video feed of smoke and explosions cracking into the buildings. The men held their own, they were awesome. The heroes were the crew, they heard the traffic on the radio, and then they did like they promised. We had been pretty much locked in position, and they grabbed their balls and did what so many men say. "If you're in trouble, we will come and get you," and they did. Looking at them coming down the dirt road, rolling to the fight, someone should have known there was nothing but bad intentions on their mind. We laid into them. The men were in support, and the vehicles maneuvered to end this Mickey Mouse bullshit.

We had accurate fire pretty much focused on our location. Hopefully the enemy thought we were what was for dinner. We were the buffet, and they were right. They got a free helping of dick, and it was all they could eat. Once the vehicles arrived, it was over. I looked at the men on the wall, and they were as happy as a puppy with two peckers. The vehicles blocked our location from any enemy fire, and it was a celebration. We were there doing an impromptu AAR (After Action Review: a discussion on what happened. What went good, what went bad, what or how to become better. It usually happens in a class room environment and not on the front line). Shit was flying worse than during the fire fight. Man, this and that, and holy shit! "Where did the vehicles come from?"

The crews told us the story and how they just happened to get lost. It was a good thing to see, and even better to live through. The men just had another event that led to them standing taller. We were alone, no one could say we didn't do this or that. The Afghan Army fell back and we filled the breach. The men did what they had been doing all the time and this time, everyone on the task force knew it. It wasn't the company, or the battalion. It was the Black Sheep, and they weren't the bitches people thought they were. We were less than twenty-six soldiers, and for some reason made the fucking assault for a *"TASK FORCE."* No officer, no hero with bells and whistles. Just a bunch of men who refused to go gentle into that good night.

SSg Fairchild stands behind the line and watches during a lull in the fighting.

One of our best partners. On the Right is Kip (note Canadian Maple Leaf flag on his arm). He was on the team training and helping the Afghans. Canada was there fighting – I saw them. Thank you for being a warrior.

Spc Gutierrez stands behind the wall to protect his drivers toe. He was with the vehicles that came to our rescue.

We ended up finding something despite all the bullshit coming from my first sergeant. I swear he was a piece of shit and won't change my mind. No matter what happened, or what we were going into, he played it off like it was nothing. He simply acted as if I was overreacting, or that I was scared. It pissed me off, and this time I had taken the bait. Then again, what the fuck could I have done about it anyway? This turd bag running that company while finishing his masters in psychology. He planned on helping soldiers. Well he could get on with it and start stomping around for IEDs. Support from our "Brothers" seemed to be getting fucking worse. Call for fire, almost get blown up. Ask for help and I get left waiting on the phone as if I were a veteran trying to make an appointment. We get the green weenie on this mission, and believe me I am being nice. We can't get help, so we have to help ourselves.

If the risk isn't getting higher, the amount of work we do does. Even the Afghans have it better. That, or at least they can say "Fuck it" and take a siesta. We seem to be the only ones sent to do the "Dangerous" dumb shit we have been doing. I don't have too much to worry about since I was dead the moment I left the States. I've been dead for over seven months and I still smell pretty good. I am wondering if all the questions and concerns from high above are ever going to do anything.

Gotta Find The Key

As we did our consolidation and reorganization, we were passed by the Afghans and their Canadian team. They pushed toward the area we were taking fire from. We had made it through the day, but the night was quickly coming upon us. We had a large engagement and had seen all the preparation in the area we had searched. We knew for sure that there were bad guys there. To their advantage, they knew the lay of the land. They were capable of using the terrain and weapons good enough to be a threat from a distance. They had made preparations and were fighting their fight as planned. The Afghans and the others went off and were going to push out to the limits of the engagement area. We moved back to the last compound that was right before the compound that we were fighting from. Now, here is where we need to understand something. Life by every other definition is different to what and where we were and had been living. We found a compound and it faced straight toward the unknown area where we were receiving fire. On the opposite side was the task force. They were pushing to complete their mission and were pretty much in place. To this point the only element in contact was us. We walked the compound and found it to be pretty good for our use. High walls, good roof, one way to enter, but several places to approach. We took a vehicle and drove it right through the gate. By having the vehicles with us, it kind of made us self-sufficient. We wouldn't need to ask someone for this, or help from somewhere else. Using the vehicle, with all its systems aboard, multiplied our effectiveness to disrupt and destroy targets in the area. Our accuracy was increased as well as our lethality. Now that they were with us, I was intent on keeping them and using them for what they were made for. With that being said, we nudged the wall and made enough of an opening to squeeze the vehicles through. Then, here comes Fabo! Old Fabo was the nickname for Fabish. He was one of a kind, and a great asset to the platoon. He was always quick on his feet, smart, and had one unique way of talking. He was supposed to be my VC but I fired him after an hour. He was funny and used his humor to break the ice. It could have been that I thought I was the funniest motherfucker in the platoon, and that was it. He made it to the fight, and by God he wanted everyone to know it too. So, the last vehicle to come in the gate, and it is him. He is the VC, and it is very easy. The driver drives, and the VC guides him. Everyone else did it, so why couldn't he? Now, imagine a wall with a gate in the middle. At the left side of the entry point/ gate, there is a room attached using the wall of the compound as the fourth wall of the room. This is the last vehicle to come in. We are on the radio and telling them to stick to the left, as they are coming into the compound, *away* from the room. Granted there are pieces of the wall on the ground and it is making the vehicle shift to the right toward the room. That is why we were going slow, and telling them to stick to the left. Fabo lines up the vehicle straight and I am looking at him and right then, it hits me. This is not going to go well. As soon as he starts moving, just hearing the engine rev up made me think, "This is a mistake." I was like, "Fuck Me!" As the vehicle takes off it hits the rocks and sure enough leans to their right and pushes into the room and makes the room into a tee-pee. "Are you fucking kidding me?"

I told him I was going to put his ass on detail and KP, whatever the fuck I could find. Then again, we had nothing. We were all alone and didn't have to worry about doing stupid shit. No sir! It was dangerous and that meant freedom. We cut into the walls for firing positions. We took what we had, used some of the knowledge we had gained and adapted. We also lowered the tops of the walls to add our vehicles systems to our defenses. Having that equipment let us move an engagement out into the open fields. It was better than the distance of our NODs, (Night Observation Device), and other devices. At night and at a distance away, the enemy wouldn't be able to tell a thing. Fairchild worked on the security and we put a vehicle across gate "Fabo." We also had a dismount system that allowed us to set up an office. With a vehicle parked near to the building we were able to run it into the closest room. All the time I accumulated working for the circus gave me good ideas on what to do. Within the hour we were looking good and had our own fucking TOC. Left to the Joes it had everything from maps, reports, supplies and had a place for a makeshift aid station. There were enough places for the squads to sleep in their own areas. Besides living in Indian Territory, we actually had a better life than what we did on the FOB. There was a nice area in front of the building and it had a hole for a fire. We went through the priorities of work, and one of the squad leaders came up with a guard shift. Fairchild was doing security and when it was done, we walked the outside. "If it was us, where would we come in at?" I asked.

Bam, wire here! We adjusted the fields of fire to include the avenues that we had no eyes on. We put our early warning devices in there and called it our Alamo. By the time night hit, we were pretty tired. A day that had a forecast of nothing but clear skies turned to soup sandwiches. No support, no nothing and we managed on walking out of that shit without a scratch. Weinel was pretty good for an FO, and he got us some targets and locked down the areas we were concerned about. We were dialed in, reset, had security, interlocking field of fire between individual positions, team, crew, and a fucking FO who was the tits. Everyone was on it like stink on shit. As the tasks were assigned, we went to work and it just got done. I didn't have to oversee every individual task myself and tell soldiers, "twenty meters to the left." No, it was easy enough to let the men do their thing. As a leader, you do have to walk the line and inspect. What the men did was make my job easy. There was a task to do, and they did it as good as before. Leaders dug into the tasks and made sure things were right. They were big boys, and liked the fact we were out there, and they were part of a team and took the responsibility head on. Fairchild had his hands full with the first sergeant. When it came down to status reports, he was good to go. Fuck, the damn reports that were needed to be sent up were put on the note sections of one of the computers. All we did was set the alarm and when it went off, get the info and send it up. The first sergeant wasn't having it. He was pissed and the CO too. They wanted us to be on the radio and relaying everything to them and what not.

I'm of the mindset, you were supposed to get us what we needed, fuckers, and that does not cover the amount of bullshit we get on a daily basis. So, they wanted to talk to me. Here we go.

"27, yak, yak, yak."

"This is 27," I respond.

"Roger, where are your reports that were supposed to be sent at (whatever)?"

"27 sent it, over."

"Well who is that? I need the platoon sergeant to send me that stuff because it is your job and..." and on and on.

Yeah, he could keep his hand up my ass and make me scratch his Vah-jay-jay. "Uh, I am the sixth element" (the Platoon Leader) "7 or 27 is the Psg."

"The same Platoon Sergeant that you told we were changing our mission."

It was on! It was on like Donkey Kong. Fuck it! From then on Fairchild did everything that was requested by the company. He was on it and we were cooking it up hot and ready to serve. Now,

I guess that Dicks wanted to keep me close, direct me and maybe feel like I was going to run and ask for help. Fuck that. It would have taken some shit for me to do so. I didn't see it happening in the near future, but if it came down to it, I would do it for the men. We heated up some MREs and burned our dunnage in the fire pit. The nights were getting cold and we said, "Fuck it, let's have a fire." The walls were like twelve to fifteen feet high and the fuckers knew where we were. We sat there and just enjoyed watching the fire and discussing the events of the day. We were safe.

We all knew shit could hit the fan at any time, but I guess we were not supposed to do what we did that day. If these fuckers were gonna come and get some, it looked like we had back up. Little did the enemy know it wasn't like that. They were going to have to readjust their plan, snoop and poop to get a plan together, and take time to implement it in accordance with our schedule. That is not an advantage because we were not planning to stop and wait. We were going to find them and fight. Now that we were there, we had time and the advantage was on our side. The nights were getting nippley and we sat around the fire and relaxed. The men were no longer in the moment. We talked and told of the events of the day, how close each one was to dying and then come the jokes. "Slap." Another calls bullshit and tells the "Real" version. "You were shitting your pants. I found you by the trail of shit. It led me to where you were."

Man, everyone was subject to a tough crowd. Then we were people being normal in a not so normal situation. It was our normal though. We were together, in danger, and felt better. We knew it was too dangerous for anyone with rank to come by and make our life miserable. Just normal shit and talking shit was one of the things we did. The subject of PTSD is pretty big today. People often recommend going somewhere to talk to someone. Well, this was our therapy, where we talked about our problems and helped each other out. If a person to talk to is fine, twenty should be better. Plus, you are talking to someone who was there with you and understands the environment and stress. But unlike a group session with some that may be faking the funk, you also have people there willing to tell you to stop whining. We had a little CP of our own set up. We were with power and had the stuff organized as best as possible. We were to protect the task force by holding the line and remember, we were the assault. So, there was a rhythm and speed to the things that needed to get done. We had twenty six men. That was to include the FO, medic, and the crews. Baron, Burk, Gutierrez, Iggy, and Fabo. As far as squad leaders, I had Vinyard, Briola, Colunga, and Fairchild. Just like that, and we are back to playing war games. Someone monitoring the radio says someone was requesting illume. They were going to be shooting in our general area that night. Now illume drifts, so we try to get it to "pop" in one area and use the wind and gravity to take it to the place we want to see. I guess that the airspace was also clear now, unlike earlier when we wanted rounds on targets. So here we are and we are admiring the ability of others to get shit they wanted, to see the area. Wow, guess we just needed to "not" be shooting to actually get help. Everyone is talking about not having this and we are talking about seeing the fucking vehicles come down the road like this and that. It's a friendly place despite the area and circumstances we are in. Men are posted on the watch. You can see their silhouettes in the dark and a little green glitch from their NODs. The hum of a vehicle is in the distance as well as that of the radio coming from our CP/TOC or wherever we put the fucking MREs. We are gathered around a small fire talking as some go to get wood and do some stuff before they crash or go on shift. Some men are in full dress and we have others in shirts or doing hygiene. That is until we hear a call come from the radio.

"Shot over!"

"Shot out!"

We start talking about a time that the men were in the Argendab and the canisters that "popped" did exactly that. I thought I gave a good description earlier of what went on there. As the stories are being told, probably by Swain, it gets quiet. As the story goes along and you see a young Joe get his shit and head over to the building, to get under cover, I realize we are being bad-asses and talking shit.

"Yeah, that was fucked up, I seen the whole thing," I said, as this guy walks away. "It would be fucked up, after all we have done to be here and some bullshit like that takes you out!" People then started to remember about needing to do this and or that, and the exodus begins. I'm sitting there thinking, "What the fuck! Are you fucking serious? "It's bad that we almost get lit up by these mortars one time, but now after fighting we have to worry about a fucking cone landing in my face? Maybe, ah, cool, I'm outta here. Then someone says, "If that shit hits me in my balls, just kill me!" That's what it comes down to, "my balls." Then, "pop," and everyone that has not moved begins to do the same fucking thing that animals in large herds do. Everyone wants to be in the middle and the pack begins to move. Then you here a specific sound that not everyone has heard, and few can accurately describe.

"Whew, whew, whew, whew, whew."

As the projectile separates it wobbles to the ground and the air hits it like if you were blowing in an old coke bottle. Then, as basic as us infantry men are, we take the fuck off and run for cover, grown men fighting hours earlier, and now running like children from a bee. Now, the odds are fucking awesome, but Murphy has been fucking shit up forever. That is why we have Murphy's Laws.

"If something can go wrong, it will."

"Tracers work both ways."

"Friendly fire isn't."

These are just a few.

Next thing you know, we are bitching and griping about how fucked up things are and that this was too much. Every now and then someone goes out to brave the chance, and we egg him on, call him a bitch, or pussy. Say he isn't a man, and others are telling him he's stupid, he's gonna die, and we are going to go through his shit, call his sister and talk to this, that, and the other. Then he runs in and we are all laughing and having a great time doing stupid shit. We were acting like small children you would see playing for the first time or at a school their first time there. Yeah we're fucked up. Go through bullshit, like shit through a goose, but we have a great sense of humor. Some of the best ones here made bad shit, funny as fuck.

There we were. The mission was off to another fucked up start. Right now, we have seen action and dealt with some good shooters. We weren't down anyone and ended the last firefight with the vehicles moving in. There were signs of someone getting ready for something, but we have not seen anything close yet. Our infamous leaders have put us as the mother-fucking assault and we made mashed potatoes and lemonade. We are to guard the main route and allow them freedom of movement for whoever wants to drive on the road. We are here for seventy-two hours, till the marines come in and fast-rope to specific objectives. Sure, all the planning and meetings were hard to deal with, but now, we are on our own. The only way things would get any better is if we were to turn off the damn radio. Since we moved into our little castle, we improve our location and weathered the night. The next day gave us something else to do and new risks to take. We had patrols out and were tasked with going back over the stuff we did on day one. Our purpose is to search over what was searched the day before. So, off we go and time to look for the fucking presents that some asshole left for us to find. However, we had a plan.

Remember the great news we received about us now being the assault? Well we got motivated. We were given the fucked up purpose of "attacking," and the only direction we were going was forward. Today, that meant that we actually had to go backward and stomp around. Well, we used that time to make charges that we would later use to clear our routes, breaches, and improve our security. We had taken the time to get these tasks done, and were planning on using them. A quick note here though. This, is no shit, what you see in just about every movie and it is never really done in a manner that catches the fucking point. EIB: it was a good thing, but let's face it, you have to do it. You don't want to do it. You are forced to do it anyway, and probably dump that shit when you get a go in that task at that station. Now, you are trying to remember everything you forgot. Here, it is about living or dying. As an older soldier, I got to show these fuckers the tricks of the trade, our skills, and our arts: GP charges, Bangalore, door knockers, water impulse charges, Flex linear, Flex linear modified to clear a one foot path. So we do that Voodoo, that only we can do, so-o-o well. I got a chance to pass on our history—a part of us that started back in the jungles. These were things that others taught me, and I passed on to my soldiers. These were perishable skills and things that you needed to know in case we all died, and you were the next "hero." The best way to enter is with surprise. What we were going through was a ghost town. But these fuckers knew we were coming and who knows where and what they left behind. At this point, we just went with the flow. We didn't have any trust in the command. We'd seen graphics that looked like some asshole spilled Lucky Charms on the map. We knew that it didn't matter what the fuck you were going to get told. Here, we were dealing with bullshit one fucking inch at a time. We planned for everything, and just figured, let's go by the fucking numbers. First, it was the team and squad leaders. They were going to lead their men; they were on point. They went through the orchards and became bloodhounds. They had seen their fill of "toe poppers," with some men wounded.

That made the squad leaders fucking tough. The men didn't mind too much, because here we were trying to save each other. As a leader, the men couldn't have been in better hands. We would move out to go clear all these places that were "cleared" before, and it was picking straws to start the rotation. If it was your time, you were going to earn those stripes today. Better pull your head out of your ass, because it's on you. Take point, lead your men, and pray to God that St. Peter doesn't smoke your ass later on at the Pearly Gates. Patrols started off slowly. We began to get a good eye on the area we pushed through the day before. We had passed compound after compound and who knows what we missed. Today we were going to clear the areas and we knew there were things there, lying in wait for someone to be careless.

The lead team moved cautiously through a village that was riddled with signs of life a short time ago. Whoever was there decided to leave for some reason. I didn't know if it was from the threats of the enemy, or knowing two sides were going to collide there. All these thoughts are in your head and you try not to wander and keep focused on the moment and you do not use the trails. If we have to go a little further around, over a wall, we do it. You might ask if we don't clear them, others might assume the routes were fine. I, in turn would ask you, "Where the fuck do you think we are? Disneyland? There's no one here! No people, no livestock, pets, turtles or fish."

I can actually hear a snowflake bitching. "I am pissed and the 'I don't give a fuck organization vs. those that provide everything while I sit on my ass' will hear about how I got shit on my shoe." Well, first off, why are you in a tiger's cage? Are you a tiger? Well then you are tiger food. No one, outside of grunts, are going to be out there. Plus, if we call and say it is clear believe me, it will be clear.

We begin to move and clear and take in the terrain. The men are moving and taking in simple shit that you didn't or wouldn't give a shit about anywhere else. We relearn something as simple as walking. We have to. Here where we are is not the same in the west, east, the forest, or up a hill. Where you are at that time is a new landscape. It could be Mars, and you need to take it that way. The learning curve is quick, steep, and maybe painful. At the same time we are making lists of dos and don'ts. We adapt and modify our formations and we stop crawling and start walking. We start off slow and then as we are learning we are beginning to move faster. During the operations, we are looking to find a baseline, or the floor level. We are looking for what normal looks like in "this" terrain. This includes erosion. If the sand blows hard, does it leave hard dirt on the bottom? If there is a watered field, what is the result when it dries, untouched? We are tracking movements and adjustments to the area. It is the constant of the entire place. It is not the specifics of the area, but the things that could be present or absent from the norm. Disruptions or what's missing, maybe what's added, that tell you the place is safe. It is the "key."

Once you find out the characteristics of the area, you know what to look for, the things that are foreign or strange. Once you have all these things and the rules that we make, then we start to go faster. There is now a blueprint to what we see and we begin to move. Yeah, we start to take this fucking place and make it our bitch. There was a time that we stood outside of the breach in fear of the unknown. Who was that motherfucker in there and were we gonna make it? Now that we are on the ground and in the crapper, we had no other option than to take charge and own it all. As safely and confidently as possible, we begin to change to our environment. We use our knowledge and replace the fear that kept people inside the walls of their base. Like everything, you have to respect what you have, know that with one simple mistake there is a possibility that you might not make it back. The enemy knows it. He blows stuff up, tries to get into your mind and use it against you. What he doesn't know, is that we would rather be out here fucking with him, than get treated like shit back at base. We were not going to back out of the task, nor were we going to fail due to fear. If necessary, we were going to die doing the job.

Out here, we are the baddest motherfuckers and you will comply.

First up, a spooky, large compound. It was just really weird. It had been gone through before we got there. We brought out a charge and set it to do a breach so we could gain entrance. We moved out about fifty meters. I had the charge and Swain was with me. We both had our guns, and fuck, there was a dual initiation system. It is two triggers to set off the charge. You should have two just in case the first one doesn't work. Here we are on the ground and behind a wall. I have the system in one hand and the fingers of the opposite hand in my ear. Swain leans over and puts his fingers into his ear and is like what's next? By the way, leaning k-pot to k-pot does not work. I'll get that out now. So, I tell Swain to pull the safety, push in the pin, rotate the pin a quarter turn, and bingo, just like it was planned, boom. We make our way to the breach. Swain hangs back.

"Uh-uh, I don't like it," he says.

I look at him.

"Something's off."

Here we are ready to go in and Swain is saying no. Here is where an asshole would start up. "Shut the fuck up, don't be a bitch. You're a fucking coward; you're a piece of shit," and everything else.

I look, and I know we can take our time. So I am like, "What are we gonna do?" Swain, well he wants to frag it, just the room we were going to enter. I don't know what the deal is. If there is something, what are the chances of actually hitting it? Then on the other hand, Swain, well he is short. Hell, he shouldn't even be here and he reminds me every chance he gets. Call it a feeling, premonition, or just your gut, so let's play this safe. I decided to go with the hunch, and we call it up. We get the green light, Swain frags it, and boom—boom!

We trusted him enough to go with his gut, and he did a one in a million shot. He detonated an IED in the very room we were going to go in. We were going to come in from the external wall, just to change it up; we knew the enemy had some idea of our clearing procedures. However, it was set up so as to get a guy coming in and sweeping the room like we do in teams for MOUT (Military Operations in Urban Terrain). Using the door, it would have been bad for someone. We would have also run into it coming out of the room. We push forward and enter the compound and start collecting random items, stuff so weird we didn't know what to think. What we really did was search. We didn't take anything until we cleared the item and checked for booby-traps (like we needed another thing to add to our continuous growing list of things to do).

It was time consuming, long, hard work. Clear to the next place, breach, clear, record, mark tag, take a shit and move on. We came across another compound that had a patch of grass in the front. It was elevated and there was like a small cave that was underneath it. When I say cave, it had a small opening, and it went down to around three to four feet deep. It was long and had some silver type of residue on the walls. I didn't know what the hell it was, and was not going to do the taste test. I had done that before, and ended up with some weird fertilizer pellets on the tongue. Fertilizer—I like to think that it was manufactured, and not natural. We decided to go ahead and clear the damn hole and threw two grenades in there. If this shit was residue from making HME, (the homemade explosives used to make the IEDs), it was going to make a bang and we were set to get as far away as possible. We called, got cleared, and cleared the area for the possible boom. Pins pulled, we threw them in and backed away. All we got was a muffled "poof". The only problem was, all we got was "a" muffled poof. It didn't take a rocket scientist to figure they either detonated at the same time, or that only one detonated. Either we are going good, or we are stuck like chuck. We sit back for a while and let the dust settle. We have to talk about options. Here we are in this clearing operation and we are sitting on a dud. We have people on the radio and we have the RTO and FO out here with us too. We called up to see what the deal was with getting EOD out there, and the wait was hours, if not a day. With everyone moving and setting in their places, EOD was kind of busy. For them, an operation like this with so many moving parts was like Black Friday for a cashier in a store: busy, busy, busy, and we were in a hurry. Here is where the momentum of your movement could slow down. You put out security, and your day is done. Fuck the mission, you have to babysit this bitch and lose your roll. Pull out the water bottles, blueberry Pop-Tarts, and sit. You might think that that's awesome. We're no longer in danger and we just get to chill. However, the tide has turned in the favor of the enemy. We had been left and stuck waiting, listening, knowing that we were going to get attacked, that we were on our own and that whatever came our way, we were going to have to deal with it. I walked over and took a look at what happened in the "cave". When a grenade goes off, it leaves a hard spot, maybe cracks the ground, and as things come out from the center, there is loose material or whatever was there. Well, there was the detonation spot, and right next to it was an unexploded grenade. The fuse was damaged and that could have been anything.

How long could we wait, to see if it was going to pop on its own? I sat there, and wondered how we could get this shit taken care of? Who was going to do the job? No one here was EOD, or had any kind of training on this stuff. As I sat there listening to the guys talk on the radio I flash back to 2003.

Here we were stacking missiles that were scattered all over the place in Kirkuk, Iraq. As a matter of fact, we were sent on detail to go and pick these rockets up, put them in the back of a truck, and transport them to wherever these things went. Some of the rockets were broken, wet, leaking, and let's just say when they told us to load them, we may not have actually done it in the most careful manner possible. There may also be some pics in the virtual world of soldiers humping them like horses, maybe suggesting that the rocket was a person's "appendage." We were also stacking mines and RPGs and anything that goes boom into big piles. Then, we placed sticks of C4 all over the pile and the whole lot blew up. We were planting and recovering stuff all the time, but through the different deployments, some just said, "fuck it" and called it up. It is actually your call, but to me I knew what had to be done. I walked over to the cave, and took a good look to see what I was dealing with. If you ever seen the initiation system to a grenade, it is pretty simple. Spoon goes off, it releases the timing thing and then boom. I was looking at the small system and it was mangled. I went ahead and called for a small door knocker that we had at the ready. Briola, Swain, and Colunga were there and had some concerns. I told them we didn't have the ability to slow down and even if we did get help, we were probably at the bottom of the list. After all, we were only the assault, but the priority went to the route. The freedom of movement to the task force was more of a priority. I could not in good conscience ask anyone to do this, and I was not going to get one of them hurt. I took off my gear, crawled through the opening and sat there with the grenade. I got my k-pot/helmet, but then again I didn't want it to fall on the grenade while I was working. That could have gone either way, so I left it. However, after so many times doing the EIB lanes, I learned that your piss pot would hit the rod on the task, and all you would hear is the grader tell you that you were a "no go!" Oh, and by the way, you died because you used your head. I sat there, and took my time and tried to get a real good look and see what was going on. Looking back, it would have been great to have a selfie stick. I would have loved the distance. There at that time, I asked for the charge, and got as low as I could. If this shit was going to go wrong, it was going to be me. I didn't think that there would have been any problem telling anyone I was dead or wounded. As I crawled up to the grenade, I made sure that I didn't have too much slack and placed the C4 on the dud. Watching this shit get closer reminded me of the fucking movies where two ships were trying to dock in space. One slip-up and your D-U-N dun, son! When I laid that shit on the dud, I waited to see if it was going to go off. I stayed there close to the ground and waited. I didn't want to get up in a hurry and have that shit blow my ass off trying to get out. After what seemed like a lifetime, I gently moved back and got the fuck out. I went back and told one of the guys to ask for clearance to detonate and we were good to go. So here we are, wondering if this shit was going to happen and here comes the countdown: ten minutes, five minutes, one minute. Then for the first time ever in my life, something happens and it makes me forget what I did, where I was, what we were doing, and we begin to talk shit. We did not get "thirty seconds." Nope. The sergeant doing the count down for some reason said, "Half a minute." Half a minute?"Who the fuck says half a minute?" We are talking and turned to yell shit at this guy and *boom*, he pulls the initiation system and we missed the whole show.

Anyway, we spent some time clearing and working back to our "palace." We noticed that the Canadians were back, and were having a pow-wow. Up until now we hadn't really engaged with them, but we were in the same boat. We walked over and shot the shit for a bit. It seems that some of the elders were coming to talk and we listened. They were there to let us know that when we engaged the enemy, we killed several of them. The bad guys were going to their houses at night and taking their food, supplies, and making them clean, wash, and mend their clothes. They had decided to bring us the bloody clothes as proof. I stood there and looked at the shirts and pants and still wondered how connected the locals were, and if they were telling the truth.

They were reporting that we killed around nine fighters and the enemy told them all to leave. They said that we were going to get attacked and it was going to happen in the next couple of days.

We were out further than we were supposed to be, but we had fought for the area and we were not going to give it up. So now, things change.

Okay, these fuckers want to come and play fuck-fuck games, well it was about time. You started it, and we tagged you back. We went back and went through what we had. We used the systems to give us a good look at the terrain in the area, and maybe see any other possible avenues of approach. We so far had our little place, and we were going to hold on to that.

Here is where you get your leaders together and we go over the worst case scenario. I did think that it was time that we adjusted our perimeter, walk the line, check with the FO and nine lines, medical equipment and the men. If we were going to get rushed and attacked, we might as well be ready. We gathered around and our leadership decided to talk about security and we talked about what we had in place, and then we wanted to go over it again. Someone would volunteer for a needed task and get it done. It's fucking awesome when it works smoothly. This is unlike the times we have to go and do some bullshit. Here, we are calling our own shots. As others are behind the security lines wondering how bad it was out there, we were out here living a life that was peaceful. Yes, the dangers were greater, but this is what everyone bitches about when they come back from Afghanistan.

"I was in danger, I saw this, I did this ... blah, blah, blah." Fuck you! Sorry, but it isn't true, there is a difference. There are those that want to find the bad guy and remove him from the face of the earth. We march to the sounds of guns. We want to see what the fuck is going on. We want to get in there and fight. We want to close in and destroy him by any means available. Usually "people other than grunts" (POGS) say we just break shit, shoot shit, and kill stuff, and we do. We do it so well that everyone needs soldiers like us doing what you are scared of. We keep you safe enough to see another karaoke night on the FOB. We do it by busting our ass in the manner that has been passed around since the beginning of time, by walking in the steps of heroes that came before us. We live in chaos and control the mayhem that others think is crazy. You on the other hand have never walked to the fight during the day, then night. I am talking about training; doing it over and over again till the Bn XO gives you a fucking go. Nothing is more trained that the fucking trench. Over and over again, you know exactly where the person is going to go and it does not matter it's a blank fire. They get pissy and make you do it over and over again if you mess with one of their pet peeves. Then you do blanks again and again. Finally live ammo, and by the time you get to this point you have lost it. You want to shoot the shit out of something and

I don't give a fuck if the target has a hole in it so huge the sensor will not let it go down and come back up. No not me, because if that fucking target stays up I'm going to shoot everything I got at it and when we stop, I'm going to yell out, "He's still moving" and we are going to do another mad minute and I am going to squeeze that trigger and "blow that target up."

Then we come to real life and we run, we move, we do the same things we have done a million times, but we have seen it before. POGS, have not, so to them we break shit, and kill shit. It's a whole lot harder than that, and you have no idea of the chaos in which we live. We volunteer to be dropped off and know we will find trouble. We think we are better than them and we will win. We choose to meet the challenge and win, or die. Not everyone does that. So how about a little respect when you see us come into your FOB?

Yes, our uniforms are torn, old, faded, and our hair is a little long. But don't throw us out because we are not clean enough. We do not have the luxuries that have been afforded to you. Instead of respect, we are treated like we are not good enough to enjoy the same stuff as you. How the fuck is that right? While you are fighting for some chick to dance with on salsa night, we are actually fighting. You sleep warm and cozy in your hooch, and we climb mountains. We live in the rain, heat, wind, and know what we have given up, to fight. There we are, unable to get a good hot meal. You saw your replacements come and go, due to the ever changing role of support. We saw a new guy show up to take a buddy's position because he got wounded or died. We still need four more, but hey, nothing is perfect, right?

Okay enough on that. We are beginning our checks and what not. We seem to remember that there was a company asset of mortars back in the rear. Yeah, with the gear. Thinking that there was somewhat of a good chance that we might get attacked, I decided to call to see if I could get them sent out to us. Does the CO answer? Nope! The first sergeant does, and we have a good idea of what might happen. I didn't think that it was too much to ask. If we were right, we would smash those fuckers. If we were wrong, they got to sit their ass here instead of over there. Like clockwork, and on cue, we were told no. We were told *no*! So, we made fucking lemonade. We pushed on and used what we had the best we could. First Sergeant Dickface did however, let them go to the breach, where Third Platoon was. They had an awesome time dude! They were by the creek or some well, and they had a little fishing hole. It was so awesome and cool man. They had a great time and made it look so nice. Wow, those guys were so special; I am so jealous. Fuck that! We continued to work and run operations from the Alamo.

One morning, we had guests. The Task Force Commander and his SgM walked up to our location. To me, it was odd, but fuck it. That's what you do, make the rounds and check out the men, see how things were going and get a little face-to-face conversation. We moved the vehicle from the front and opened up the wire to let them in. I stood there and welcomed the two battle buddies. I had no personal experience with the Battalion Commander and just a ride or so with the CSM. What I did see and knew was that they were out and about, and that is more than I could say for our leadership. We walked into the compound where they would get the tour. I took them to our makeshift HQ. Straight off the bat, they were impressed. As a matter of fact the Cdr said we had it better than he did in his place to our rear. They looked at the maps and the way we were tracking stuff in our area. They took a look at the compound and what kind of shape our security was in. I don't remember too much more. I was just surprised that they took the time to walk out to see us. I was also happy to know we were right on the money. We were complimented on the work we had done. That, to me was all the more reason to keep on doing the job, and forget about all the bullshit. I told the guys we got a good pat on the back and looked professional.

Shortly after the visit, we were called up to do something up at the breach. I remember going up there and I had to fucking do it. I am a dick, and I should have known better, but I did it. It was something that I felt I had to do. I talked to the first sergeant and asked him to come on down and check out our area. After all, he was running around with the others, but had yet to be where we were. Maybe, asking him to come on out and see how good the men were doing, the men would see him in a different light. He had a chance to be an example. In this operation, that would go a long way. Remember careful, for what you wish for. Don't open your mouth and insert your foot. Keep quiet and do not fucking do it. I do not remember how the fuck the plan went, but I guess from the good reports from the task force guy and the CSM he was inspired to come out and visit as well. We were ready to receive our leader, and expecting for the better relationship. So he said he was going to let me know when exactly he would visit.

I was headed back to our place and we were notified that there was a meeting. Some of the elders and local leaders from the surrounding villages were wanting to talk again. Colunga and Briola were out and about working the crowd. The senior squad leader would talk and discuss whatever was talked about. We started to play their way, and we changed up how we did things. Most of the time, they would bullshit about nothing. Water, food, Taliban, and shoot the shit. Meanwhile, the HMFIC (Head Motherfucker In Charge) sat there and took in the info, learning from what was being said if we were going to be dicks and or just some people willing to give out free shit. So, when in Rome, right? We stayed in the back and felt out the crowd. Colunga and Briola were pointing out the religious leaders, who the head guy was, who the leader of the village was and who was the big fish, the one that spoke for all. They sent up a smart, healthy, well dressed guy and he was the speaker. The Canadians were running the stuff with the Afghan Army guys. They were talking about who knows what; I just wanted to see who was who. There was talk about the bad guys coming over and wiping us all out. The enemy was pissed and wanting to inflict some damage of their own. They were using scouts walking in the fields like farmers. I was wondering if any of those bastards had a free lamp we were supposed to give away? Maybe the battery from the lamp used to make an IED? The fake farmers were the look outs. They would bang their shovels to warn the fighters when we were close, or when to move up. They were operating during dusk when most were coming back from the fields. Kip (who was the Head Canadian) was on it.

He asked about their dress, where they were coming from? If they had burn marks on their necks from rope slings? Just anything that would set them apart from regular civilians. He was good, and they were good company to have around. We had been warned about an attack that was supposed to happen.

We wanted to be ready, be prepared, and so we did what we could. Right now, we were trying to get their team players figured out and we were good at it. Colunga or Briola were able to point things out here and there. We would hang around and as the talking continued we made our way around to the cheap seats, the places in the back where the leaders would hang out and observe. We were looking at some old men. In this area, and through the years, they had to be smart and tough as nails to survive all the fighting. I made my way to one of the old guys and with the use of a terp and one of the guys, we would begin to bullshit. Introductions, and then some joking around. It was a good thing to have something that was catchy or flashy. You would have it out, and noticeable. A leatherman, a lighter, flashlight, or some good old-fashioned Copenhagen would do. We sat there and chatted, sat there spitting and jaw jacking, talking about how old and strong he had to be to live this long, how wise they must have become after so many years of knowledge. Then, they asked what I had in my mouth, what was I chewing on that kept me spitting and what not? Oh, this? In Iraq we called it *schweeka*. I don't know what it is in Afghanistan. These old dudes, well they had their version of hard shit. I don't know what it was, and I sure as hell was not going to find out.

There was a time when the war first started, and it was about the tea. Sure, I'll sit down and drink some tea with you. Why not? It's a hundred jillion degrees, and hot tea makes complete sense at this point and time. I'm seeing UFOs, Leprechauns, and that llama needs to pass me the sugar.

Tea was a good thing, and it was respectful. So, we drank tea. I was living with the commandoes and they ate loads of onions and garlic. I do not mind onions, but these guys believed that the onions and garlic helped you in the heat. Now, even to this day, If I smell onions, it reminds me of the sun being so bright you couldn't open your eyes, the sand so bright, you have to have glasses. The poor conditions that we lived in. The way people stank. That makes me think of the iron smell of blood. Then pools of blood, dried up in the dirt. Flies, and the pools of blood on floors, or in the back of a truck, real thick and chunky because there are brains in it. Yeah, onions. I'll pass.

Copenhagen: every now and then someone will try it out. It isn't poppy or crazy drugs. What it is, simply, is a psychological tool. Here you are in an argument with someone, and you turn and spit and it adds to your persona, adds to the message. Then, here you are and you ask to step away and get a quick message from one of the guys. Maybe, create a gap in time or a break in the dialogue to think of a good response. Either way, you are one little thing closer to being like them. They see you more like them.

I'm sitting here with this old guy and he and I go back and forth. I tell him I know who he is and that he is the man. He acts bashful and what not and we joke and bullshit. We start to get more info and we start talking about the families and where they were. They were told to leave and to get out. War was coming and those that stayed were mainly those who were elders and were going to take care of the place. I just thought that the elders did not want to leave and get replaced. So, that's why they stayed and were going to try to play both sides of the fence. So, the elder and I talk and we bullshit. We want to find the bad guys, but then again, it would not matter. We had our mission, and were now support. Fuck, I mean security. He pointed out that he was in the next village over and it was dangerous. Bad guys were everywhere, and that they were planning on killing us there. What the bad guys did, was involve the local population. They warned the local people in order to minimize civilian casualties. The bad guys were being more socially aware and doing things like this to get approval or acceptance. After all we were not able to do it like them, and it was their politics to maybe grow the ranks while changing their image. It was pretty simple, and it gave the people a choice on what to do. Stay and you might die, or get the fuck out! We talked about his town and tried to get as much info as possible. What was the count of bad guys? Was there any specific location? What was the time frame that we were looking at? Anything, from possible weapons to caches. The boys wanted to find a big cache, especially Briola. If you get to find the weapons, you have bragging rights. They did find some in the Argendab and had a fair share of excitement. Briola wanted a *dishka* to take back to the States, a souvenir, a memento from the days we were in the war. We gathered all we could and passed it up to the command. There was a possible attack on us and what information we had received from the local population. The info was not 100% but worth the consideration. We didn't have to drop everything and overreact, but it was worth taking note and watching our surroundings better. We went back and we organized for the following day. We requested permission to snoop and poop. A little bit later we were given the green light to push up further and take a look at the old man's town. After all, there was going to be a great show and we wanted to get out and have some fun too. We did our maintenance and worked on some of the tools of the trade. We made plans and selected who was to go out and who were we going to leave behind. After we checked out all the systems and did our checks, we decided to roll out. We stopped with our neighbors and told the Canadians what we were going to do. It was just going to be a basic patrol and we thought possibilities were slim of getting into a scrap. We said we were going out to their front. Just to make sure we were not shot at (like that is another problem we could use).

We had our run in with the enemy on day one. We were good but I don't think the other guys did so well. Besides being screwed over and hung out to dry in front of the whole company, we played the part we were given.

As we go back over things that were cleared before, we take our time. It was all over the news that we were coming and intel said that the enemy had prepped the battle-field. So We stop and look for booby traps, bombs and mines. I take a look at a small cave and wonder why a generator/pump was left behind. It could be a trap, or someone left in a hurry.

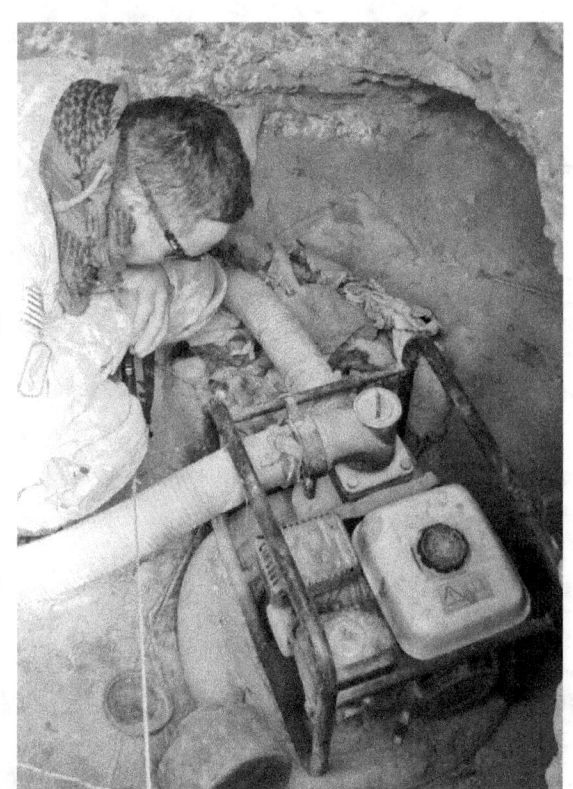

The search continues and we check everything. We look for maps, drawing, or anything that can give us a look at what we might be facing. Then again, it might just be a trap.

Time to recap the days activities. With security up, we begin to unwind and talk crap about the crazy events of the day. There is no reason to try and hide. We whooped their ass and took their place. They know we are here and they know where they can find us. Come get some!

After we took their HQ, we do a little area beautification. We end up burning almost all of the weeds, except for one area. In those weeds, we find this: three gallon jugs filled with hand made explosives (HME). We tried to put it in the lost and found, but no one ever replied.

I had experienced some of the things others mentioned before and now there was no more pretense at civility. People seemed to think that I didn't need to know shit. I had no say or input and was left holding the bag. Usually I would expect that there was a rotation, and it was someone else's time to get fucked with. Nope, and all the little bullshit games that went on before were just a warm up to a potentially deadly game being played. I knew I hated this motherfucker, my first sergeant, and yet I wondered if maybe we could change the way we were treated. Maybe I'd been too harsh on this turd and needed to show him how good we really were? It was because of my willingness to try to do the right thing that I ended up making things worse for all of us. Instead of thinking only about the men, I want to mend and make bridges. You know every time I tried, I ended up giving him another opportunity to screw me and the men over.

The biggest problem was this guy not helping me do my job. I didn't give a shit about the enemy. The biggest problem I had was begging to get anything from my command. Actually, I can't even say that. It was not even the company commander, but the first sergeant that fucked with us, just because.

Well, we were sent into fight, so we did. We controlled what we could, and I can say I pushed the envelope in combat. I did all I could and then some. I had more fear of failing, than getting hurt. That would have ended me and any righteous or holy mission I felt obliged to do. I felt a need to prove to everyone that the things I had been taught were not old and outdated. Not only was I right, but it still worked. At this point, I was written off, sent to a shit hole, had my own personal torturer, and should have been dead eight months ago. I was sitting at "Death plus 230" days.

"Who Did This?"

Colunga was up in the front, and Briola was in the back. Fairchild was to the rear with the weapons. Vinyard stayed in the rear, back at the compound. We moved out a little slowly at first. After all we were going to our deaths and we didn't intend to get there early. I remember that there was some open terrain and we were going through a place where there were ruins and a kind of castle to one side. I wanted to hurry up and not spend too much time in a choke zone. I called up Colunga and asked him what the problem was? Why were we still moving slow?

I asked who was on point and he said it was Swain. Swain was supposed to be on leave. No wonder we were moving so slow. With all the stuff we were being told, he had a right to be nervous, and he'd had some bad experiences too. I did however tell Colunga that we'd better get a move on, before I went up there and took the point position. He went ahead and chewed out Swain and we began to cover more territory. We passed several sketchy places and made our way to the village. We reached a creek and saw a farmer in the field.

He was called over by one of the guys and Colunga started to talk to him. Briola started to talk to the local cleric, and both men stated that we were supposed to stay off the road. They had seen something in the road and had placed a log on the bridge to keep us from going there. They said there were "people" in the village and that it was dangerous. I believe Colunga gave the farmer like $20. He was going to come back and try to give us more information. So we went straight for the log and tried to see what exactly we were dealing with. Being focused on the threat on the road, there was a good chance that "people" would come out and play. We decided to move back on the road and go straight to the bridge. We reached the bridge and we all got into the prone position. On the other side of the bridge was a compound to the right of the road with a large wall that went parallel to the road for twenty meters. On the other side of the road was a single wall, as we use to divide the lanes going and coming. The road split into a Y with the barrier in the center. It came to an intersection that had nothing but an open field in the top right, a large compound at the bottom right all the way to the creek. On the far left we had a compound, across from an open field. In the field stood a house at seventy-five yards. At the bottom left we had two compounds and they were about thirty feet away from the road. Basically, it was your typical choke point. Nowhere to go but forward or back. I for one, couldn't see a damn thing. We all looked and couldn't see anything, so I asked for the grappling hook. I couldn't throw it over the creek and get too much on the other side, so I told everyone to stay put, and me and Colunga went to the bridge. I didn't know too much about the bridge but the sides had curbs, so we walked on them to the other side. We stood there and tried to get a good look at the ground. I was on the left and Colunga was to the right. I was facing toward the barrier and saw something that didn't look right. Colunga, moved up to the wall and I wanted to take a look, so I started to fish with the grappling hook. The first time was scary and so was every other attempt after that. I was throwing toward a change in the surface. That way I could hook or catch anything that was wired, going to the bomb or away. It was a dirt road, but there was a place that was not like the rest.

It was more rocky or gritty. It looked like someone had been loading up a flower pot or wheel barrel and then they'd moved it away. Whatever fell off the end stayed there. It looked like it was dirt, but then spread all over the place. I wasn't able to latch on to anything and wanted to get a better look.

I threw the hook to the men and told them to stay there. "What are you doing?" Briola said.

"Let's call it in and report it," he said.

"Report what? Dirt?" I said.

We are supposed to confirm then cordon, so I worked my way up to the place that was "off." It just didn't look the same—there were these cracks that had formed in a ring, to me that said *I'm here*. I knew what or where the thing was. It looked like someone made a hole recently and covered it up. They packed it down, and poured water on it to make it smooth. Then someone grabbed dirt clods and broke them in their hands and spread the dirt to make it blend into the surroundings. What they didn't know, was once they put the water on, it had soaked into the ground. It then settled the dirt in the shape of the hole and in its form. When it dried up, it cracked and left another shape, but of what? I grounded my weapon, got on my belly and worked my way to the site.

I remember looking back and seeing the eyes and helmets of the men on the other side of the creek. They were thinking, "This motherfucker is crazy" or "This motherfucker is going to die," or even both. I turned back to what I was doing. Hell, I had done this before in EIB, and this time it was for real. I also had something else going for me the others didn't think about. Here we have whatever someone threw in the dirt, in the middle of the night, then threw dirt on, and then water and more dirt. Chances are that they were not the smartest or most delicate of handlers. I then reached to my gear and pulled out my paratroopers knife. I'd had this thing since the war began and I'd wanted a reason to use it. Yes, I know that some of these things are magnetized and can fuck you up. However, if things here are like they are in my army, they are made by the lowest bidder and not the very best.

No heat sensors and it was all in the ground. So I began probing first. I started with a rock. Then another one, and then, "Tink!" not a rock, but something else. It sure as hell was not something that was from there. Whatever it was, it was wrapped in Saran wrap and tape. I kept on going and trying to get the whole shape uncovered. One little bit of rock and sand at a time. I would barely touch the ground with my hand and let whatever was loose roll away, off of the object. When I would hit a hard spot, I would run my knife across it but backward using the top spine of the knife and not the actual cutting side.

There was no real reason for this, except I would sit there for hours trying to get that fucking knife sharp and it never would get an edge. While I did have the knife still, and if I ever lived to tell the story, I figured I shouldn't fuck up any work I may or may not have already put into the damn thing! Once I did that, I started to go down the edges and remove chunk after chunk. While I'm doing this, I'm thinking back to grade school where we had those electric switches that turned on the light in science class. I would glance over to the men and see some eyeballs and the top of K-pots and think that they were saying two things. "What the fuck is he doing?" and, "Is he still fucking alive?"

Every now and then, I would find myself getting faster and faster. At that point, I would look at Colunga or the men at the creek and spit.

What the fuck am I doing? I'm a fucking idiot! I couldn't see how I got myself in the fucked up situation that I currently found myself in. Once I got settled again, I looked at what was right in front of my face, spit, and got back to work. I would pull up some rocks, and some sand, and rocks. For the most part, I felt like someone should have smoked the shit out of the fuckers that put this shit in the ground. The amount of rocks that were in there to fill up the hole meant that they were fucking up the task and taking short cuts. To me, this was put in by fucking privates on extra duty, and not someone who knew what the fuck he was doing.

Seriously, here I am with my dick in the fucking dirt picking at a fucking bomb, and I can see two privates rushing through this task to get their ass to the fucking hay barn for man-love Thursday. Then again, thank God for that.

    I make my way down to the bottom of the board and see two wires coming out of the corner. Okay, there has to be something on the end of this, so I uncover a nine volt battery. I grab that fucker and pull it off the line. I knew I had the initiation system, and the power source. There are usually three parts to one of these: the box or initiation system, the power source, and right under the plate should be the charges of HME. On the other hand, it could be offset to fucking hit the striker like the lieutenant did. So I have the battery off of this fucker. However, I know how much of a fucking dick I would be. Again, Sarge (I'm being sarcastic) would tell you to dig all the way down. Do it right, don't just lift it out. No shit, E-I- mother-fucking B! When recovering the anti-personnel or anti-vehicle bullshit, you're supposed to go to the bottom of the mine. Why? Just in case someone did exactly what I just did. In case people like me dig up your shit, put a fucking grenade under the son of a bitch, just to blow up the guy recovering the system. I worked my way down to the bottom of the complete pressure plate and made sure there were no other wires and with the greatest of care I separate the whole enchilada. Just like that, I was finished. I wanted to fucking scream and piss all over the fucking place! Instead, I lay there, and went over my work. I didn't move, and I looked back and touched the plate, battery, and at the end of the wires into the ground, found the blasting cap, in a big fucking "yellow" shitty plastic jug. Just like the ones we'd seen before we crossed the line. I pulled everything apart, placed the battery in my pocket, grabbed the pressure plate, stood up, and we began to move again. We had our first souvenir. The look on everyone's faces was one of amazement. They had a gleam in their eye that had been long gone. Their smile was back and we had a win on our side. However, we were around fifty meters from a fucking danger zone, the intersection. Colunga and I bounded forward. Swain came across as well as others for security. The next IED was right after you crossed the bridge. You were faced with the left side, where I pulled it up from, or the right side, so guess where we found the big boy? On the right side, same as the other one. Now I had the "key" though, and it was on. I had enough to call up EOD, but all they would have done was send out a fucking robot and blown the thing up, which would have taken a while. However, we had secured the first one. It wasn't a problem. Plus, there were some fucking bitches here that wanted to make us fucking dead, and fuck that "telephone tough guy" shit. I was not going to stop till we were beyond this obstacle. So, I grabbed my dull as hell paratrooper's knife and crawled back up to the plate. Just like the last one, I started from the outside of the crack and worked my way in. The pressure plate from the first one must have been ¼ of an inch or less. This motherfucker was the real deal! I don't know if that makes sense, but this bitch was fucking big! I heard how the IEDs were targeting specific targets, but it was not till I was on number two, that I knew what the hell people were talking about. The first pressure plate was small, maybe a foot wide. This one was at least two fucking feet long. It was about, maybe two inches wide? Whatever, I decided to take pictures. This time, If I lived through this shit, I was gonna have fucking pictures as proof. Just like I did the first one, due to the intense training of the EIB and other classes, I worked my way, inch by inch to uncover this plate. I found the wires and traced them to the battery, and then to the jugs. I worked and again, found myself in the same place that made me wonder out loud,

"What the fuck am I doing? Why the fuck didn't I just stay in the rack, and sleep?" There was no reason to go on and push to find the bad guy. We were alone and could sit and wait till the whole thing was over. What the fuck was wrong with me? Then I remembered all those crusty bad-asses that pushed. "When in charge, be in charge!" Those men that had us do it over and over again. The ones that wanted us to do it better, faster, and be winners! Somehow, I was not alone. I was there, and everyone that was in my life was there too. I was more afraid of letting down the men I was with, those that were, and those that had been throughout my time in the Army. My family, soldiers, and leaders were all on my mind, and I didn't want to fail. I couldn't, and was going to finish what I started or die trying.

Most people say this and that. Some say that they would die for this and blah, blah, blah. Here, we separate those that do, and those that talk. I didn't want to just bullshit. I had the opportunity to show others that I meant everything that I said. I wasn't going to run from no fucking Taliban. I might get blown up, but we were not just gonna stop.

As I worked and identified the three basic systems, I would take time to spit and look around. I saw Swain off to the right pulling security on a fucking wall. I called out to him. "Swain! Come here; let me show you something!" "Fuck that!" he said. "I'm not even supposed to be here. I'm supposed to be on fucking leave!"

He had his dick in the dirt off to the edge and was concerned about what the fuck I was doing. Surely, I was gonna get it this time? Nope, not this time, and I found a little humor in the serious situation that I was in. I couldn't help but laugh while Swain talked, and I saw the beat-up cigar still in his helmet band. It was serious, and here we are laughing and bullshitting as I am lying with my face inches, and I mean inches, from a fucking bomb. I finished the job and was surprised at the size of the thing, but before I did anything, this time I took the whole mother-fucking bomb, still wired up, and put the fucking wires in my teeth and took a picture. I did it, and I gave the Longhorn sign and said, "Cheese, bitches!" Mother-fucking cheese from Afghanistan. How about that for a postcard?

"Hey mom, we are having great times out here in the sand and we get to play needle in the haystack. Look, here is a picture of me before I got my head blown off."

Yeah, that would have been awesome. Once I had cleared this fucker we moved people up. Fairchild came up to take the plate back. We put the grid, date, and other info on the plate. Some of the guys took a look at the thing and who knows what they said. It was their first time to look at something so simple that you could make it at home, something that had taken the lives of so many others. To hold it for me was a major win. We worked our way to the intersection and since the right side was a field we chose to go left. This time it is Colunga, Swain, Sellner, Wynell, me, and Doc was around too. Briola moved to the left flank and took up security toward the area we were clearing. Fairchild was to the rear covering the building and the open area to the right. We sat there and Colunga asked what we were going to do. After all, we kind of hit pay dirt and we had a good catch so far. I didn't want to stop there in the intersection and not clear out to the next building, or road. We had to push out past the intersection and take a look at what was out there, and we had to secure the location. I think we were set. Once we cleared the danger area then we would call it a day.

Colunga and I walked out toward the left to the end of the alley. He was on the right and I was on the left. Basically I gave him a quick class about ant trails, and what was noticeable and things that I saw on the last two IEDs. He had been on the ground and was experienced enough that we pushed forward. While we were clearing the alley, I thought of something. Here we are like hounddogs sniffing and looking at our feet, but who the hell is watching our back? We need another man and we need to get our asses back to the fucking group. As Colunga and I reached the end, we did a quick halt. We stopped and just listened for a while. We took a knee and just listened and it was quiet. I was getting nervous and I didn't want to bite off more than we could chew. We hustled back and we took a look over where we had passed before. As we approached the intersection we stopped again and we talked a bit, set in security better and called up the IEDs. This is where we called up Swain. "Swain! Check it out."

That was my platoon sergeant from the 173rd's favorite saying. Back in the day when I was in the Dirty 30, SFC Beldock, Alpha Company First Platoon, 1-508th, Red Devils. Since he always had these great ideas back in the day, I figured that I had to mention that's where I got the saying.

"Swain! Check it out, we are going to go up here along the wall to clear the area. We're going to do the 'Longhorn Formation!'"

Swain was like, "What?"

"Two of us up front, one on the left, another on the right. That will make up the horns. One person to the rear, that would make the head. We're going to clear the remaining area of the road. You can pull security as we move. You got our back while we do this. We already found two. If we find three, we can take the day off."

I said this as if there was a fucking bonus plan in the organization. It was a bad attempt at a joke at the wrong time and we looked at each other. I gave the Longhorn sign. I was looking at Swain and pointed to where we were going. We did the same as last time, except this time we had Swain watching our six. Again, I take up the left and had the wall to my left. We were walking down a road that had nothing but a fucking open field to the right. Up ahead was a little creek or wash and the plan was to clear up to there and return. Colunga had the open area to his right. There was a house further up to the right and it looked like a house, but it was made of fucking weeds or tumble weeds stacked up to form the walls. There was a door so, it looked like Afghanistan's version of the American double-wide. As we went around the corner, we carefully walked forward. I think that knowing that we had done enough and EOD was on the way was settling. There was kind of a rush to finish this small task and get back to babysitting duty. To this point right here, we just didn't stop and cancel the mission. We progressed forward and continued. I never heard of anyone doing what we had just done and considering it a good day's work. So, we went forward, toward the light at the end of the tunnel. We are about fifteen to twenty feet out and blam! Just like that, there is a fucking crack-a-lacking going on. Shit is popping off everywhere. Swain is shooting first and yelling. This is good; Swain is a bad-ass. He did not hesitate, returned fire, and started to yell out the 3 D's: Distance, Direction, and Description. A lot of fuckers faint, take a knee, run away, hell, they fucking hide. Not Swain. That motherfucker had our back, and he is dealing out an ass-whooping. Here, is the second time ever in my life that I can recall time starts moving slowly. The ambush we went through in Hawija, Iraq, and here. I'm listening to the yelling and firing and I lift up my head, parallel to the wall. As I do, I see the impact of the rounds in the wall, right in front of my face. I heard Swain's info, and I remember the image in my head, and I swing right and start to suppress the target. Swain and Colunga empty out their mags, reload on the run, and I continue to suppress. They go back, and I cover their movement. I reload a new mag, and fuck the trigger finger, I use the "Fuck Your Couch" mother-fucking middle finger and spray that fucking hooch. I work back to them and when shit is this close, charge, motherfuckers! Swain sets up on the left, I bound over to the right. We are at the opposite corners of the intersection and we lay into them. Sellner is popping off 203s at these fuckers and we hear them scrambling. Colunga and Sellner take off down the middle. Colunga however is saying that he can't see. I point out the direction and he and Sellner take off. They are bounding through this open field and me and Swain are shooting the shit out of the place. We've hit a machine gun nest and we are knee deep in some ass. Sellner is lobbing off 203s, Colunga is shooting at whatever he is shooting at. Swain and I are trying to hit these fuckers talking shit about our moms, and it is on like Donkey Kong! Once Colunga and Sellner are in grenade range, they begin to suppress. Swain and I bound over to their left. We didn't want any squirters to go down the road or cross it and here we go. Meanwhile the FO is like, "Fuck you! I'm going too!"

So Swain and Wynell are covering the left flank, Colunga, Sellner, and I am going after the bad-asses that tried to fuck us.

Fairchild and Shaftner are coming off the right side and it is on. We are on the move and we have just changed the momentum to our advantage. We are shooting, moving, and communicating. At first, things were slow and smooth. Now it's as if you hear everything, and nothing loud hurts your ears. The crack of the guns, the 203s, grenades, everything is like on low. Your heart is going, you're breathing, but it's as if you are holding your nose and are trying to pop your ear drums. I tell Swain to hold it down and I go to get on line with Colunga and Sellner and we advance. We throw everything at them. I yell for a grenade and Sellner says, "I got it." I'm like "No, fucker, throw it over here so I can throw it," and he says, "Nope." He pulls out the grenade, takes off the safety tape, pulls the ring, goes to one knee and in a not so manly voice yells, "Die, motherfucker." Colunga and I start to laugh. What the fuck? Here we are in the middle of a firefight, and we begin to talk shit. "Oh shit! You didn't pull the safety?"

"Yes I did."

"No you didn't."

"OK, if you did, where the fuck was the boom?"

"I hope these fuckers don't pick up that shit and throw it back!" While we are engaged in a conversation about nothing, Swain opens up again. Squirter! Bam, bam, bam, bam. Swain is fucking playing peek-a-boo with a fucker running across the street. Somehow, we get through to the house and find just blood and shit tore up. I hear that EOD is out there and they need to know where they are needed to go. So, we are on squat hold for right now. I gotta go get these guys and we need to adjust to the area. Briola is inching his way off to the left side. I go back, by the IEDs, over the bridge, and back to another irrigation ditch and run into the EOD. This guy has his shit all spray painted and cool. However, he reminds me of the first douche bag that tried to get rid of a soldier named Leffers. He is a cool guy, S.F. and we chat a bit. He said that there were some Airforce rookies with him and that he was wanting them to get their feet wet. So, he was going to let them handle the

"Robot." At that time I am like, I fucking knew it. I knew that this shit was going to happen and I simply responded, "It's done!"

He's like, "What is done?"

"The IEDs. They're confirmed and they're waiting to get picked up or whatever you do with them."

So, he responds that they need to make sure, because most of the time they get called out and it isn't, blah, blah, blah.

"Not only are they confirmed but they're disabled."

'What?" he said.

"They're confirmed and not operational. I know this because I dug them up, took off the pressure plates, and the batteries. They are just in the dirt, you can have them." Just like that–boom! The whole shit opens up again. We are talking and I see the Air Force guy take up some real estate and jump in the prone. I stop the conversation and say, "Uh, I think he is in an ant pile?"

It didn't matter, I tell him if he wanted to take a look at what we had, to come along because I gotta go back to the front. Then the Air Force private stands up and starts with, "I have ants all over me." Or, "I have poop on my shoe," and notice you are in the tiger cage. I took that as a cue to go back to the fight. We go down the road, over the river, and through the woods to the intersection. The guys are engaged by fire coming from down the road. Colunga is telling me what is going on and I asked if the compound that Fairchild went through been cleared? We had squirters running around and the last thing we wanted was to get outflanked and shot in the back. So, I told them to hold tight and said I would take a peek.

There are rounds zipping around and coming from all over the place. The EOD guy is looking at the jugs.

"Who did this?" he asks.

"I did." Zip, zip, zip, zip-zip-zip.

"Who are you guys?"

"We are the Black Sheep, second platoon."

"Uh, you are just regular guys? You are not special or... Special?"

"Nope, just regular guys. You didn't think we were just going to stop and sit here and wait for you? No, that's not our job, we are supposed to close in and destroy the enemy, by any means necessary. I'm going to go and check this place out."

"Are you going to go alone?"

"Hell, yeah!"

"No you're not. I'm gonna go too." So we took off and made the rounds. We cleared the compound and made the way back. Then, here come the Canadians and the Afghan Army. They are wanting to pass friendly lines, but need to conduct the link up. So, off I go again to the back. I start to talk to Kip, and he is ready for the fight. I am explaining what we have and how the area is set up. We know there are squirters around and we have not made it entirely to the end of town. Just then, bam! Shit opens up again. I tell him to move forward to our forward location, and we can let them push forward.

"Oh, by the way, watch out for the bombs on the road."

"What?"

I tell him about it, and I said we have to go. I needed to get back up to the men. So here Wynell and I go running up the fucking road, past the bombs, and bullets coming toward us, no shit, *at* us, and I think, "This is the most perfect time of my life."

This moment right here, bombs, guns, bullets, and I'm running to the sound of the guns and my men, The Black Sheep. No matter how long I may live, I will never reach this perfect feeling of person, place, and time again. I am running down the road with the FO and everything just lines up. Everything is the way it's supposed to be and where it's supposed to be. It all happened in combat, on a road where there is so much going on. At that moment, I felt peace. It was a calm, that I felt only one other time. There was no noise, things were moving but not like normal. It was as if a picture was taken and everything froze. The feeling of running and hearing your heart beat, your breathing, all the gear bouncing around was not there. It made me feel comfortable, and safe. I understood what and where I was, and could realize that this feeling was special. The first time, it was like a dream. This time, I didn't know what it was, but I knew it wasn't going to last long, and I smiled. I felt like everything was like it was supposed to be. The fucking stars, planets and everything else were in place.

It was a confirmation that all the bullshit and fucking hard times had paid the fuck off. My moral compass and the belief for looking out for these men, was right. I finally get back to the corner of the intersection where Colunga was, and it is on again. Just when you think it is over, shit is starting to pick up again, and me and Colunga talked at the intersection. I figured we should bound up and get online with Swain. Colunga said we had to wait. He said he lost his glasses and could not see. I looked around and didn't see anything, till I looked at my boots.

There under my boot were Colunga's glasses. It was like a bad fucking joke, right on time, so I reached down and gave them to him. Colunga responded like a broken hearted child who was refused his cookies.

"Oh man!" I knew where this was going to go, so I pushed him and said, "We gotta get going." We went forward and came up to the entrance of another compound. Colunga turns left and as I make my way through the turn, I tell him to go over it. We went through, stepped high and cleared the compound alone. I hurry up and make my way to the entrance to look at something that was out of place. There on the ground is a black top. It was a shirt top and actually looked like something the Viet Cong would wear. It was not just a shirt though, there was something inside, and it was big, I looked at it and there was a fucking trip cord attached to it. It was coming out of the shirt and it was long. Just then I hear boots coming up running and the words, "Friendlies coming in!" I turn and it is Wynell and Fairchild. I tell them to stay very still and not to step on the cord.

In the shirt, was a fucking bomb. It was a metal pipe with a water bottle attached to it. The whole thing was different. It was not like anything that we had seen at all. It did resemble some of the objects that I had seen before, way back in the day. It looked like something that we could have found in a fucking jungle. This however was fucking out of place and I looked real hard at it. Its initiation system was a fucking water bottle. It didn't have a pressure plate, but it worked by the pull string. If you pulled the string, it would bring a wire to touch the opposite wire and complete the circuit, and boom! There had been some talk or rumor about this kind of switch, but till then, it was all hearsay. We took off the battery. I sat there with Colunga and explained how it worked. There was a little bit of commercial explosives that was used to run into the bottom of the bomb to set off the main explosives. That would propel the charges forward out of the "pipe" like a gun. After it was taken care of, I wrapped it up and gave it to Colunga. "Here you go, it's yours. You can have it." Colunga was like a proud father. We had gotten our three, and fuck, the whole day was done. When Wynell came in, he had just missed the cord and we told him what was up. I asked him what the hell was he doing there?

"It's the radio. Command wants you to stop. You have gone further than anyone else has ever gone before."

I thought to myself, *what? I haven't heard that shit before. The bad guys are right here. We've got them on the run, but we have to stop?* As a matter of fact, we were ordered to stop and hold what we had. We were to secure the area. I told the guys the war was over. We stopped and let the Afghan Army do their passage of lines and we did our squat hold. Once we got told to stand down, we attempted to consolidate and work on what we had. We were going to focus on the area that we were shot at from. Maybe they left something so we were going to explore the whole site. With the Afghans pushing forward, they were going to have to do so without our assistance. We set up the security for where we were, pointed the guys out, and went to work. We wanted to explore the position they had and see what the hell we were looking at. So, Wynell, Fairchild, Colunga and I were going to cross the road and join up with Swain, and the others. At that time EOD is out there, and they see Colunga walking with his little baby, the bomb that I said he could have. Once they realize what he was carrying they yelled,

"Stop! Don't move! Drop the bomb and walk away!"

Colunga just kept on walking. Then his response was comical.

"It's okay. The sergeant said I could have it!"

These guys were fucking freaked.

"What the fuck is that?"

"It's a fucking bomb!"

They were shitting their pants. They didn't have nowhere to run, and didn't want whatever Colunga had there. So, we stopped, opened the shirt up, and showed them the bomb. After a bit they got a little closer and were excited. This thing was common in Iraq, but not here. The initiation system that was used was the golden ticket. After they saw that the "baby" was okay, they broke out the camera. I guess we'd helped with their intel. We gave them the water bottle and we removed the top of the charge. This bitch was homemade, and these just don't pop up anywhere. I guess that EOD took Colunga's baby.

After all, a buddy of mine was doing work in country. Sergeant E was the head NCO for the local program there, and they were the local CSI. We talked about this before, and I was comfortable knowing that at least someone I knew would be able to check on this shit, instead of it just getting lost and someone else taking the credit for it. I trusted him, and still do. There is a lot that comes with being side by side in war together. Hell, we started the war together as "Sky Soldiers" and "Red Devils," that means a lot. Once, Sgt E and I turned over a dump truck to the fuck-faces who later were in the papers. That truck was carrying gold, and Sergeant E and the men were the people who found it. We never heard a thing till it came out in the paper, then it's some Major posing, standing on the loot. That probably got him a good report, and made him a Light Colonel. Meanwhile, we were kept outside, dragging our knuckles in the dirt. Hopefully this would be different and maybe we would get something back. We were now in the reconsolidation and reorganization phase, and were going to have to look at the area. First off, we were going to look at where we were taking contact from. Plus, someone had decided to throw a grenade and nothing happened. We were curious if he did pull the pin, or if he just threw it. We walked the compound and saw the leftovers from the battle. There was a locked building near the ambush position and we decided to kick it down and check it out. As I stepped back to kick it the EOD yelled "Wait!"

It was too late though. We made our way into a room that looked like a grain store. Colunga and Briola start to check things out and they find a book with crap written in it. As that is going on the EOD is telling me that we should have checked the door before we kicked it in. In their perfect world of everything being death and a mistake, we simply live. They are so full of knowledge that it actually keeps them moving at a slow pace. We're not moving dangerously, but have been in our area and have seen what is common here. Hopefully Colunga's baby bomb isn't the new norm. There were no bodies in the firing position. That kind of left me thinking we were not hitting shit. There were casings from the ammo, trash, and blood. There had been someone there, but we knew that they had some type of recovery. We walked in search of anything, but we found nothing important. Me and Colunga walked around the back of the hut and were scouting for any trails or tell-tail signs. We were getting out a little away and were looking at a compound that was right next to the hut. As we are snooping and pooping, we hear a yell.

"We found it!"

They recovered the grenade and yes the pin was pulled, but the thumb safety was not. We heard the others talking shit and laughing. We ourselves were talking shit, and we hear EOD. They said that they were going to blow it. The plan was to pull the safety and throw it to the back way. Colunga and I didn't care, and said okay. Me and Colunga were looking and it hit me. Premonition, extra sense, I don't know or can explain it. Then, I look at him.

"Hey, what's the chance of them throwing it our way?" I ask him.

As soon as I said it, plop! Right off to our side. We turned the nearest corner, hugged the wall and boom! We came back and were a little hot.

"What the fuck? We were back there and you almost got us."

"You dug up two IEDs, got ambushed, found another bomb, are kicking in doors and you think you're going to get hurt?" the EOD guy said.

"Fuck yeah! Our luck, we'll get it in the shitter." As we made our way back to the IEDs, the Canadians came back. They said they ran into a hornets' nest and that they were taking fire from different directions. They were going to pull back and that would leave us in the front again. We were getting pop shots from here and there and were waiting to blow the IEDs. Briola moved up and set up security to cover our withdrawal. He had the gun teams and was going to get him some action. Shots were heard and bullets were zinging. The machine guns opened up and began to spray and suppress suspected enemy locations. Once we were back at the new position they were going to do a mad minute and pop smoke. This would let us know they were fixing to move. It was to signal their withdrawal and movement to our location. We bounded back and then came the guns. We positioned our twelve to fifteen guys and waited to blow the IEDs. We put our charges on the first one, but it didn't go. EOD was going to have to hump back and get more, so we hunkered down and waited. I was lying in a ditch with the FO, RTO, Wynell and the special EOD guy. He was still trying to figure out what the hell happened there and how we got so far, or did what we did. He asked again.

"So, you all are just infantry? You're not some other different unit?"

"No," I said.

Wynell interrupted. "Have you got the munchies?" he asked me.

"Fuck yeah!"

By this time it was late in the afternoon. Wynell said that he had some summer sausage someone had sent in a care package and we began to cut it up and chow down. The EOD guy was looking at us like, "What the fuck?"

"You want some?" I asked him.

"Sure, I guess," he said.

The picture of us sitting in the ditch was not complete without a couple of zings going over our heads. We maintained security till they were ready to blow the bombs in the ground. We pulled back and watched as one by one they blew them up. To make things worse, there were seven other possible bombs, and we had to maintain what security we had. I remember that we did get a call on the radio from the CO. He wanted to let us know that he was sending out 1st sgt Dicks over to be the "on-site Commander." I had never heard of such a thing. Most of the time it was the men out there fighting that were running shit.

Then again, I was not too interactive on the radio with them. I had the RTO doing his job, and I was doing mine. On a trip back with EOD came our leader, in his new vehicle, with the gun pointed at us. Hmmm, that kind of makes you feel a little warm inside. We were in a huddle and talking to the EOD when here he comes. We are on the ground in the prone position. We had been out all day on a simple patrol and now it was dusk. I remember blowing one of the suspected or known IED positions and a fucking huge rock hit me in the wrist. I was cursing and what not. The first sergeant is laid up next to me and asks me why we were not wearing clear lenses? Yup, we were wearing sunglasses and now as it was getting dark, he wanted to know about our eye wear. He didn't ask what was going on? What happened? If anyone was hurt? All he asked is if we had our clear lens glasses? I told him no. We took off at 9am, we were gonna go for a walk, and here we are. I guess that made us not look good, or it was piss-poor planning, but we had dealt out somewhat of an ass-whooping to someone, and that was okay for me. I lay there and felt sick. We wrapped it up, and headed back to our patrol base.

After the day we had, we ended up with a load of guests. Just as we were trying to get involved in our little piece of the pie, my invite was accepted by our leader. First Sergeant decided to visit in and he didn't come alone. He brought an entire squad from Third Platoon, and the mortars.

Here you have it. We are doing the same thing we do every day. At the end of the day we sit and bullshit about the day's events and tell stories of the crazy shit that happened during the day. We sat there and had a conversation in which we all shared and recounted the foolish and dangerous events of the day. Like most things, everyone had their own version and telling that version was unique. We talked about other units we had been in and we shared the difference in the enemy's tactics. We talked about those that were not as lucky as we were. It felt right, sharing experiences and remembering others in a group of soldiers, a tribute to their memories and carrying them on forward with us. After all, we were waiting for the main effort to show up and we had already been there a week or so. It seemed that the timeline for the marines to get there kept getting pushed to the right.

How lucky do you really want to be? Some paid the ultimate sacrifice. Some were injured, and others well, they just weren't there. Another thing, if you ever felt that the world was a small place, you have no idea. Talking and hearing others' stories tells you a lot about the man. You find out that many of you were in the same place years ago. You begin to talk about places and then times, operational areas, maybe even battles and next thing you know, you were practically shoulder to shoulder in the same litter box. You might talk to someone at work about the carnival that came to town, that awesome ice cream place in the mall, hell, maybe Six Flags or Disneyworld. For us, it was the very same thing. It was just a different situation and in some dirt pile thousands of miles from home. Again, we are all talking and shooting the shit. We have a small talk about the guard shift, and the next day's events. While we are all huddled around the fire, all we see are eyeballs from the visitors. They had nothing really to talk about and for the most part just stared blankly into the flames. I talked with the squad leaders and we wanted to be sure things were planned to go good while we were entertaining, make sure everyone was in uniform and had no bumps in the road. Like usual, we would alternate and check out the positions. I would walk around before I hit the rack and let the others get some sleep early. We had a spot on the main roof and we had a 240 positioned there. You could see over the wall and check out everything on the outside. You could hear the crap that groups were talking about as they are cozy and in their rack. You could hear the sound of the radio coming out of a speaker box somewhere. That always reminded me of the movies.

"Bravo 27, Bravo 27, this is Reaper, over!"

"Bravo 27, Bravo 27, this is Reaper, over!"

It was the same thing, and it always sounded cool. Over the walls you could see the distant lights and the terrain in different shades of green.

The night vision glasses we had were okay, and it made everything a green or black color. When it was quiet, you could look at the distant houses or others doing their stuff out there where they were. Sometimes you could look up and see a million stars in the night sky, and it did seem peaceful. I would go up and chat with the guys. Maybe hear about their plans or a crazy conversation about something that they did before here. Some would argue and some would stay quiet. I thought it was part of my job to go out there and actually spend some time with them. I remembered when the lieutenant and I made the rounds during our time on perimeter security, back on the FOB. We had several towers on the FOB and we would run batteries out to them and just bullshit with them. We coordinated to have hot soup and maybe coffee and would relieve the guys to rotate and get their fill. I didn't like the coffee because it tasted like turpentine. The soup would taste like it was made out of a boot, and salty. We took it up to the men and we would talk about soldiers' plans and what was going on then. I did not have that now, but knew how much the men were important to him. I swore that I would watch over them and that is in the NCO creed. It states that everyone is entitled to good leadership, and I will provide that leadership. Well, sometimes you get the opportunity to listen and be approachable, and that was good in my book. Being away from my friends and not having a platoon sergeant to listen to made me feel like I was lost. I never thought I would be out and alone, and here I am. All my buddies were spread all over the place, in the Army or out of the Army. The crusty old platoon Daddy was not around to ask any questions too. It was just me, and the Black Sheep of 1-17 Infantry. I hated to be alone, but this was what I was dealt. I was told that there was a lieutenant waiting to join up with us, back in the rear. That didn't help me out too much, and under the conditions we were in, we were out there and alone. Until tonight, and that was crazy. To see the others act like they were zombies and not even interact with our guys was crazy. Most platoons would share stories, but we were less than the others. It was as if they didn't want anything to do with us, and were just helping out the first sergeant. We had a place for them to sleep, but they chose to go somewhere else. The soldiers didn't talk to us, and the NCO's just gazed into the fire. First sergeant told the men to make sure to wake him for the 4am shift. I did not know what that was about, but I figured he wanted to make the rounds. I just figured that he was going to get involved and see the men. So, I pulled out my fart sack (sleeping bag), and laid it next to the fire. I took off my boots and all my snivel gear (warm clothing), put it under me in the fart sack and went to sleep. Over all it was a good day, and we knew the enemy's plan, and would deal with it in the morning.

Since I was near the fire, I was woken up after the guard shift at 4am. I figured it was the visitors walking around and getting oriented to the place. Then I heard some low voices. Next thing I know, the first sergeant was waking up the whole place. He was pulling up the squads and waking up all the men. He was telling the Third Platoon squad to go do this. I am not a morning person. I do not like to hear loud shit, especially if I'm asleep. Here I have the one person that I invited out to our location, barking at my guys and using his pets to boss the men around. What the fuck over! I lay there in my fart sack and knew that I didn't want to start the mother-fucking day with a fight, an unnecessary fight at that. I listened to the bullshit and figured out what the hell was going on.

My fucking leader and mentor, was in the mood to start making me look like shit. He wanted to show the platoon that he was the "Master" and we all were sheep. To top it off, he was using NCOs that were subordinate to my squad leaders.

"Boom!" it was on. I came out of the sleeping bag.

"Who the fuck is waking up my guys?"

I sat up like a freaking vampire and started to put on my boots and smoking jacket. I asked the question, even though I knew the answer. "What the fuck is going on?"

The reply was simple. "Sergeant, we are doing stand to."

"Stand to, what the fuck? Well if you want to do stand to, go ahead and do it. Our guards are up and we are fine. We have been out here this long, alone, the Canadians are right there, and what the fuck?"

By now I was standing at the fire with the sergeants that were barking out shit.

"Back the fuck off! We did not invite you out here to fucking fuck with us. Maybe we just wanted you all to get some time in the front and see some shit? Since you all had a fucking swimming–slash–fishing hole and haven't done shit!"

Then, I get some smart response from a buck sergeant.

"We have seen some shit and we are…"

"Zip it! You've been coddled too long and I am not your friend, buddy or pal. This is a one way conversation and you need to learn respect."

They just stood there, as well as my squad leaders. The men from Third said they were just doing as first sergeant wanted and directed them to do.

"Not in my house," I said.

The first sergeant walked up.

"It's about time you woke up," he said.

"Really? Hmmm, like I wasn't hearing you waking up the whole camp to do 'stand to?' Like this is what you all do in the rear?" We started to go back and forth.

"This is what we get," I said. "I go out of my way to invite you out here to visit the men and you want to make me look like a fucking dick? You wake up everyone, and leave me there asleep. Last time I heard this was my platoon. You were visiting, and last night when we talked about the guard and preparations you didn't say a damn thing. Now, you're being Mr. Helpful and doing something that goes back to the French and Indian wars. We are not in France, there are no fucking Indians, and *we* have got this." Here we are hundreds of years after all that shit and what? Are we supposed to throw away our rockets, guns, gun systems, and communications to wait for the fucking Mongolian hoard to come at us on horses? Fuck that! We would be having meat for breakfast, lunch, and dinner. They would be some stupid bitches to do that. Back in the rear, you can play Army and do police calls, stand to, and every other stupid thing you want to. Do it, and feel like you are part of the mission, like you are in the war and fighting. Here, I don't like stupid and do not like one squad running around treating us like shit, in combat, even if it is the first sergeant telling them to do this or that. My men were off and resting, and I needed them to be that, rested.

He just said stuff that didn't fucking matter and I got it. He didn't want to be a first sergeant, he wanted to be the fucking emperor himself. I told him that we were trying to do our best. I wanted him to come and spend time with the platoon, and everyone had said no way, it would just end up badly, and we'd get fucked. They were right. Now he is fucking with the flock, and using his position to make life miserable. "What do you want?" I said. "What is it?"

"You have a nice place here," he said, "I'm considering jumping to this location with the company command."

"You have to be joking?" He had taken in our request for additional help and was thinking about leaving us there with them, while he jumped third platoon to the next town–where we were supposed to have been waxed. Now, that may sound good to some. It would take us out of the frying pan, and pass it on to someone else. However, we had made connections, and we were the ones in this shit from the get go. We were put into the "Attack" position for the task force, and like hell were we going to get taken off just because it was not as "dangerous" as they thought. They wouldn't admit that was the case, but they knew. We didn't know about the whole thing, but would later find out. So I told him, "Fuck it! You want our place, fucking take it. Take the whole fucking place and like hell are we going to fucking be around you if all we are, are pieces of shit to fuck with." I called in all the squad leaders and told them they had ten to fifteen minutes to get packed up and we were leaving. We were not going to stay where we were not wanted and we were going to go find us a new house. Dicks stood there and didn't understand what was happening.

I walked around and wasn't seeing the whole picture. Yeah, I'm admitting that I was pissed and not even thinking straight. I had nowhere to go. The only place I knew about was where we were tied up and in contact with the enemy. Back to that town and the house just across the bridge. It was on the other side of the wall where I had dug up the two IEDs.

However staying with this command would come at a price.

Being there to do chores and take supplies to others was worse than facing the enemy. We are supposed to be winners. You cant win if you don't finish the race. Being made into support and doing what no one had done for us made us less than them. This is the life of the Alpha male. It takes away your reward and makes all your efforts and hard work mean nothing. If anything it proved that we were good to start a difficult or dangerous task. We were good enough to get thrown into the breach. We were good enough to work hard at something but we would never be allowed to finish or win. We could break our backs with the heavy lifting but the end results and knowledge of a job seen completed and accomplished would go to someone else ten meters from the finish line. Sure, there was a castle, but that had been there for years. If anything, the locals and or bad guys probably took that place while the Russians were there. If not, they knew exactly what the avenues of approach were, blind spots, and probably had the damn place booby-trapped. Hell, thinking like that, any damn place that we would have picked would be the same. It was their back yard, and we were at a disadvantage. I just knew that we were not going to be used as bitches. So, I went back to the problem.

    The first sergeant and I moved into a building and talked. I wanted to finish what we started. It was out of our hands, and we did the job that was fucking dirty. Now, we were going to get passed by another platoon. We had a little more than nothing in terms of a relationship with the locals. It would not be starting over, and every close bullet that whizzed by was not for nothing. First sergeant said that our mission was to secure the travel route. We had to maintain the security and it was better if we stayed at our position.

    I reminded him of the fact that he wanted to jump the company there. That was stupid and would put the company on the front line. I'm not a rocket scientist, but I'm pretty sure that wasn't the way things were done. It would place them smack in the center of our platoons. However, if I was to move forward that would create space and a speed bump for anything coming their way. Yes, we had a task to do. No one is saying we didn't. I knew there were bad guys out there, and I wanted to let the platoon loose on them. Overall, we were there to find the fuckers that came to America and blew up our shit in the States. Here were bad guys and we could remove them from the face of the earth. That is what we were all doing there, and I would rather do the fighting there than back at home. I told him of the leaders we talked to, information and possible informants that we could develop, and taking the fight there. Out there, we would know what was going on, instead of having our back to our forces waiting for the enemy to work up to us. We had met them and fought on day one. We pushed forward and despite the fact that they were going to kill us, we met them again, and we dealt out an ass-whooping to someone. Now, I think it made more sense, because they were on their heels falling back, we could take a step forward. Whatever plan that they had to do their guerrilla tactics and get us in a trap didn't work. The Afghan Army took the next bound and dealt with it. Good thing because we were only going out in nine to thirteen man patrols. First sergeant started to listen. He wanted us out of the way and to continue to make us squirm? Well he had the chance. I do think he got some kind of pleasure in having us out there. However, he said it was the CO's call. That was the plan that he was thinking of, and it was pretty much set.

I then did something that made me feel sick. It still does today, and I regret it today. I told him that I knew how things worked. I said that I knew he was an experienced NCO, and that we both knew that the CO would ask him for his opinion. When he did, we both knew that the actual call would be his to make. I apologized for whatever happened and admitted we had to work together. He was the first sergeant and his opinion mattered and would be the way things would get done. So, after the talk we were okay. Now, at this point, we were getting the boot from our palace. We were actually going to go to a worse place. We knew we were going to get into it again and be in enemy territory. I had made the worst deal in the world. We had done our job, and did it well. There was no shame in getting passed over and getting to stay in the rear. So far, we had not lost anyone but that could change at any time. I walked back to the men, and I told them what was the plan, and my offer. This was different now. Before, we were handed a box of shit, and forced to make lemonade.

This time, I was wanting to look for trouble. I wanted to do all the things that we sing about running and calling cadence. I was tired of being a day late and a dollar short and everyone wanted to go. I don't know if it was due to the conflict with the other platoon. I didn't like the fact we were first just thrown to the wolves and then getting passed over. It was as if they got the nerve to join in the fight after we settled their nerves for them. Maybe they felt bad for letting the half platoon go out there and make it look easy. Maybe it was shame?

The squad leaders felt the same. I needed to ask them and tell them what I did. They felt the exact same way I did. Fuck those motherfuckers! Nothing mattered any more. Tomorrow may be the last day we got to breathe air and I did not care. We were a tested and proven platoon. We didn't have all the things others may have had, but we were good at making it. Out there somewhere were some bad guys, and we wanted to go. Why not? What were our options? Get used like toilet paper or continue to fight? We chose to fight. Let us do it and finish it.

I didn't know if I was going to ever get back home, back to my family and to the state that I loved so much. I erased all the plans that one builds while deployed and knew that I was going to live with the scars from the past. If things went wrong, I might not be the one who would die. Someone else in the platoon might and I would know that it was because of me. On that day, I did it, and I made the call.

I could have chosen for us to stay in the rear, but I didn't. We were chosen to do the job, and we did. We didn't back down, but the way things were getting done was wrong. Who would you talk to anyway? If anyone could find out how things were, it would sound too hard to believe. Since we started this and were doing good, I thought we were invested already. To go along with the idea of us getting left in the rear seemed crooked. People don't give a shit who started here or there. All people really remember is who was standing at the end. We did some stuff, but to take the easy way out seemed like we were quitting. It made sense to me that if we were thrown in to do the job, we should finish what we started. I didn't want to hide out. I didn't want to have any regrets.

At the time, I knew that it was a double-edged sword. There was no way that I could know everything, but I did know that bad things could happen. I wouldn't be able to run the platoon forever. I couldn't make sure we received all the best missions, or best men to fill the ranks. What I could control was our say in what we did in this battle. If they wanted us in for whatever reason, all we could do was fight. On the other side of the coin, that meant they were responsible to support us. That would be nice. The time to get the word didn't take long. First sergeant said we were a go. We were going to push out further, and we were going to have to do it alone. We would not have any vehicles, just men, weapons, and whatever else we could carry. We were not going to have anyone cover our movement. We were not going to have another platoon in support. Once we stepped out we either made it, or we would fall back to the Alamo.

We did what we usually did. We got together and we made our plan. We did plan on having fire support, but didn't really count on it. Oh, and in case I forgot to tell you, the CO was going to join us. We should try to not let anything happen to him. Maybe, it was because we didn't have a lieutenant? Either way, we were going to bounce and push out within the hour. So, we packed everything that we needed. Weapons were cleaned and made ready. Once the officer came, we got up and got it on.

Bad Infidel

Since we were all going to get killed anyway, we went looking for trouble. Here was a large, weird site, like someone made a hole recently and covered it up with different dirt, spread all over the place. Could it be gold?

I think it might be gold! Let's hope EIB (Expert Infantry Badge) was worth it. With my Paratrooper's knife, I begin to search. My radio is off. My shadow is not going to touch the mercury sensor. I got this!

Bingo! I found something. Weird, it's all wrapped up. Hmmm???

Maybe it's a bar of gold all wrapped up? Little by little just like Old Sarge use to make me do, I uncover this thing. I don't think its gold anymore.

A large IED. This is only the power and initiation system.

IED – Improvised Explosive Device

Maybe it is gold after all? Aren't you supposed to bite it and taste it? Yeah, I did it. So let the shit talking start.

My first trophy. No, we are not going to stop. We are not going to stay. The enemy will not hinder or stop us from finding them. We will remove them from the face of the earth.

Doc recording the find and writing our name on our trophy.

Me and SSg Fairchild. He couldn't believe what just happened.

After the second IED, I told the men that we would stop once we reached 3. I never thought we were really going to find 3. Of course we had to get ambushed, fight thru the ambush, attack, chase and then find them. So, this one was special.

After removing the detonation part, I gave it to Sgt Colunga. Its his baby. Inside were large pieces of metal which would tear thru the target. That meant one of us or our vehicle.

SSg Colunga and me. Texas, Baby! Oops, sorry I squashed your glasses. Oh, and we almost got blown up by one of our own grenades. Thanks engineers.

Our improvised Combat Outpost signs speak for themselves.

It's hard to do your job in a dangerous profession. It's even harder when you are prodded and poked any chance it can get done. You may think that you would get to the point that you would stop asking for help? Maybe get to where others start to do their job? I too would expect the same. Being a dumb ass, I wanted to give people the benefit of the doubt, another opportunity to prove me wrong. I thought that I had to keep trying. It sucked a lot, and made every bone in my body boil with hate. Then again on some higher plain of enlightenment or psychological and moral perspective, I was doing for others what had not been done for me.

I go from one game to another. It's a tough time. Now we just so happened to have our own little bubble and live as best we could. Soldiers had a place to relax and be themselves. These are the times when stuff that happens will be made into tales and urban legends.

Respect Goes Both Ways

We snooped and pooped all the way to the next village. We moved and it seemed like it took hours to get the distance we needed. Finally, we reached an attack point. At that point it went as if we planned it. We dropped our rucksacks and began movement to secure and search the target. Once secure, we began to move in and establish security of the compound. Fifty feet away was the intersection where we came into contact and found the IEDs. The building we were moving into had bars on the windows. On one wall, someone tried to pull them off and took the whole wall out. Part of the outer compound wall was knocked out and it was on the side where we were ambushed. As a matter of fact, whatever remained of that hut was straight in front of the hole. It was big enough for Fabo to drive into and was a vulnerable spot. On the other side of the hole was the same field that Colunga and Sellner moved under fire. There was a stairway leading to the roof, and the roof was flat as shit. There was no fucking cover and it looked like we were going to have to do some work. We set in, and began to build up our defense. Hell, if we were out in front of the task force before, we were way the fuck out this time. The Canadians didn't budge from the last place that we called the Alamo. We were out in the front and there was really no way anyone would be able to get to us in a hurry. We had crossed several ditches, one that was about twelve feet deep and had a shitty road on it to cross, and another water crossing that was not as big.

At first glance it didn't seem like we would be able to get anything across, like our vehicle. Then, there was another water crossing that was the cement bridge that me and Colunga walked across to get to the IEDs. There was an adjoining compound that ran parallel to the creek. We had thought that there were squirters that went that way the day before. It was an avenue of approach and we couldn't get eyes on it. We had too few personnel, and we would have to come up with something to keep anyone from coming through there. We walked the perimeter and came up with some ideas. Since we humped all our stuff out there, we had to find the most dangerous areas and deal with them first. It just so happened we took razor wire on pickets when we went out. As soon as possible we went ahead and set it up. We found cans and rocks and did it like in the movies. We set up flares and divided the sections to squads, came up with patrols and shifts for security. All in all, we were not going to get too much sleep at night, but we would offset it with down-time during the day. We began to build and make the place a home. Like before, we were out there and alone. The CO enjoyed the walk out, and shortly after, went back to our old Alamo and their new Hilton. We had a radio and we had bullets and beans. Everything was very simple and we would now control the area.

Once we were settled in, we began to walk and do our thing. We met with the locals and searched everything that was out there. The town was abandoned and there was nothing. It seemed that the warning that the Taliban gave was serious enough to get everyone out. We began to learn the terrain and the village. In one place, we found what seemed to be a tunnel that was started in an effort to link up several compounds. The nights were cold and we were a little tired of freezing our ass off at night, so we built a fire pit. Where the wall was taken out because someone wanted the bars off the window, we made a pit out of the bricks and socialized.

We were good at scavenging for stuff and soon we had heaters and some pipe. We collected some rugs and pillows that had been left behind. This would prevent anyone using them to plant a bomb in or what not. We didn't want to have the people that were scared out of their homes to lose their belongings, so we secured them. By doing so, we figured that they wouldn't mind us using the stove. Plus, they would come to us when they came back. The men had a nice big room to lay their head and get off the cement. We had a stove to warm up the guard and those on patrol. So literally, we had to have a fire watch.

As for our new building, it was not as awesome as where we had been, but it was bad-ass in its own way. There were writings on the wall and pictures like cave drawings. I asked one of the terps what it said and he was a little hesitant. It said that the "freedom fighters" or bad-asses were there. It was actually a training area or school. There were pictures of helicopters flying or taking off, then off to the front, in the direction of flight, a mark that anyone would recognize. It was crosshairs from a gun. It was used to train people on where to aim and shoot aircraft. So, we reported it up and waited on whatever the higher ups wanted to do about it. It didn't take too long before we had a visitor.

Starting a short time after we moved in, we were getting sniper fire. The guy would shoot in the morning, using the sunrise at his back. Then again in the evening. He would shoot with the sun at his back again. We had this guy out there and he was actually dialing in his weapon. After a couple days, we were on a mission to find this guy. We began patrols and setting up counter-sniper positions with our sniper. The shooter in our village was not a fucking champ. He did know a bit and with every shot was getting closer and closer. We knew that there were only a handful of people in town. Either he was one of the local population, or he was not. If he wasn't, someone knew or saw him coming and going. If we didn't do something, we knew before too long, our luck would change. One day we met up with the elder of the village and talked to him about it. He acted like he didn't know a thing and I simply told him that we were going to get this guy and he was not going to be okay. I told him that we were going to tear the village apart and search every fucking nook and cranny and get him one way or the other. He told me that we could not go into the houses and disturb the women. I said, we would have female soldiers out here quick to search them. We had found the firing positions used in the evening. If we got another shot, we were going to come in. It didn't matter and we were not going to play politics. So, either he gets a hold of his village, or we would. That evening I was called out to a meeting. There was going to be something happening and it would not be relayed over the net. So, I stepped out with a squad. Swain was in the lead, and as we were moving, ping. A single shot went right through the middle of our formation. Swain whipped around and started hopping around. I laughed, and told him if you hear it, you are good. He went off about the sniper while we moved.

We arrived at our old location and prepared to get our next mission. During the brief we were joined by the Canadians and talked about some mission that they were going to do. I whipped out my colored detailed map and was promptly asked where I got it at. I told them the Canadians had passed it off to me. It seemed to have a lot of stuff that the maps I was getting didn't. Must be different in their military? They always seemed to have better stuff.

We went through the brief and the CO offered various support and resource options to Kip and he said he didn't need any help. All he did ask was that our platoon be there with them. "All I need is the Black Sheep," he said.

I was surprised and knew that we were going to get it one way or the other. I acted like I didn't hear a thing and looked up to see people looking at me. The Canadians were asked about EOD and he said, "Nope." "All I need is him," he said, nodding at me. If things had been okay between me and the first sergeant, they weren't any more. The brief ended and everyone mixed into their groups. I stayed talking to someone and swear I saw diamonds and gold. It was lickies and chewies from the rear. Third Turd, Simple C, was walking away with pogie bate. Here is where things are split up and everyone has their own little pile. As I made my way into the building I asked for the platoon supplies. "Sorry sergeant, we don't have nothing." There was evidence of material and much needed snacks and rip-its everywhere. Maybe I just have to go to talk to First Sergeant Dicks. Again, here I was thinking the best, but the answer was "No!" I told him that others were carrying stuff out and asked if there wasn't something for everyone.

"All that stuff?" he asked, "Oh, that was special order."

Why did I even bother? He then said that if he could, he would try to find me a diet coke. He knew I liked them, but it quickly turned into this for that. I did an about face and took off with things to do. Man, something like that can really end up with someone getting fucked up.

I was chit-chatting and checking out our vehicles. I wanted to see about getting a vehicle to head out with us and add to the security. I wanted to have it there and be able to use the equipment and add to our defenses. If anything, it would stick out like a sore thumb and deter any ground attack. I also wanted to take some stuff back and check on the crews that were left behind.

I found out that the crews were added to the security of the compound and used as if on detail. The guys in the HQ were not going to get used that much and our guys were on permanent guard. As I was walking to one of the vehicles I noticed that there was a group of terps huddled along the wall and talking. Hell, it was noticeable and it seemed as if they were talking about me. They were looking at me. They would look at me and point and then turn away. To tell you the truth, it made me fucking nervous. So, I walked over and asked what was up, and what were they talking about that was so important? I had to take the shit from all directions, but if I'd caught these guys in on the act I was going to address it.

"No sir!" one of the terps said, straight off the bat. It was kind of respectful, in a good way, and caught me off guard. Then he said that he was telling them of what he had seen. I didn't know what he was talking about. Then he filled me in. He was a terp that came with my platoon to fill in for Bizzak, our regular guy. He was with me the day we were ambushed and saw me take up the IEDs. He saw us charge toward the hut and spend the day in a skirmish and he was telling them all of this, and with a respect like I had not seen in years. He said that I was brave, one of the bravest people that he had ever seen. I was embarrassed, and shrugged it off. I told him that is what *we* do. The whole thing caught me off guard and that didn't happen too much. This was the same terp that was bitching and whining about living in a tent and gave us all hell before. He was different now, sincere and respectful. I stood there and we all talked for a bit, but I had to go. It wasn't just me, obviously. All of us were making a difference and it was still nice to get a pat on the back. It wasn't from my command, or other soldiers, it was from some local people who let me know that they were grateful, and that made a difference. They all stood up and shook my hand before I walked away.

I finished making the rounds and we packed up whatever we were in need of. We were then given an asset who would collect info from the battle field that would paint a better picture for the higher ups, an officer and a couple of his men. Straight off, I told them that this was not like anywhere they had been before. Shit seemed to pop up and if so, they needed to take direction from one of the men and not be wandering about. It was a serious place and we would need participation. I handed them to Colunga and Swain and they briefed them up, then got them ready for the night move to our location.

As I was saying that, I remembered an occasion I was on the receiving end of such a conversation. That was a different country, time, and place. I was in Rhamadi, Iraq, about to head into the actual town.

The CSM from the 503rd grabbed us in a huddle and told us to be careful. His eyes were intense with pain and exhaustion. When he first called us into a huddle, we did so half-assed. He said to bring it in closer, in a voice that commanded respect. Now we were in a tight huddle like a football team. He wrapped his arms around us and began to talk. His voice wasn't yelling or gripping, but soft and full of emotion. He called us in and told us to take care. He said that Rhamadi was a real serious place and the people there played for keeps. He said that there were a lot of people who were killed and injured there. It was more than just his words; it was how he said it. His eyes and the emotion in them scared the shit out of me.

We loaded up straight after and began movement through the town. We were shitting bricks till we made our destination. I don't think that I was that intense, but then again, who the fuck knows what people see when they look at me.

I remembered that trip, and quickly focused on our movement in Afghanistan. Once dusk fell, we rechecked the new guys, and then we moved out. I looked around and saw little green eyes from the NVGs/NODs (Night Vision Goggles). It's funny, but after so much time out and about, you learn so much from the soldiers you are with. I said it before and it's true. At night time, you can identify people just by the silhouette and the manner of their movement. I could see my guys plainly, and sure as hell could see the new guys. They were uptight and reacting to everything. These guys get so fucking intense with what is going on out in the distance, that they forget to watch where they are stepping or where they are walking. Now you are moving out and all you hear is people tripping on rocks, or stumbling on their own feet. Walking in an open area, we are spread out and you hold your own lane. New guys, they try to stay close. They're worried about getting lost or left behind. Something you pick up is using both eyes. Yes, you have a night vision device on one eye, but the other one is used for depth and basically your own night vision. We made our movement and approached the Alamo 2.0. We let them know that we were out there, and that we were coming in. As we got nearer we began to see the glow of a nice fire waiting for us. We passed in, dropped our gear and I got ready to brief the rest of the platoon. The men gave our guests the tour and showed them the pictures and writings all over the walls. I settled in and sat on my stoop in front of the fire. The lieutenant pulled up a spot and we began to banter about what had happened and our ideas for the following days.

As we'd settled in, we now had some pets hanging around. Some of these men were young, men none the less, but some of them have never been away from home, and this is their first outing. You have city folks and country folks, some from the islands and others from the middle of America. Wynell and Williams were those kind of people. They had found two chickens, and like people who have never really been around animals, were being curious. I looked up to these men, as young as they were. They had a lot of responsibility and were bad-asses. What I found them doing made me realize where they were in life. Despite what I had seen or asked of them, they were young, innocent, and kind.

They grabbed thin string and tied it to the animals' feet and gave them a whole large length to walk around. They put a stake in the ground and just watched them in amazement. They would get them grass and feed them food from the bread out of an MRE. It never crossed my mind what they might have missed growing up. I asked them what they were doing and with huge grins on their faces they said that they had new pets. One of them they named Mister Kluckers. Seeing their faces and expression, I felt it to be genuine and true.

So, having got back from the company area, I'm sitting by the fire and something is off. There is a silence and it is thick enough to cut with a knife. We are sitting by the fire with our guests and something just isn't right. I don't know what it is, but it's there. I look at Briola and he has a trash bag under his arm. He is moving and rubbing this bag and being polite. We are all talking but all I am getting back from the guys is, "Yes, no, ha ha ha," and that's about it. So finally, I ask.

"What the fuck is up, and what the hell is in the bag?"

Now the men are creative and jacks of all trades. So this is new and I am not aware of shit.

"It's Mr. Kluckers and company," he says.

"What the fuck? Those were the fucking pets of these two over here, and if you want to fucking warp someone, you hit the damn nail on the fucking head."

So here I am with guests in our place and I am told that these guys butchered the pets of the other two, who, by the way, were not too worried at the time. I think it was actual hunger and the thought of barbecued chicken that outweighed the master-to-pet relationship. But they'd blown any chance of fresh eggs.

We had been out way longer than what the original plan was. We had MREs, but really started to feel the need for real meat. The noodle stash was just about gone and we were about to run out of pogie bait. It is well known if you want to see real primitive action, start by making people hungry. Loss of sleep gets you quicker results, and it's just as bad.

Now we are talking about grunts, remember that. These men dug through the fucking MRE's and collected hot sauce. Briola probably had some freaking soy sauce somewhere. Hell, we are talking about men that had noodle parties and not just ramen. Nope, these guys had shit that came in bowls, cheese whiz, Mrs. Dash; they were sneaky and amazing at times. They used what they could get their hands on and mixed it in the freaking bag. Briola was tenderizing Mr. Kluckers and had a weird look to him. On the other side, we had the terp making bread and what not from rocks and shit. No yeast, so he covered the stuff and set it close to the fire to see if it would rise. At this point, all I could do was say "fuck it." Then quick fast and in a hurry there was food cooking on the open fire.

All things seemed to return to normal and the wait began. That night was cold, and I remember eating combat bread as we chatted. When it was time to taste the bird, Bizzak gave me bread, I whipped out the nacho cheese with jalapenos and took a piece. I took a bite and it got quiet. They asked me if it was any good and I chewed and started to shake my head and cough a bit. Without replying I took a big bite and with my mouth full, told them it tasted like shit. At that point the need for jokes was not necessary. Knives were pulled out and it was a massacre. The men looked like they were fucking ninjas and it sounded like a fucking blender. There, out on our own, I knew that it was not the Ball, or Superbowl. No championship and no lottery winning, but it was the little things, the small moments that you have to recognize. Stop, notice what you have. Take a look at where you're at, and remember these moments for how special they are. Time is cruel and often takes moments like these. You begin to struggle with names, and places, so I was shown to enjoy them when you are there. The men with us warmed up to the platoon. We shared things with them and helped them out as much as we could. Colunga turned over a book he had found. Hopefully it had good intel and possibly stuff to use. We were given information from the locals that during our last attack they were told we had killed the Taliban commander along with several others. They said the enemy lost nine and that they were really mad and looking at killing us all. We would go out and the new guys were welcome out with us. After a couple days, they returned to base, off to check out other places and people. Our days of entertaining were over and that could be a sad thing. For the first time out there, we were actually with someone. The night first sergeant decided to get everyone up and wait for the charge at first light didn't count. We actually lost what we fought for and had to leave.

Life went on and we began to see exactly what our predicament was. What we did have, at that time was a shit load of weeds around the place and we implemented our own area beautification project. After all you are supposed to improve your positions and make them better. So were we going to pull all these weeds, or were we going to improvise? We decided to burn the shit, and the goal was to do it in sections and do so with a small fire and use firebreaks. Now some say that in the Army, our job is to kill stuff, and break shit. This, is not one of those times. No, it was not. What it did turn out to be was a cluster fuck and shit got intense. The weeds lit up like fucking roman candles that had been pissed on by an old greasy platoon sergeant. The flames went from nothing to intense in a fraction of a second and all we could do was watch it go. I stood there chuckling to myself. *We are so fucking done! Man, are we gonna get into trouble!*

However, it was glorious! Not only did it get the job done, but it was like gunpowder. There you have a Joe and he is in the same position he was when he lit the fucking thing. But now there was smoke on his face and all his facial hair was gone. He looked like a fucking cartoon character, wondering if what just happened was real. It was freaking awesome!

Despite my concern, there was no one around. If anyone had seen the smoke, no one said shit. Nothing on the radio. No one asking what the fuck just went off like a bazillion watt flash? No, just crickets. Then shit got real, real quick. Two yellow jugs were pulled out of the weeds on the other side of the house. Inside was a gray silver colored powder and in the top, tucked in, was the same mother-fucking commercial det-cord that were on the two IEDs we found in the front and on Colunga's baby. Of course, we moved them out of the way and continued the job, but this house, well it seemed to have been used not as long ago as we thought. To add to the art inside, there were jugs cached right outside the place. Bingo! We got a winner!

It was obvious we interrupted whatever was going to happen and they left their crap behind. Somewhere close was an ass-clown. He was out there, he knew where we were, what the place was like, and that we had his shit. Better than that, he was scared, and we made whatever opinion he had for the future in the area, disappear. We showed up and had taken the town back from the bad guys.

Perhaps he was the sniper and then, he might have had some balls? Nah, he sucked at that job too. Plus, I had an idea to get his ass next. First, we would have to test the crossings and see about getting our vehicles out to us. Things were good for the time being. We were out and no one was around to fuck with us. We were active out on patrol and combing the areas. It seemed like we were becoming some of the better type of neighbors that the locals would have met in recent months. For the most part bad guys were somewhere, but not too active in our sector anymore. They remained active further out, and intel was becoming more available to us. The little stunt that I had pulled with moving the platoon out further seemed to work out in our favor. Security for the route that the task force was using was good on our end. We had that sniper thing, but for the most part it seemed that the town had dealt with their end of the problem.

It started to get busy where we were. If you have ever been in the infantry, it's always about security, security, security. We had fixed our location and continued to modify it. It's just something that we did, constantly making it better. Back in the early days, we had to camouflage the o.p. by clearing old vegetation that we used to conceal it every so often. Here they knew exactly where we were and we just improved on our defenses. This was life, and it was a daily grind. If you are not out and about checking things, you were basically a construction worker. When you were not doing that, we were humping it back to get our supplies like water, food, ammo and company meetings. From somewhere, the idea came to push the third platoon forward of our position. So, we meet up and sit down to plan this huge movement. It was funny, because when we moved out, we were on our own.

"Don't ask for shit! That way you won't be told no."

But we were actually going to cover their movement, as well

as the Canadians and our first platoon. All I could do was chuckle and say "What the Fuck?" It's good to know that things had not changed. Looked like first sergeant's babies needed to get walked over to their new school.

This time there was a reporter back at the company and he had been talking with the command and such. We noticed him on a supply run, and saw that he was busy getting all the good stuff from the guys in the rear with the gear. He was joined at the hip with the CO, doing his job, writing down all the info he was getting. I could not even begin to imagine what the hell he was told; tales of glory and fame, stories of pain and despair. These people are usually with another guy and he takes all the pics. Don't think that this is okay. Sure, people want to hear the stories of how units are doing and the price that comes with winning a hill or sand dune. However, that lens and the opinions of a reporter have often hurt more than anything. Anyway, we were planning for the next company mission. "Support Third Platoon" was what I was given. Great, got it. Back in our area, I had my hands full with other things. It seemed that as people returned to their homes, they would find their way to our location and want to socialize. Sure, that word, "socialize" in our language seems harmless. However, to them it's different. These people can read bullshit and know the type of person you are by looking at you and reading your expressions. After a while talking to you, they would ask something important. Usually it was as they were leaving and at the end of a meeting. I found myself bullshitting with some of the best bullshitters around. It all started one day early in the morning. I was in the fart sack and it was a cold morning. Guys were rotating on and off guard and keeping warm by the fire all night. I slept alone in the room where the wall had been pulled away, the same place we had the fire pit in front of. I also do not snore, but did awaken at night time by someone who did. I never caught the guy either. It would stop and he would leave the minute I would wake up. Then again, yeah it was me.

In the morning, it seemed that the wind would change and blow smoke into the room. This happened especially if the fire was left to get small. The rotation of the guard shift and keeping an eye on the fire usually had me sleeping a couple of hours and tossing and turning throughout the night. I think I already covered that I was not a morning person. Today, there was a need to wake me up. It seemed that there were a group of people outside our wall, waiting to talk to me. Of course, that meant certain death to the messenger. So right off, it isn't a good start.

Anyway, these people could wait out there. I had a foot-long rip in my pants leg that needed stitching and I don't think that they would understand the idea of going commando. I would reach over to get some water, wash my fucking face and make ready to see what the fuck was so important. What, didn't they have fucking poppy to grow and bombs to plant? Shit son, I like to take a morning shit and didn't like to do that till the fucking sun had warmed the sweet pile of crap, piss and frosting in our slit trench.

These talks followed a pattern. I would act like the Grand Poobah, and when they got to me I would make nice. We had an old coffee pot and the terp had some tea.

We would get started, which meant getting down to bullshitting. If they were serious, then be direct and serious. If the topic was religion, hell yeah, bring it on. I would admit to being a red-blooded American from the State of Texas. There is a God and Heaven is Texas. We even got all the pretty little angels running all over the place. Now over the course of my time, I'd learned a little Arabic. I was pretty good and the terps were good teachers. So the locals would ask my name and I'd answer. They would like to banter and talk about good times. To them, age was a big thing.

What I did not do, was all the bullshit that we were taught in our classes.

Like what, you might say? Well like everything. If you were to do things like we were taught, that would give them an unfair advantage. They would automatically get respect and a position of authority and I wouldn't get shit. They expect you to bend to every demand after that. Nope. You have to take the high ground—stay on the high ground and bring them up to your level. Then you're only smelling the stench of bullshit instead of standing in it.

Sure, they would be polite, but respect, well, that came from the eyes and they didn't volunteer you a damn thing. If you start off giving them anything in a negotiation, right off the bat, you couldn't get anything else done without giving up more. That puts them in a comfortable place to be nice to you, and makes you feel strong and powerful, but everyone at the table knows you are going to fold.

Another thing was to have a good terp. He had to be kind of like you or understand you and the way you were. Basically, I had a team, I never went at it alone and always made sure that Colunga, Briola, or another person was with me. Colunga had his spider sense, and Briola was slow, patient and experienced. Sometimes I thought he was dead, he was so slow. Since we were out there and on our own, the terps did something crazy. Somewhere they heard me tell of how I was adopted by a Sunni General in Iraq. So, they figured it would be good here too. Hell, with the sun I looked like a heathen and so it began.

The story was that my father left Afghanistan and went to the US. There he found my mother and got hitched. She was from the US and Mexican. I was born in the US but still grew up in a traditional way. I don't know if they ever questioned why I was Baptist, but it never came up. Then we said Colunga and Briola were from Afghanistan as well. Next thing I know, we were getting information about the littlest things.

We were greeted by the elders of the village we were in and those of the surrounding communities. Most importantly, we were kept in the know about things that had been happening just outside our reach, like bad guys, a long gun in the area, and roads to stay off. Let's face it though, we were not too good at following locals directions. So, we began to develop places to go and people to see.

During one of the first meetings in Alamo 2.0, we were told that in the last attack, we had killed the Taliban commander. Elders from all the villages had decided to come and share the news. Requests were made for us to go to other villages and do the same thing. It was evident that in that engagement it had struck a devastating blow to the cell unit there. Plus, it also let us know that there *was* a cell unit operating there. That meant leadership, communications, support, intelligence, and organization. Of course, this was good news to us and we reported it up. We received information that there had been no known cell in the area, and any cell leader was unknown as well. The information, along with the book Colunga turned in, the devices on Colunga's "baby," and the Alamo 2.0 with all its artwork and writings was making us a pretty big deal.

Probably not! It was the company sending it all up. I doubt anyone really knew that one small platoon was getting all this intel. It was all about the company and its leaders. As far as the locals were concerned, I was having tea parties like the Republicans back at home. The morning of the Third Platoon movement we dressed up and walked out two hundred meters to the forward edge of our village. We stopped in the farthest compound in our area to cover the other platoon's movement. It was cold and wet. There we were with the CO and the reporter who was shadowing him. We went up and set our stuff down, took up positions and watched. One squad was left back to do a counter ambush in hopes of getting the shooter in town. At this point I believed that he had moved on and hoped he didn't come back. We sat there for some time and the picture guy was out taking snaps and shots. Some were taken by the reporter while listening to me tell of Colunga's baby and how it was set up. He took some pictures and I ended up coming out in a paper. The funny thing is I came out like the leader of the EOD, which I was not. It did end up coming out in a local paper back at home. Too bad at that time my home was not in Texas. Along with that one, several others were taken and printed during our time there.

Once The Third moved into their area, we headed back to our Alamo. On the way back, someone decides to walk in the mud and got stuck. He didn't walk on the little wall that goes all the way around the field. Instead he walked straight and plop. I hear the ticks of the camera and was getting angry. Without the story of what was going on, it kind of made or told another story. In another place and another time, there was a picture taken like the one in Afghanistan. It was the picture of A Company, second platoon from the 508th. We jumped into Iraq and it is pretty famous. That soldier had a huge rucksack on his back and was taking a knee or bent over. It was a bad night and we were really weighed down in the mud. It looked like hell and I can feel my thighs burning like they did that night. In it was a Red Devil and the unit was out of the 173rd. That picture captured a miserable jump and the results that followed.

Here, it was the complete opposite. Now we are going to see this shit all over the place. The two had some similarities, but the back stories were different. It was out of stupidity and looked totally different than what really was. Because of that, it did kind of piss me off. Once we made it back, the reporter stayed with the CO at our area. He took pics of the walls and talked to some people. He was always writing down stuff on a note pad and looking out in thought. Maybe he was writing about a recent patrol where we ran across some little fuckers giving us shit.

We were out and about. I had walked by some kid and talked to him for a bit. After all my attempts to be friendly I was still getting stink eye from this fucker, and asked him what the problem was? I didn't want a response but I told him that I gave his elders more respect than what he was giving me at the time. I told them there was a sniper out there somewhere and to be careful and we bounced out of there. No, I did not want a response, because him knowing that I had seen him as being disrespectful to me was not going to go down well when the older men found out. He would be taken care of by his own. The way things were going, I was probably going to be woken in the morning by his elders anyway, and it would happen again. I didn't remember the reporter being around at the time, on that patrol, but come to find out, he was. Ooops. That also came out somewhere in some paper too.

The next time I met with the elders, I did address it with them. Come to think of it, that same kid was there. I think that they brought him there to show me that they knew, and wanted me to see that he was all sunshine and rainbows. It was the little things that mattered. I thought about it, and they did too. It was a sign of a relationship and working together. It seemed like we were heading in the right direction. It also made me feel as if everything we were doing was turning out to be good.

Me thinking that I will never see my sweet Texas again. Plus, this looks like west Texas, ughhh! Let's go Cowboys!

Locals would come and like to chat over nothing. Usually it took long amounts of time for them to finally ask for what they wanted. These were some of the best negotiators I had met.

Another early morning. Members and leaders from surrounding villages come to see what they can find. I'm not all about giving away free stuff just because your feelings are hurt. They get what they want from the my higher ups. I'm just here to get the bad guys.

Hosting sit downs became a thing. So we get tea, get out the fine china and see if we can find out more about the enemy.

I tell them about my family. Rumors are that my father was from Afghanistan and my mother was Mexican. That couldn't be further from the truth. I'm 3rd generation Texan. How 'bout them Cowboys, baby!

Behind us is the kill zone where we were ambushed. It's also where we found all our IEDs, a bomb, and yeah, we were going to die.

I didn't have to do anything. After all I was told that I was going to die. I should have already been dead. All from someone, who wanted to make others as scared as he was. Then again, that isn't the type of person I am. I think others didn't know me. I wasn't going to let them tell me what I was. At one time, I wanted to just go with the flow. Then, here comes my conscience and pushes me to get the fuck up. It is a bad thing, and to fucking piss me off more, it was in my buddy's voice. Freaking Weaver, Kip. He was the boy scout, and we always had to do this or that. Now, this voice has me testing my limits and pushing the boundaries. How much stuff can you do? At what point is enough, enough? Living like this is normal to me. The word grunt *has associations. It also has the implied task of fucking around, getting into everything the enemy has and ruining it.*

We are beating every task and still, we continue to work and bullshit while others are sitting on their hands. The company sucks. Our conditions suck, but if you are actually having a good time is it really work? We are doing what I think is right, but I didn't see others doing it.

You really don't know this, at the time. Then you get some visitors and can see and smell the difference. A simple thing like walking, what we do as grunts, is so dangerous to others. You see the difference, and can be proud of it, or realize where you are in life. We lived together, and that lets you learn more about the people in the group. Topics come up and the discussions could be seen as violent or offensive. It's a group of alpha males talking passionately. Yes, the topic was ghosts and that led to another experience.

Guns, Ghosts, Bullets and Bombs

So here it comes again. Third was going to end up pushing out further and they were going to be out and about. The next village was a good klick away and we were going to have to move again. So, we went to the following village that Third took some days ago. Straight off the bat, we were made aware of two places to avoid. The first was a compound that was the community shitter. We would get the hell out of there ASAP. The other, right where there were IEDs. We were told that there were booby-traps around the whole place and to stay away. So, we went out there anyway. It was better to go than to be left in the shitter.

We had been told that there were markers like weeds put into position where the bombs were. We were told not to use the doors where tumble weeds were located. So here we go, I pull up to the weed in the door and take it off. There are no ant trails and no tell-tale signs that I can see, just an open doorway, but there are too many places to hide the thing. Knowing military stuff, we use the path of least resistance. So the edges of the doorway are about two feet out. That would be where I would put something. Then again, these guys don't know what I know and could just put it with in a three foot radius of the door.

The mine detector we borrowed was returned. We tried to use the one issued to us, but there was too much iron in the ground.

So what to do? Okay, get me a grenade over here and let's see about setting it off. First time didn't work, so we go for the second. This time two go out to either side of the door. One goes far, but straight ahead, and one in the door way, four in all. Three explosions? Uh Houston, I think we have a problem. Do not tell me that someone didn't pull the pin or safety? So the shit-talking starts. What we didn't see was that one flew back over the wall and right behind where we were standing. How do I know? Because of the fucking video! Rewind that shit son, oh shit! There it went. So do we call EOD which will be a freaking camp out, or do we practice the "pin the C-4 on the donkey?" I yelled for some stuff and did it myself. Boom, it's gone and it's game on again. So here I am at the door and there are a few guys with me and I can't figure this one out. Where the hell would this thing be? Then I start thinking that it was just a fucking diversion. I stand in the door way and as I am talking to myself and others I said it has got to be right here. At the same time I have my foot on the ground and sweep away the top sediment and bam! I am looking at my foot uncover it and it scared the shit out of me. No knife, grenade, or grappling hook; just my balls, which have detached themselves from my body and gone and hidden in my rucksack. Briola, who was behind me, and everyone else has disappeared, kind of like in the movies where the guy is facing a dinosaur and everyone behind him says, "Don't Move!" So those fuckers are a terrain feature away waiting for the boom. I stepped back and swear my heart skipped a beat and then went into hyperdrive. Shit, I needed a smoke! We gathered and began the shit-talking.

"Where the fuck did you guys go?" I asked.

"Ah, hell no sergeant, that scared the shit out of me."

"Damn! I can't get no emotional support or what?"

I went back, grabbed the knife and went to town. I took the balls off that bastard and kept them.

We walk into the compound and there are three doors, two in the front of the compound wall and another one to the rear. Briola and I are walking to the back door and there is another bush. "Uh, let's call EOD?" Briola says.

I told him we had to confirm that there is a bomb to be sure. So we move up close and Briola gets a sick feeling when he sees the knife come out of my kit. I start to poke around and bingo—we've got another one, and I take off the plate. We walk back and call up for EOD and guess what? It's going to be twenty-four hours before they can get to our location. Fuck! Well we can't take back that call now. Thinking about it now I should of called it off. I didn't think of that till now. So we sit there developing a plan sitting by the building, minding our own business when we began to hear fire.

It is Third Platoon and they're in a skirmish. We pushed out to their direction and we got in a trench. Me and Wynell were taking a knee and rounds were buzzing by. Wynell got into the ditch and asked me if I was going to get down.

"What for? It's happening over there?" I said.

Just then, a burst came by and one round came so close to my head that I didn't hear a crack, but I heard the fucking spin on the bullet as it twisted through the air by my head.

"Scoot over, fuckers!" I yelled.

Me and Wynell were talking and I told him that the last bullet was closer that anything I had ever remembered hearing. Then I figured that coming from that direction, and the bad guys are over there, it had to be one of our guys watching out to their flanks. Fuck! One of Murphy's Laws states: *friendly fire... is not.*

Wynell is talking on the radio and we let them know we are out here to their right. Our 240 is set up on our right flank and toward the enemy's direction of travel. We see nothing, but remain there and notice the fire dies down. We pick up and head out to cut off their escape route and it's a click out. A thousand meters in full battle rattle and there are irrigated fields in the way. So, we get dirty. We make it out to a piece of high ground and Colunga and others head out to take a look at the next village. At this point we are a thousand meters out from our last location. Colunga and his team are another eight hundred meters out and checking out shit. Colunga gets intel but we really can't do anything. We have two bombs to pop, but have to guard them till tomorrow. Colunga thought we would get gold, but we really do not have the ability to do anything right now.

Colunga and the others have always been able to get good intel. It goes with having boots on the ground and knowing people. The only bad part is that we just don't have enough people to cover everything we have going on, much less act on some new intel and fuck up these bad guys. At this point I have twenty guys spread out all over the place. Some are at our base, some are guarding the IEDs, some are out on the high ground with me, and more are out on patrol with Colunga. He comes back and we are sitting there watching and observing for now till we get a call to bounce back and Charlie Mike (Continue Mission). Directly to our front we have a row of houses to the far right coming in our two o'clock position, and a road that is further back that seems to be parallel to the houses. To our left are some trees and another compound. So basically our sector of fire is 10-2. That right there is some funny shit. Why? Because when we train in the States the team leader gives out sectors of fire. The general directions given are 10-2. Then we usually say, don't be a dumb-ass and say from this point to there. Of course here, we are basically set up as a range, and we can only shoot forward. Sure if something pops out, bam! We engage it and it is gone. However here, we were set to shoot straight out. Between the houses and the compound to our front. It is a textbook set-up and that road to our front seems to be the likely avenue for escape. It just doesn't get any easier and just as it is set up in training, here we are doing the same damn thing.

So here we are and we get reports of motorcycles moving on the road. We are in a transition, and that slows down our reaction time. Remember we are to be going back to the old location and sit on the bombs. Then, something happens that changes everything. Now roads are normal methods used by the locals to move.

The problem is that due to that, it is also used by the damn Taliban. In front of me, I see two bikes and there is a cart in between them. They are circling the wagon and it hits me. There is the mother-fucking triage that we had heard about. Some said that they got their wounded out quick. So I'm like, let's open it up. But first I want to call it in. Crickets, crickets, nothing. So here I am watching a parade of bad guys leaving and probably something I thought I would never ever see, I will probably never see again and it's an open target. Then, it's gone, and I have nothing.

Finally they get through and I am asked for info and I report it but it's gone. Then, they say I can't shoot because that is the marines' area. The only problem is that the marines aren't there yet. They won't be there for days, hence the fucking freedom of movement of the enemy. So we leave a gun crew and squad out there and head back to the shack that we figure was used for a shitter. I get there and the Catholic Priest is there and he wants to give Easter mass. Being a Baptist I don't do Catholic mass. I don't know the customs or prayers, but hold the idea of Easter as the most important of the holidays for me. I don't want to offend anyone, but I was willing to attend this service. I have had the pleasure of sucking up deployments with those of different faiths and could call some of them my friends. They always told me Catholicism was the best religion, because you were forgiven at confession every week. After all, no one was perfect. I took it as a chance to remember in my own way and give thanks for saving this crazy-ass boy from Texas. Well of course we have soldiers that are of the faith and to tell you the truth, I didn't see any other ceremony so we received a small message and bowed our heads in Afghanistan. As crazy as things were going, I wanted to make sure God was at least going to get us out of this area in one piece. As the service ended, we hear the regular sounds of fighting as well as news that one of the guys is sick. There is gunfire and we got to get. Just like that, we put on our kits and get ready to head out. The priest says if there are men out there, he will come with us. I look at him.

"You need to stay. We'll get everyone back and I don't want God pissed at me because you wanted to come along. I don't want to be in the dog-house if something happens to you. Hell no! You don't want to go out where we're going."

So, we went back out a klick to the 240 position and there was our sick man, not sweating but in pain. I was thinking it was his appendix. Why not? That seemed to be the one thing that was going around. We checked him over and had no choice. We were going to have to drag his big ass back, and get transport from where we were to some location in the rear. This was going to suck! All the times we had been assessed a casualty in training was fixing to pay off. Hopefully we were not going to get shot in the ass heading back.

With Barron in tow, with his shit and stuff, we took him back and put him on a truck to the rear. We had not seen too many go back and not return if it was serious. To me, it seemed serious and I was a Combat Lifesaver! We know everything. Doc didn't know what the hell the deal was either so Barron was gone. I agreed with his assessment and it was done.

At this point we had no casualties. That was fine with me and we would take it as long as we could get it. We'd had a few other things. We did have one guy fall off the roof while putting up sand bags for a gun position. We were placing bags of dirt up there to give the position some cover in case we came under fire, not to mention that was the time we had a fucking sniper taking shots at us. I guess Pait wasn't concentrating and took a swan dive. He ended up being okay and coming back. After all he made a soft landing and his head broke his fall. He actually left a dent in the ground where he landed. That gave us something to laugh about for a while. He was okay though.

Goot, our driver who was a pretty good soccer player (and shot his load from the driver hatch on our first contact) had a problem. His toe! Yeah, he drank Monsters as often as he breathed. He had to get out and get seen for his bunion. He did return and to this day we still talk shit about his driver's toe.

A funny thing about Gutierrez was he was one of the guys that could have done anything else. However, like the rest, he wanted to be with the platoon. Prior to getting deployed he showed off his skills in Seattle. Most grunts enjoy the time and opportunity to get fucked up! Instead, Goot went to an international soccer game with Colunga and got fucked up. I really shouldn't say any more but yeah, it is as messed up as you think.

There was a thing where they would allow you to kick a goal shot. If you were able to score, you would get a case of beer. So, here enters Goot and bam, he scores, then he does it again, and again, and here is Colunga acting like his agent collecting all these cases of beer. So they ran out of beer and then did bottles of this or that. Now it didn't take long before they sent in the professional goalies and bam, in your face, Goot keeps on scoring. Well it went on until he was offered a tryout for the Sounders FC. Yeah, this guy had a shot.

Instead, he decided to go to war. At that same game I believe, he also did the "naked man running on the field" thing. Colunga said they put him in the jail there in the stadium, but he was released. Then, all Colunga remembers was getting to the jeep full of fucking alcohol and a dog. Goot was lost, no phone, and it took some triangulation to locate him and get his ass back to base. How about that? But then again, you get some grunts out and about, and you are about to have a crazy fucking time. When time allowed, we tried to break the constant grind of being in war.

The following day, our sick guy returned. He didn't get a finger in the butt, however he did get a shit pill which unclogged his pipes. How did he feel? How about, how did we feel carrying him, his gear, and all his poop? That was a fucking story that we used for a while. We had our damn MREs and usually that stuff makes you shit a brick. At times they might clog you up sure, but what the hell was he eating? We went on at him about being full of shit *and* bullshit. His eyes were brown because of the same thing. It went on and on till the "shit" was not really that funny anymore. I recently visited with some of the guys and I think he still finds it pretty unfunny, so I won't mention Barron any longer.

Back in Afghanistan, we were there waiting to get relieved and it should have been any day. We were reading about the marines and all they had been doing. Most of the info we would get on my way back to the company, or other people dropping by like our guests and reporters. Here we were going on a month which started as a three to seven day mission. We were at twenty-six guys and had taken on a bigger piece of the pie than any other unit. Hell, I didn't know what was going on, and that didn't bother me. We are supposed to keep our men informed and let them know what was going on. Most of the stuff we got was from our Canadian brothers. To me, and the others, they were good in our book.

Fairchild was dealing with the first sergeant and we were told that we were going to have to help at a position in between Third and Second platoons. Hmmm, not cool. I had to do the damn math. Without our vehicle crew we were down to three squads. Having to pull our own security and rotate on missions left people tired. Now we were going to push out another squad to help a platoon that had been sitting on the breach the whole time and had more men than we did. Not to mention the whole switch-a-roo before we attacked. The whole deal of "letting me go to earn a Bronze Star." It sounded like fear to me, but we'll do it. We split to help out the others, and we continued on. Oh, but there was the problem of us still waiting for EOD to come and blow those IEDs. For that, I had to keep a squad and a gun team there for security. That way no one would get blown up. Yeah, that made sense, *not*. The locals knew that they were there and stayed away from that shit. It was not theirs, and they didn't want to deal with the guys who put it there, so they left that shit alone. So, tag! Colunga you got that deal. We were helping out another platoon which pulled a squad. Then a squad plus gun team on the jugs/IEDs. At this time we were located way past the creeks and had three vehicles. We were pulling security at different locations and spread out real thin. I mean, third wanted us out there because they pushed up. When *we* were out and about, no one helped. We didn't have to set up a lifeline just in case something happened. Well, whatever they need. Even though they were the largest and best platoon.

As far as Colunga's mission went, well what happened was something that we talk about to this day. I like motorcycles and had bought one after my second deployment, because that is just what I liked to do. At that time, there was a soon to be very popular show that had just started. SOA was a new show on Fox and I started watching it back at the beginning (not later, on the band wagon, when it got all crazy and full of soap drama). I had the first two seasons and would watch it every now and then. Yes, even in the field I would sit and watch that shit late at night. Soon, it became a regular thing. We would get together and we started to watch the show together.

Due to technology, even out in the middle of nowhere we had the ability to watch the series that I had. I also had a cell phone I had unlocked with a chip that we all used to call home. Others had something different and would either change up shows or sit and talk. That's when the subject of the "paranormal" came up. There were shows we would watch and or read about. Then people would talk about their experiences and stories that have been passed down. Some of the men had some freaky stories and we would all listen in turn. When it was our turn, we would talk about what we heard or thought we knew.

Briola, in his turn scared the shit out of me. He had some local stories from back home and it seemed pretty legit. He explained about the culture and areas that were said to be haunted. He talked about the brutality of the Japanese and places where many were killed.

He talked about superstition and some of the characters from his culture. To me, I compared it to some of the things I grew up with. The stories were interesting and a lot of the details were similar to other creatures I had come to hear about.

Briola turned into a scary little guy as he talked and we listened. He knew his history, culture, geography and some events he had experienced himself. I used to look at him like a wise little Yoda, but then he turned into a scary story teller. I had also experienced some stuff at an early age. I'm Mexican so the damn *cucuy* was always coming to get me. I'd heard of *La Llorona*, others might have the version of a banshee. Maybe the tale of a woman crying looking for the kids she killed. I'd heard of *Lechuzas*, or witches who turned into owls, *multos*, or shadow figures, both versions black and white, *El Diablo*, and just about everything in the Mexican *lotería*. Witches, cats, dogs, goats, and the *chupacabra*. I knew that some were used to get a bad kid to behave, just a story told to someone young and impressionable. Instead of being something that you needed to know, it became a joke or something to tease a person.

Now, there were people actually looking for the experience. I knew enough to stay away and not kid about it. I didn't care if someone did or didn't believe, I wasn't having any of that. I don't playing with stuff like that and will go another way. I had strong feelings about it. This came from living in a haunted house as a young kid. There cannot be good without bad. There is right and wrong, good and bad, light and dark. These are things that I believe that people do not fully understand and therefore are ripe for the pickings. It is often the ones that are all hard and fucking pig-headed that get made an example of. Just like Bigfoot. So, we have Bigfoot and ghosts. Colunga had never heard of any of this. I started to tell him of Ireland and all the stories there and how they have the banshee. Guys are all telling their stories and Colunga is telling people to "Fuck off!"

I told him that if he didn't believe in what we were saying, he needed to ask his grandfather. Colunga respected him and he was from the old country. If anyone had a story or experience, I knew it would be him. He lived in Ireland, and the land has had its experiences through the years, so much, that it's impossible to believe that there wasn't something left tied to it. We talked about how many years that the country of Afghanistan had been in war, how many innocent people had probably died. The U.S. has had some places where people who experienced tragedy have remained locked in time, either experiencing the same event over, and over, or wandering through the years without knowing that they have passed. Other countries, and different places have the same results. Cemeteries, burial grounds, battlefields, hospitals, camps, houses, and some towns. Yet we have turned it into entertainment, people wanting to experience firsthand that there is something after death, another place and the continuance of one's journey.

We kept up the conversation until it was time to set security for the night. Teams moved out to their positions and the night shift began. Vinyard was helping out Third Turd, Colunga was sitting on the IEDs I pulled, and we were at our makeshift base. We had to leave the Alamo 2.0 and settle for less secure and not the community shitter. Late that night we received a call that EOD would be gracing us with their presence and they were not going to be alone. They were coming with a camera crew. That meant that somewhere, an officer was involved and we were going to represent the military fighting in Afghanistan. It would not be good to have a simple soldier talk and speak of what is going on, on the ground. No, therefore we have officers to guide them and answer the big questions. Our reports are read and the officer comes out smelling like fucking roses.

"What a soldier!"

"What a specimen of the American fighting man!"

No one wants to hear the real story so they church it up. Add to that, we were having problems. We were told to stop requesting so much stuff and water. Food seems to be MREs and it's the box that has the same meals 1-12. However, our first sergeant is driving by and visiting the Third Platoon and the Canadians. Since we moved to a more open area, we had requested sand bags to improve our defenses, and nothing. He would drive by, and drive back. No stopping, no battlefield circulation, no checking in on the platoon. We had no option but to bust down some mud walls and stack the chunks of rock as cover. Then we went old school and began to dig fighting positions. If there was support out there, we were not seeing it. It's not bad, if that's all you had, however.

I once watched as the Third Platoon sergeant walked away from the first sergeant with a case of Cokes and RIP-ITS. I thought supplies had come in and decided to ask about our supplies. He was tending to his own and playing favorites. Others were getting the new Tactical Rations, but we were getting the poop. We were strictly on a basic diet, water and MREs. It was as if we were living on Spam, and everyone else was having take-home Chinese food. The next morning the small package with EOD and the reporter showed up. We were up and waiting to get this over with. Colunga had been checking in trying to get a sitrep to the estimated time of their arrival. He sounded tired, but he had been checking in all night. As soon as the package arrived they looked around.

EOD just happened to be these Air Force guys in a fucking Buffalo. They looked clean and wanted to get the party started. Little did they know that we were not the destination. We were going to walk out to where Colunga was. He was making radio checks often and throughout the night so I knew he was tired. He kept asking what was their ETA? That should have been a sign.

There wasn't really anything where we were, hell it wasn't even worthy to take pics. Nope, nothing to see here and the reporter and camera guy is whisked away. Instead, they take snaps of the nice clean soldier that came with him as an escort. The soldier is shitting his pants and that makes him look battle fatigued. We just stand off in the distance and watch as this is going on. By this time we are probably more animal that human.

I wish we were as clean as these guys but it really didn't matter.

These are the tourists and what is important is that we get this over with as soon as possible. It didn't take long for something to pop off and at this point if it did, we were undermanned. We never had anyone of our own come out to give us a hand. Whatever did happen, we would have to deal with it all on our own. I didn't give a shit about their show or what they wanted to do. We had to get them over there. I only hoped no one was out there and counting us. It turns out I was going to take them out to the spot, and anyone else was free to go.

The new soldiers need to pose, click, click, click, okay.

"Stand here. Right. There are the IEDs. Pose like this, then get the fuck out."

Every second that they are there, time counts down till one of the men does something that is normal shit, for us. At this point, we had not been around normal and we were off a bit.

Being out for so long, you can literally tell the difference in people. You have been in your group and away from civilization. We are thinking, talking, and developing a different sense of humor. When someone new comes out, you can smell the soap that someone used to take a shower. Men, women, it doesn't matter. You can smell the difference. Right then, it becomes evident that we may get paid evenly, but our lives are not the same. We are wrapped in the definition of hero, but we are not. There was a picture I remembered seeing on Facebook once, and it simply read, "experiences vary." After being out in the wild, nothing was ever going to be the same. People don't care about how important your job is. What you went through, how you are living, or the fact that you are being told you need to conserve your water better. Grunts are grunts, the lowest in the military food chain. Those that fight are no longer important to those that support the mission. The strong are now controlled by the weak, and kept in place with ideas that we are all equal. We are told that it is one unit and one fight but that is not correct. It is easy for the infantry to live the good life like those of support. It is not easy for the support to live ours. As we are standing around watching I am reminded of this difference.

We got our stuff on and decided to take a walk. Air Force was wondering why we didn't drive. We took off walking, and they followed us, in their truck of course. It was eye-opening how dangerous that these people thought the ground was, and here we are walking them to the location. I don't remember seeing them take any pictures. The glass must have been too thick and how would that look?

There was an officer with them and we were told to direct them here and there. I kind of wanted to see him directed straight to the IED and watch him shit himself. We fucking pulled these things out of the ground and here EOD was creating a safety bubble. We started to get orders and being told what to do. No radios, send in the robot, pull out the mine detector. Bro!

"We have been dragging our ass all over this place. X marks the fucking spot, fuck the bells and whistles and get it, blow it, and get the fuck out with your bullshit rules."

Fear had them riding in on a fucking Buffalo and letting us know that "they" didn't trust us. It is crazy how there are these rules that these guys bring in with them. We could have blown the shit out of the IEDs by now and moved along, but these guys are doing the extended version and posing for every opportunity available. Meanwhile Colunga is there and ready to go. I'm sitting there and figured if someone was going to talk to the reporter, it should be him. Hell, he had a way with words and he was either being a dick, or he was crazy. Colunga didn't want any part of it. Every five minutes he was asking to leave and get the fuck back. I finally pulled him over and asked what the hell was going on? With a thousand yard stare he said the place was haunted. I asked him again, and I got the same response. I looked at the guys and they were all on the same sheet of music. They just wanted to leave and get the fuck out. Okay, Yallah!

We entertained the crew and they were doing a piece on the Air Force guy. He swept his way out to each bomb and looked very professional. We then watched the Air Force blow it and the reporter goes to talk to the tech. Us being out there in the front and locating and disarming the things was not important. I'm sure the reporter didn't even know. The guy went through the process and why not, the story would have lost its pop. Then outside we found an unexploded 203 round… and here we go with the dog and pony show all over again.

Hell, we were in contact around that area and one of the men had marked it. After all was that not what we were supposed to do? Now, that we have the bomb guys out there with a reporter, they are ready to do their job. The only thing that came out of it was one badass picture for one of my guys, McKeen. He will be getting ass for the rest of his life on the perfectly taken picture, a pic that proved even in war, shit isn't what it seems and can be used to enhance anybody's career. Those are mostly people who are officers. NCOs get used and then thrown away when their knowledge is taken.

After everything was said and done, we made our way back to the new Alamo and there is Colunga. I asked him what the hell was the deal and he said the fucking place was haunted. So, I sat there and heard their story about the night's activities. Colunga and the others talked about how they watched as shadows entered and walked back and forth down the wall. They swore that people were peeking in and out of the entrance. It was happening and noticed by a couple of the men. After looking in a couple times, this figure would then walk in and move up and down the walls. I asked about the night devices and if the kit was working or messed up. They said no, everything was working and good. They would flash lights at it and it would disappear. Once they turned off the light, there it was. The group stayed and repeated their story. Some might say that they were convinced and probably just repeated one story. For the most part, I gave them the benefit of the doubt and didn't want to prove anything otherwise. That would put me way too close to something I don't fuck with.

Bad guys, okay we can do that. Supernatural, hell no.

What made it worse, was that the men were saying that there was a dog out there and he was going crazy. He would bark and not just bark, but bark like he was scared. Then he would run down the wall and then stop. He would start barking again and then head back. Over and over again. Watching how they talked and reacted showed me that they'd had a fucking moment. Some may simply say that it was a group thing and maybe they all talked themselves into believing the story. I don't know if that is true, but I do know that I had seen these guys go at it with some real bad people. As a leader, I would have to say that I believed in what they were telling me. It is okay for me to have faith in them. Sometimes that means I don't have to question them anymore. Listening to their tale was hard to believe, but their words and actions made me laugh. I don't have to go prove them wrong either. I believe them and that's good enough for me.

This is the Taliban version of taping off the area. I didn't know what it was yet. However I grew up in Loop, Texas, and I know tumble weeds don't eat rocks.

After several attempts of trying to blow up whatever was there, I decide to lightly move the dirt with my boot. Here is what I find. When I look back, everyone has left me all alone. I swear my heart stopped for two seconds. Now it's time to dig it up and make it useless.

Left to right: Sgt Colunga, me and Sgt Vinyard sit and wait for E.O.D. At this point I think we all felt like we had pushed the envelope enough. SSg Vinyard looks at a video and we catch a miracle.

This is a smaller anti-personnel IED. The pressure plate is smaller and easier to initiate. It soon became clear that this was all part of a bigger plan. We started to notice similarities in the different IEDs and assumed them to be all part of a bigger picture.

Left to right: SSg Briola, me, SSg Fairchild and Sgt Colunga. Yeah, we are the main effort for the taskforce. We are the assault.

I guess I can call this "Task Force" Black Sheep. This was the assault element for the whole enchilada. We were actually less than this, but those damn crews showed up to get into the fight.

Sgt Colunga and myself. Normal Soldiers with one hell of a sense of duty, loyalty, and courage.

Spc McKeen was caught in the right place at the right time. This picture was in some papers. We joked that he was going to get laid for the rest of his life. Then again, that might be today.

How About Them Apples?

Going into the fourth week of the deployment we were beginning to make preparations to be replaced by the marines. We had cleared the old castle we'd noticed a long time ago. The new unit was supposed to be bigger and needed room, so we went in, cleared it out and made it ready for them. The platoon was still broken up and in different places. We had patrolled up to the furthest area that we were allowed. We had an OP with the largest and best platoon. I had not figured out why we had to share the thing since they were close to twenty men stronger, but who cares, right? I had another place over a klick away. If something popped off there, they were screwed. It was the same place where we had seen the motorcycle escort on the road, where we also ended up picking up one of the guys from the overwatch position at Easter. We were everywhere and operating in small teams. Everyone else in the company stayed together. As for my men, the platoon was broken down and sent in different directions. We did have some good news though. We had picked up a local who was willing to tell us where all the IEDs were. We were out and in unfamiliar territory so we took his help.

Other leaders and elders had made their way to our location. Word had gotten out and we were asked to go to this village or another. It seemed we were having meetings and conversations with locals. We didn't have the numbers others did, but we sure did cover more ground. Someone would give us some information, and before too long, we were on our way. Other units seemed to move out and when they got there, dug in and waited for the Marines to show up. When we were out patrolling the other villages, we were shown the bad places, areas where there was something bad or just wasn't right.

I didn't know who the people were, or who they were loyal to. I would think if I were in their shoes, I'd do whatever was necessary for the survival of my family, especially my children. I didn't have to be rocket scientist to know that when it came to IEDs, no one wanted to have them around. That, to me, made us team mates for the time being. I didn't want to lose anyone to an accident or being careless. As a parent, I wouldn't want to be scared by a loud blast and wonder where my child was. So, if it wasn't the locals, it was some guy who didn't give a shit about the bad guys. So once again, I ended up confirming the devices and collecting a couple of pressure plates. We started to build our collection and noticed that some of these things were exactly the same. They had the same material and characteristics. It looked like they had come off the same assembly line.

We should have had several but EOD took some, as well as the task force command. What I had done was one of the craziest things I could remember. After I disarmed them, they were collected up and were now being given out. I didn't like it and felt that it was our intel. I could understand it going up to the research and science people for DNA testing. What I thought was happening was they were being used as a trophy for those who had nothing to do with anything we did. I would come back from patrol or doing something with the men, only to find out my stash was raided.

Another thing was that no one had an idea of where they were found, how the systems were defeated, and what one washed-up, old turd was doing on the job. No one knew that they laid there in the ground, that they were hooked up, disassembled, and collected, not just disarmed, but disarmed with a paratroopers knife. I thought about all the stories I had read and veterans I had talked to. They too were out somewhere and learned how to take out booby-traps and mines. Their times were in the jungles and rice paddies and they had adapted to survive. I had done the same thing, and no one knew except Briola who was usually right there with me, along with those of the Black Sheep. On one of the last days there, I was on the ground and getting started on an IED. The local informant started to make his way to my location. The men stopped him and asked him what the hell he was doing? He asked them what the hell was I doing? They responded that I was going to make it safe. He was surprised and said he wanted to learn what I was doing. He wanted to learn, so he could do the same thing. He thought that this was something he could do, and he was willing to learn. Then again, maybe he just wanted to set it off and get rid of me? Either way, the men kept him away and let me do my thing. Since time had passed, people from the villages started to return. We were getting more visitors and the families started to come by. At one point, Doc was running a sick call and treating injuries and burns. Most of these patients were children and it was fucked up. There was one that had burns to her body and in real bad pain. Another had some infection and cracked skin on his ears. It was real troubling how these small kids were so bad. I couldn't stomach seeing them and let Doc do his thing. Of course, we dealt with the drug searchers, adults that talked about generic symptoms and looking for meds. Real life hippie Antifa from Afghanistan. Those we told to lay off their own supply and pound sand. Then again if I lived there like them, I would be high all the time too. It sucked and their lives sucked as well. Going back to Doc, I reckon that Doc Pilgrim had his hands full and did more help than he would admit.

With so many new people in the area, we were having to wait again on EOD to show up and blow the bombs in place. Of course, that meant that we had to separate and pull security on another location. This location was as far as we could possibly be. When I said we were spread out, I mean my platoon was holding more territory than the original outpost had, before we began the whole mission. What was good was that the five to six man teams were not going to have to do it much too longer. Our replacements were going to be there and word was that they were moving in our direction.

I was out with Colunga's team and with the local snitch. He was pretty much right on the money with the intel and keeping me busy. Before I headed back to the Alamo, we watched as the marines pulled in on the same road I had witnessed the enemies medivac parade. We had waited way over the three to seven days that we were originally told. It was a good sight, and that meant that we were going to be out of there before too long. As they made their way, I couldn't help but think that my lieutenant was right on the money. We had talked about getting out there and staying in one place long enough to make a difference in the community. It was messed up that we couldn't do the exact thing in our own neck of the woods. It would have stabilized the area and that was beneficial to us. I had heard about experience and now the platoon was complete. All the talking was backed up and we were a solid team. The possibilities of success were 50-50. I think that it was reasonable that we could do the same thing anywhere else, especially where we lived. The constant thing there was our commitment to the area. Of course, we never stayed out there, and were always coming and going. That was turned into the enemy's advantage. That was where we multiplied their chance to blow us up.

Here, we were doing the work but going to pass it off to someone else. That left the question: if we were seeing these kind of results here, would it continue with the relieving unit? Would they be able to step into what we were doing and remain successful? Would they allow the people to handle their village and support them? A lot of the times the incoming unit would arrive full of piss and vinegar. Shit is torn down and it creates a bad situation. We were fair and strong. We fucked up some people and stayed. Establishing a relationship with the locals and talking moved both of our causes in the same direction. Therefore, we were not seen as invaders or bad guys. Our problem was the same as the locals'. I was often asked if we would stay there and keep the bad guys out. The elders knew if we were to leave, the Taliban would return. I knew if they did, many of the people that asked me these questions would no longer be around. They put their faith into my country's uniform, but I knew that it was only temporary. I think in their minds they knew the same, but hoped for better.

No matter what we did for these people, there wasn't shit going to stay safe unless they decided to fight for their own peace. You could tell them the story about every great nation that had ever been. How the US started and we fought for what we wanted. To them, it wasn't about a country. It was about the dirt they held in their hands. The only kind of patriotic people there were the enemy.

The locals there didn't care about government or politicians. They quit that long ago and only focused on what they could hold and touch. On that point, I kind of agree about the politicians. Politics had 90% to do with the bullshit we all were going through. Unlike us, we at one time as a nation wanted to be free. Real patriots who took a stand for an idea that would become America. These people didn't want to stand up, no they would rather take a knee. So as a grunt, I only ask what nation has ever became great by taking a knee? Could any one nation stand against an opposition while living on their knees? Hell no! Then again, as a grunt I am the kind of guy that ends up getting killed and it gets blamed on some bullshit lie like a video tape. Not to mention probably getting left out there alone without support. This is just me, but where the hell have I heard this one before. Seems like patriots and heroes can die, as the crazy politicians continue to lie. As far as the marines, they were coming from their piece of Marja. We were in Marja but the place was actually known as Badula Qulp. This was their mission and we were holding our own in our area. As we assumed our area and the task forces freedom of movement, we started to disrupt the enemy's plan. As we were fighting, the marines were fighting their way to our area. We were out as far as we could go. We watched as they pulled up. We were stopped from going any further because of the territory. We, the Army, had up to here, and they had everything else. In order to not get the wires crossed and have green on green, we were told to stop where we were. That is the term for force on force.

US units on US units. With technology as it was, you would imagine that things like this didn't happen. It still did at times but it wasn't as frequent as in prior wars. If they said stop, we would stop.

The marines were in a convoy and on the one freaking road that we had seen the fucking parade of motorcycles on, protecting what I thought was the evacuation of the enemy. We witnessed the first three vehicles stop and the marines get out. Before too long, there was a dismounted patrol headed in our direction. This was a good opportunity to let them know some of the info we had. The road that they were on had IEDs on it. They had stopped right in front of the location where they were. We waved, but they paid no attention and ignored us. Despite radio and everything else we had to communicate, it was pointless. Again, as Colunga settled down with his men for the night, we returned to our CP and geared up for that night's security. Come morning, we got dressed and headed that way. It was a good hump and we were hoping that they were not morning people. We had to go toward another village and then use an old road to get to the following village where Colunga had set up the day prior.

As we approached, their vehicles started and they began to move. It wasn't too long before the worst thing that could happen, happened. The rollers on the vehicles went flying in the air. As I was walking into the small village we heard the sound and knew exactly what it was. As I approached, the soldiers told me what they had seen. Next thing we knew, there was purple smoke and birds in the air.

As soon as we saw it, we knew that they were a medivac. We watched as people scrambled and could hear their noise in the distance. Not too long ago that was us, and the very same feelings were right there in an instant. There were three vehicles and a task force behind them.

I remember seeing the choppers come in. The birds blew away the smoke and then kind of sucked it around the blades and down through the top. They were there to pick up and carry out the wounded. That day sucked. It was fucking ridiculous and not necessary. Communications were like the red tape that we dealt with on a regular basis in the rear. After so long, you kind of prayed that no one died, but this is the world in which our work was pursued. Either it is others, or it's you. You see or hear it every day and feel it in the pit of your stomach when you are alone. You can take showers and never get the stink off you. It's there all the time and it's your burden to carry.

That was near the end of our time there. Soon we would get replaced by another platoon, to hold down what we had held together and built up during those thirty some odd days. Our final mission was to back up the Canadians and that would be just about it. Our task was to oversee their movement and provide overwatch while they went in to kick in doors. As we were wrapping it up, there was light at the end of the tunnel. What we did was a lot and a pretty big deal in my book. It was like the last days of any school. All the big stuff was done, and we were basically dotting all the I's and crossing all the T's. After sitting on the overwatch for what seemed like forever our northern friends wanted to show some hospitality. We were rewarded with them buying us breakfast at their foxhole. We pulled in, relaxed and talked shit. We got to know the guys a little bit more and partake in their rations, or did we?

No, we were again reminded that we were the shit on the end of the stick. For weeks we had not been able to get sandbags or decent fucking food. There seemed to be something, but we figured we were good enough to get the MRE's. We saw with our own eyes as our fucking first sergeant made his rounds to the other platoons. We knew he was giving them the new larger meals for the other units. I remember hearing a conversation on the radio and went out to kick a tire. However, till the day we left, we were given the basics and thought of it as being just bad luck.

As we sat down we were served American rations that were given to them from our fucking company. Yeah, the other platoons had their shit and the Canadians did too. We were left out of the supply line and I guess our stuff ended up with them. It made me fucking sick to my stomach. They sat there and told us that they had been getting regular supplies, including drinks. They were given the sport drinks of choice and we sat there sucking up bottled water we either humped in or stole.

While we were sucking down bullshit the whole time, they got T-rations. Meanwhile we sat there trying to be cool about it. Fucked again! Woo hoo! We were just having a blast with the Canadians while they were there. I couldn't hold it against them, but I sat there and saw their supplies which were ours. We did work well together and they seemed to look up to us. They were a big part in what we did and were more friendly than our first sergeant. They really didn't like our first sergeant too much, but he was willing to make sure they had enough to eat and drink.

I swallowed it all down and was polite till I left. Then I cussed that motherfucker all the way to my bullshit area where we'd been told to stay. It was around forty-eight hours till we were to move out and I got into it with the first sergeant over the radio. I told him that it was fucked up to get American supplies from the Canadians, supplies we couldn't get from him, but that he was easily giving to them. Our supplies were cut down, to include ammo and basic things like sand bags. Now even our food and drinks he just gave to others. I said it was bullshit and he blamed it on supply requests. I'd had my fill of this man's excuses; to get our own food from soldiers from another country was crap. People get pretty bent out of shape for shit like this, but it didn't mean shit to him. So, I told him, it was fucked up.

He got so pissed off he showed up to our location in a fucking truck. He brought all that was left and dumped it on the ground. They drove up, put the truck in reverse. Then they gunned it and slammed on the brakes. Whatever didn't fall out, we had to unload. That's the kind of bullshit that gets people hurt. He dumped it off like he was dropping trash off at the dump. We didn't care. We jumped on that shit like animals. We ate and celebrated the end of a successful mission. To him, he was getting rid of rubbish. He probably didn't want to deal with the headache of turning it in. The last hours we had there, we had food. We ate like a big family and began to dig a burn pit. There was so much that we had our pick of meals and we were not going to leave anything for anyone. As we burned the stuff, I sat there and thought it was such a waste. He had told me that he was not going to take anything back and I was stuck with it all.

Now, we were burning this and it was fucking up my head. People say what doesn't kill you makes you stronger. I think if you go through enough of it, it will crack your brain. I had seen enough crap and bullshit to know life was less than fair. Being dependent on the system and having to put your trust in someone left you vulnerable. That system should be stronger. It should be more reliable than the mail man. The things that happened to us, will never be made right. By the end of it all, if someone wanted to know my opinion, what did I think of the overall outcome, I would say it was a success. Despite the word of mouth, orders, being fair, against the odds, and any other way you can sum it up or put it, it all came down to who had the cards and how that hand was played. After all is said and done we can say I was an idiot, brave, a dumb-ass or just lucky. We can talk about it. We can say, "You should have" or "I would have" but I am just showing you my hand. There are not many people I know who would have done what I did. Despite what was supposed to happen, we had everybody. That was our biggest accomplishment.

Everything was kept simple, we dealt with our piece of the pie as one unit. The other stuff we had no control over. We adapted and did what was necessary to be successful. The bullshit games were wrong, but served as a tool to bring everyone in as a tighter unit. We dealt with more scenarios than NTC could have thrown at us. All of it was possible due to everything the platoon had gone through prior to this. Each person brought experience and knowledge to the table. Controlling that, letting them do their job, and supporting them, gave the leaders confidence. It was my soldiers that were the biggest contributing factors.

There was a time when this platoon was at the top. They beat out others and were recognized for it. During that time they had leaders that saw how special and good these men were. They knew that they were a great platoon and thought very highly of them. For those who did, you all were right. The men know your name. They will remember it was all of you. Thank you for taking care of them, way before me and this little book. The platoon was a place where communication was allowed to go up and down. Everything was war-gamed. I took time to listen to the men who had been on the ground. Their knowledge was invaluable and lead to respect and even faith. Everyone contributed and every one of those leaders led when it was their time. It was demanded of me in my days, and I in turn held them to the same standard. They took up the lead and marched into battle. They became confident in their abilities, were able to make decisions under fire, and continued to the end. If they did good, or if they fucked it up, we were going to go together. I hoped that they felt I was there to support them and be there till the end. Overall, as a unit we defied some bad odds. We managed to kill a sniper, located and took out a gun team, including taking out the bad guy's leader in the same ambush. I had pulled up around seventeen IEDs and the intel we gathered was substantial. We had discovered another cell in the area. The pics from the house we stayed at were useful. If not, it was cool art. We discovered an explosive initiation system that had only been rumored to exist. We managed to witness their version of the Shriners doing a parade, but missed out on their medivac. The book Colunga and Briola found would be used for future good. We had over 60% of the population back, helped to distribute some medical aid and helped the locals in re-establishing their lives. Most of all, we lived to tell the tale. Not a fucking scratch on anyone. (We can't say that about some buildings, thanks Fabo!)

We locked horns with the bad guys and we were the baddest motherfuckers in the land. What seemed like a fucked up situation, we dealt with it for good. It would be years afterwards that we heard it was a fucking suicide mission. We were sent in as bait.

Colunga was contacted by a reporter who said there was a 2.6% chance of survival. People wanted to know if we had known the risk. We didn't know a damn thing, but the company did. The command thought it was acceptable and decided to send in the "Black Sheep" instead of a full platoon. It was later told that the assault was being discussed up higher. People were taking a look at the whole event. They were looking at the company and what it supposedly did. What no one told anyone was that the company HQ didn't do shit. It was a little ragtag group of undesirables that were given to the overwhelming odds. They slapped the shit out of the bear, and then made a rug out of it. After I left the company Colunga would deal with all the press. Officers in training discussed the assault. This was done at either the battalion or higher up. They talked about us facing the odds and were questioning how did we do all that we did? Why were we going in like we did? It looked to be a lose-lose situation.

Opinions went two ways, either we were lucky or stupid. Well I for one would go with that. We had to be one of the two. Whatever the reason or questions, it was about the actions of a small group of men. Colunga was questioned and asked to tell how we did this or that. He didn't know the significance of things as everyone else did. We had not heard anything ourselves. Others had the parts of our story and we all wondered why or how Colunga filled in the blanks and got pissed. How were people hearing and learning anything if no one talked to us? If it was so great and awesome, why were we treated like it was nothing? Everything we did seemed to disappear and got swept under the rug.

Other information made its way back to Colunga and as soon as he heard it, he would call me and give me an earful. Not only was the unit that was there unable to go more than five hundred meters from its compound, but there were other units sent in before us. This is info he received from another reporter telling him that these units were sent in and they didn't make it. Their equipment was captured and supposedly used against us. This was seen as another threat that we didn't find out till almost a year had past.

Some of the threats were machine gun teams, and a sniper. I guess using our stuff was bad luck. On day one, we killed him. Maybe it was a .50 cal or a 203, but he was done, thanks to the fucking crews showing up. Those glorious bastards. The machine gun crews were a concern to any operation to be held during the offensive. People were trying to find these machine gun crews, and we fucked them up too. Not bad for bait. With us not even being in the know, we went anyway. I remember hearing the first sergeant telling me that the plans were changed as if I was in the conversation, playing it off like it was no major thing, then saying he'd told Fairchild, like we were dumbasses. I don't know if what we came to hear or find out was all true, but it made sense.

It goes with everything that happened the whole time out there. To think that these fuckers knew all this intel and were keeping it makes you want to go insane. If we didn't scrounge and get maps and equipment from others, shit could have gone the other way, not to mention denying my request to have the vehicles cover our movement. If we were bait, I guess they didn't want us to lose so much equipment. It seems like they knew something the whole time and planned for us to die. They knew enough to not tell us the truth. Not sending out a full platoon controlled the number of casualties. No vehicles in support meant less equipment and supplies at risk. I think it was more for our equipment though. They were worried about the vehicles and the supplies aboard, rather than about their men.

For some reason, what we did was getting talked about to new soldiers. They should also have to study on "What not to do, ever, ever, ever!" When new soldiers came into the unit, they didn't think any of us were around, till they ran into Colunga dragging his knuckles and club behind him.

They told him of the scenarios that they went over and studied. Colunga sat there and listened as one officer used us as an example of how to adapt and work together. That's Colunga's story and he can say it better than I can.

It would be two years later after that, Colunga would get a call from Afghanistan. One of the largest missions to date was carried out on the info that was pulled out of that book. Our snitch was still getting used, and he was right on the money. I was told that the operation was called Black Sheep, but can neither confirm or deny a damn thing.

Well, I ain't dead after all. After it was done, we fell back into the crowd and became invisible again, just like it was before. Right after we get back to our tents, the focus goes from fucking us up, to getting me the hell out of Afghanistan. Usually things are getting done to piss me off or mess with the platoon. I think the same way that Dicks wanted to screw Colunga over in the beginning, was just like this. He wanted me out of there quick and by doing so, helped to erase what we did all together. How does it all end?

Things were never to be the same again. We united for an AAR (After Action Review). We met in some big building and expected for there to be questions, information and feedback. As I walked in, there were only chairs for our leaders and some from other platoons. We were directed to be there so I pulled a seat with my platoon who were on the floor. We sat on the floor and listened to everyone say their part. All the main "Officers" or people in the rear guard being professional being important and talked about the success.

After all, our success as a platoon was seen as the company being successful. It was not the mission but just extra credit. I didn't once talk to the CO about anything and only talked to the first sergeant. There was no planning for what we did alone. Once we were on the ground, I was responsible and would have been held accountable if it had gone bad. I had been given enough rope to hang myself with. I knew that we were to clear to a point, but then it was hands off and left to me and the platoon. As far as purpose of mission went, it was just "kill the bad guys." Not to mention that we were to find the sniper, gun teams, and IEDs by being a target.

I'm listening to people that didn't say or do anything when we needed help. Now they were basking in the moment of success. As far as the overall mission, yeah, the task force did okay. There were no big problems and it was pretty smooth. They all had their chair at the table as the men and I sat on the floor. We sat there like bitch-ass monkeys ready to hear each one stroke each other. This probably led to several of them getting promoted or awards for valor. We sat there and we were not even asked a damn thing.

There are some things that you see in the movies every now and then, that make you tear up, moments that you wish you could experience in real life, and then it happened. The one officer that came out to take pictures and get some intel says his pitch and then adds, "Especially to the Black Sheep for doing an outstanding job.

The info was valuable and is going to pay off big dividends for years to come."

True to his words, it did come to pass and he was right. Then the one EOD guy that couldn't believe we were just grunts, did the same. He talked about being out there with us and how we went beyond. "I wanted to thank the Black Sheep".

Then another, and another, till it got to the point that my company commander told them that it was enough. We know about the sergeant and the platoon. This was an AAR and was focused on the companies working together as a task force. If there was anything else about the platoon, it had to wait till the end. After all, his success had to do with our platoon, and he would not want to be left out of the limelight. Just like that, our company did this. Hell, we were the turd bags and not supposed to outshine the command. We were the bait. We didn't know it at that time and he was going to keep that a secret forever. I guess he just wanted to downplay it all. For that meeting, we were part of the company. That would only last as long as the meeting. I wish I could put every one of those bitch-ass fuckers in the same position. It was bad enough to hide the truth to not tell us, but serious enough that they so easily decided to sacrifice the lives of my men and me. For me to do the same to anyone else, I would be wrong. It would be unfair, I would be a dick and be dealt with.

To tell you the truth, I would have probably gone anyway. I remember a time when teams were wanting to take the hard jobs and wanting to take that test. It let you know where you stood concerning your profession. I did it in the 173rd and never had I said no way. I had great leaders with me there. Putting it like that would make people question why the strongest platoon in the company didn't want to meet the challenge. Even if I was told I was going to go and the "better" platoon thought like that, it would have been easy to say, "Nope, we got it! Let us show you how it's done!" That did not happen. That leads me to believe that they knew of the possible risks and more.

I am a firm believer that you should not make anyone do something that you yourself wouldn't do. I have to forgive them for the sick stupid bullshit that we all went through—my religion demands that—but I do not have to forget anything. I was very adamant about keeping records of the events that had transpired. I wanted it recorded to show appreciation to these men for the valor and courage that they displayed. Let's also say this. Average soldiers do incredible things all the time. As leaders, we do not take time to record their actions and share in their exemplary deeds. We expect more and being better, quicker, and faster. However in this life, we are too close to the picture to notice everything. We see things as being expected, normal, it's your job. We forget that there isn't anything normal about any of us. Those that are rewarded, it seems that only happens when you are in the good graces. Every day soldiers get forgotten and quickly passed over.

These events and actions should have been put down and sent up for our command to know what happened there on the ground. I wanted their actions to be recorded in our history books as being valiant, loyal, and brave, that their efforts were not insignificant.

I wanted them to receive acknowledgment of their roles, something to hold in their hands and be placed on their chest. After all, this was our tradition in the military. It would be honor from high up, to the men who were actually on the battlefield.

In the infantry, you shoot for expert, because you'd better hit what you shoot at. You do PT (Physical Training) and get 290 or better. The Army standard is 180 to pass. You go to combat, and start patrolling, get into firefights, take down some bad guys. You have to do biometrics, then additional duties as driver, gunner, air missions, QRF, medivac, pulling out the wounded, the dead, take care of the enemy, pull security on the Airforce, operate with locals, other countries, save your buddy's life, be an electrician, carpenter, cook, EMT, run drones, do site exploitation of events, the communications to various radio systems, a mechanic, run the weapons systems on various vehicles, and different weapons carried, as well as a supply guy, having to run the mail room, running an arms room, and tons of other stuff you got "voluntold" to do. Instead of getting a simple pat on the back or a ribbon, some lazy ass tells you, "You're just doing your job." You are the go-to team every time shit gets real. When it's do or die you make it happen, but you can't even be given a little time to be acknowledged or thanked. That was not gonna happen to my men. The men's actions embodied not only the examples of so many heroes who served in conflicts before, it also identified the existence of the American spirt, to fight and push through against adversities from all directions. They were the underdog, and behind the eight-ball, a day late, a dollar short, and a couple of cards short of a full deck.

The men stayed true to their moral compass when so many others were not. At this time, rules and social beliefs seemed to outweigh the traditional values in the military, always told to suck it up and do as you were "told", not as others "did". The reasons for our beliefs were understood as was the purpose. After basic, they are shown the life of working hard and fighting as one team. The code is hard but simple, loyalty, duty, respect, selfless service, honor, integrity, and pride. There you learn it and live it. It isn't done as professionally in other jobs. These ideas and words are what gets you through war. To those outside Combat Arms, they are trivia questions. To those who fight, they are our code and life. Why do you think someone like me doesn't trust just anyone? It is because these words mean a lot to someone like me. To others, it's cool to say this or that. They never depend so much on simple things. It's socially fashionable to agree to some bad-ass words from great people, but they do not know. These values were the same throughout the years of conflict. These were the traits of our country's champions and heroes, characteristics that we were to copy and repeat. Pillars of our moral foundation and the highest levels of commitment to our teams and nation. Yet other examples were set in positions of respect and authority. They were wrong but supreme. I have been to Fort Benning, Georgia, and stood there looking at "Iron Mike." He represented a generation of fighters, a time where being American was worth fighting for. He represented the type of people that served then. I think that we were of the same ideas and values. We did our part and played the hand that we were dealt. I represented our generation. As a Soldier, I had to do the best I could or die trying to represent my generation. A generation trying to fill the shoes of real heroes who did it better. All the rest of the crap and bullshit is something that everyone will experience. I would never think something like that would happen in the military. It did, and despite every damn thing, I stayed strong in what I was taught to be right. I received what I wanted and more. I was given another chance to test myself and the teaching of my leaders. I came to know that despite the new methods and ideas my predecessors were right. A different war, in another land, different threats, but conducting business as taught, applied, and followed, was successful. I had felt bad for being blown off and set aside for not adapting and giving into a system of favoritism and fear. I was willing to give my life to do otherwise. To prove all the new shit didn't mean a damn thing if you didn't have heart. At least I wasn't hiding or fooling people. I wasn't pretending I was a dirty nasty grunt. I sure as hell wasn't doing it from behind a desk or behind young soldiers.

Way after all this was done, our Plt was talked to by military historians. Everyone got a chance to tell their story. What happened out there and what they all had experienced. At the end, I walked in and shared what I tried to put down in the pages of this book. I was so impressed with the outcome and how successful this small platoon was.

We as leaders never really speak or say stuff like this. I chose to do so, because this was real. It was a pearl in a sea of shit. There is no basketball coach or professional player that deserves to ever have the title of hero, compared to the men who fought for our way of life. Were things fair? Nope! Did we face death? Fuck yeah! We still did our job if we liked it or not. We stood and faced it together as we chose too. Even if I didn't give a crap about some in my command or the president. What I didn't do, was take a knee. All of us from the "Black Sheep" proved to everyone we were better. Better than what they said about us. Better than the way we were treated. Better than them. We could take all that they could dish out and still stay standing. We could deal with their crap, still do our job, and even take on the enemy and win. Better than any ending I could have thought of, it just happened.

After the AAR was done, there was to be a dinner for us. We had to attend a celebration at Camp Leatherneck. We were given a combat patch and talked to by a General. Afterwards we were to have chow with the Afghan Army to share in our accomplishments. After the ceremony, as we were walking on our way, I noticed the West Point kiss-ass that was out to get me back at the beginning of it. This was the same guy who Sampson would get pissed with, the same guy who wanted to see me step on my dick. He wanted me to mess up so bad, he wanted to see me get screwed and kicked out. He was from my last company and a snotty little shit. He was a lieutenant in A-52. Once he finished his time, like most officers, he was sent to do something else. He had been promoted, made the handmaid for the Battalion Commander of the operation, the same guy who made it out with the CSM that visited our Alamo.

I noticed him as he was walking, fiddling with paper and pens, just like a fucking clerk. He did his little time in the bullshit place and served the fucking "Evil Emperor." Once he got a little time in combat, he was never going to have to lead those men ever again. No more line for him, he will be directing from a safer place from now on.

Now, he was a handmaid and he saw me and was kind of happy. I really couldn't tell and didn't give a shit. He looked over and noticed me and asked what the hell I was doing there. It was kind of in a bad way, and he mentioned that he was in the battalion, the same battalion that was in charge of the operation. Uh, okay. Good for him.

What was I doing there? I left the old company and was working for Brigade last time he saw me. I had a bad reputation. He probably thought I was hiding out in Brigade and there for the fiesta. Nope, not even close. I wanted to burst his little bubble. I told him I volunteered again and went to get another platoon sergeant job. He asked again what I was doing there? I guess it was not really for me to be out and about. This was their thing and all the higher ups were going to dinner. I just seemed to be in the pack walking with the group.

Since he wanted to know, I told him. "I was the platoon that did all the shit he read about. You know, all the action and stuff going on out on the battlefield."

I don't know if he believed me or knew what I was talking about. He just looked up and said, "What?"

I guess he didn't believe it and before he could ask anything else, I said, "Oh, and by the way, we did it with no officer."

I pointed to the staff sergeant and told him he was the platoon sergeant. Therefore, I was holding down the fort as the platoon leader. He stood there and just about shit his pants.

"You don't have a PL?"

"Nope, and we didn't need one. We were just fine."

He asked what company was I in and I told him, "Hell no!"

Somehow, maybe some way, I didn't want to have him politicking with all the other ring-knockers and surprise me one day as a new platoon leader. I knew that he would ask around and find out anyway. That was going to be a hoop that he would have to jump through. I just hoped that I was able to get him thinking and searching for an answer. That would be the last time that I saw his dirty, lying, back-stabbing ass. I kind of hoped he made it back in pieces but he stayed in one. The real bad news was I heard his ass-kissing, dick-sucking, traitor ass went to my beloved 173rd. That is where you'd better be a man when you get there. Hope to become a man before you go to war, because they don't fuck around. Then again we were Red Devils from the 508th. 173rd was hard back in the day, but politics even started to creep in there. How the hell would I know? Well that is another story. Maybe for another time. I love that fucking unit, and it is a fucking shame his bitch-ass spoiled that place.

Nope, that's what the NCOs and a butter bar are for. We are born there, and we die there. As others progress in their career there are changes and better perks. For us, it's on the line and that's where you are going to stay. I was probably the only dumb ass that said, "Fuck it, I'll go."

I did and was grateful that I had. We ended that fucking party and we returned to our place. Swain was the last person needing to go on leave, then I was going to do my time. It was almost nine months and I believed the platoon sergeant was always last. Everyone ate first, before me. I refused to go anywhere till all the men had been home. That was my example growing up. As we got back to the shitty tents, I was summoned to the head shed. It had not been three hours and a call came in. At that time we had been given a short timeline to submit any awards that we felt were important. I was working with all the squad leaders putting in all the men for their just due awards. I had to stop helping out, when I was called to the principal's office. I went in and the first sergeant told me I had six or nine hours to get on a bird and go on leave. I had to take it, or I was told I would not be going home at all. I argued about Swain and how I expected that he should be on the next flight out. Despite my plan and what needed to get done, he didn't budge. At this moment, I felt like shit having to tell a soldier that he was going to have to wait. I also believe it was due to the awards that were getting worked on. I do not think that they wanted any of the stuff that we had done to get out. I was going to give the men my best efforts for all that they had accomplished.

I also knew that there was going to be nothing but red tape to slow the process. We attempted to meet the requirements but were told we had to add more. I was told that soldiers were not of enough rank to be put in for certain things. Then we had to draw diagrams and witness statements. It was all a waste of time and a shit load of crap. I knew what was in store. I knew that while I was gone for two weeks or a month, it was all going to disappear. Despite having years to submit them, I was told that there was only a small window, a window that ended during the time I was to be gone. The company would no longer accept anything. So as it was said, so was it done. To this date, you will not hear about shit. Check it out, look it up, nothing happened and all the focus was on the marines. I have heard of people getting Bronze stars for fucking crying in battle. The support element for a raid get stars for support, and the door kickers get nothing. People have even written up their own awards and have others sign them. All of this was not like any of that.

I felt that the system had to be trusted to work, even after everything that had happened, so I worked at it. These awards were going to be for those who refused to stop, for the soldiers that never wanted to quit. It would be for what others called average, not good enough, even bait. To me, these were soldiers, and worth all I had and more. I felt it was my job to make sure that I let people know what they had done. I felt I owed it to all the crusty badasses that scuffed me up and pushed me to "Do it again." I had to see if they were right so long ago. Damn it! You bet your ass they were. The old ways still worked.

As for the men, I had led them and expected them to follow. With that came the responsibility of leadership. Despite what I believed was the right way we tried to let you and your loved ones know about real heroes, it all disappeared.

So this is my follow through. My story of you. My shitty effort to tell people how awesome and out-fucking-standing it all was. Most importantly how great you all were. It sucked but we won, we won like champions. I considered it an honor to be there with you. I only hope to do you all justice.

Near the end of the operation we take time to relax. We had intel of IEDs in the area. Before we move out in order to confirm the possible threat, we relax and lower the heart rate.

With the arrival of our source, we begin to ready ourselves for the task at hand. SSg Briola stands behind me. I dig into my pocket to see if I had any Blueberry Poptarts. Sgt Colunga looks happy to have his hands in his pockets.

Another IED blown up without incident. There were several dug in on the same road, this one was close to a small hut. When it was blown, it tore the wall and was big enough to damage the hut structure. It could have endangered more than just the vehicle. It was dangerous to the locals as well.

With a constant flow of information from locals, we stay busy. For the most part we got rid of all the bad guys in the area, they did however leave IEDs all over the place. So, we get ready to go and make the freaking donuts! We also have word that the Marines are closing in.

Left to right: Spc Gutierrez, Swainee poo, Mongo, Spc Shaftner and Spc Sellner (walking out of the frame). McDougal is in the back, photo-bombing.

SSg Briola and Spc Gutierrez at one of the Bn. Formals.

Mission complete! Left to right: Spc Barron, me and my date, then Spc Hatfield. We are at the Bn. ball. This was after our deployment, back in Ft. Lewis.

*Spc Kyle Coumas, US Army, "BlackSheep"
KIA 21 October, 2009 Afghanistan.
"Must Go Faster," the Schnoz.*

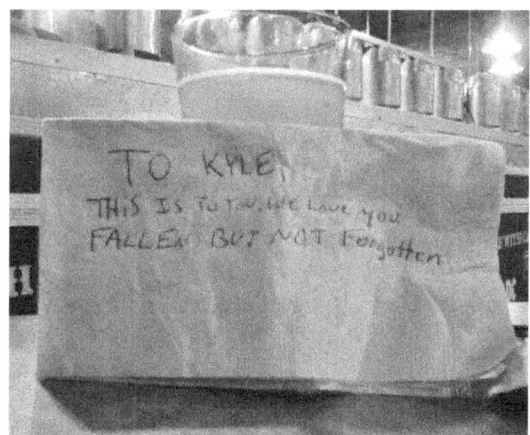

This wall bearing the names of those who paid the ultimate price stood stood in front of the entrance to the Bn.

Afterword

In the shade of distant hills stands a memorial. It stands on the crest of a hill, at Fort Lewis, Washington, surrounded by the tall green trees of the Northwest as a reminder for all to see. It faces the elements, time, and the people of our nation. The cool temperatures and damp lush terrain hold back the modern foolishness of the world.

Protected first by nature, the strong trees stand off in the distance. The silent sentinels stare at the monument in honor, as if they themselves are able to read the epitaph and know what was done. What these Soldiers have done goes back to the origin of humanity. Their deeds are so great, all that is living remains in reverence. Not because of the loss, but because of their oaths fulfilled. The Holy Bible stands as a record from the beginning of time. Written as the word of GOD, it verifies the selflessness of their actions. In the pages of that holy book reads this one sentence.

"Greater love hath no man than this, that a man lay down his life for his friends." – John 15:13

My only request is that we will endure the current social temperament. We must never forget the price that is attached to freedom's cause. We must never move so far ahead that we forget the price at which Liberty was bought.

As we move into the future, let it be under the same ideals that have worked for hundreds of years. Let it be under our own freedom, which no one provides for us except GOD, and those of us who believe. We are still One Nation under GOD, Indivisible, with Liberty and Justice for all.

These are the things that separate us from the world. Loyalty in deeds and action that have paid for everything. No matter what the future holds, we are rooted in the call to fight. As our forefathers fought to exist, we must as well. History demanded it, and history likes to repeat itself, over and over and over...

For warriors like me, if I should fail in this honorable task, let it be because I too paid the ultimate price. Like the heroes of old, let my failure be from death. May I be remembered for believing in our nation, and its values so strong, I was willing to fight and die for it all.

For when I do fall, I only hope to be found among the bodies of my enemies. I pray that I meet my fate surrounded by the wolves at the door. May I be faithful till my end and die with honor. That my body may not lay in a pile of flesh, but rest on fur... up on top!

This memorial, at Fort Lewis in Washington, was made for the 5th Brigade 2nd Inf. Division as a reminder of those whose lives were the cost of war. May they now rest in peace. It is placed on the crest of a hill and kept safe. The cool temperatures and damp lush terrain hold back the modern foolishness of the world.

Here, we acknowledge greatness and hope that as long as freedom rings, a nation, its people and our warriors will remember our fallen. Our lives and our future are better for that which has been paid for.

This place not only stands protected by nature, its stands protected by our own people. Those who experienced life and death. Families that lost their blood, their family. Other Soldiers, who were witnesses to the horror and shared their last moments. "We" who shared this one blink of an eye in time. We remember, and stay on watch, giving protection with respect and honor. It is here and will remain here until future generations forget.

Military Terms and Abbreviations

1Sg: *The highest ranking enlisted soldier in a company. This is his position, but his grade is E-8*

AAR: *After Action Review*

ANP: *Afghan National Police*

Arteps: *Army Training and Evaluation Program*

Article 15: *Nonjudicial Punishment*

Bde: *Brigade*

Bn: *Battalion*

B/X: *Base Exchange (see also P/X)*

CO: *Commanding Officer*

Cdr: *Commander*

Cherries: *New Recruits*

CLS: *Combat Lifesaver*

Class 6: *Liquor store on base*

CP: *Command Post*

Cpt: *Captain*

CSM: *Company Sergeant major*

Doing the 5's and 25's: A *visual sweep for IEDs / booby-traps at 5 meter intervals*

DRASH: *Deployable Rapid Assembly Shelter. (New version of a tent)*

E-7: *The grade for a senior enlisted Soldier. Also referred to as SFC (Sergeant First Class)*

EOD: *Explosive Ordnance Disposal*

EMT: *Emergency Medical Technician*

ETA: *Estimated Time of Arrival*

FDC: *Fire Direction Control*

FOB: *Forward Operating Base*

FM 7-8: *Field Manual 7-8. Infantry Rifle Platoon and Squad Description. This manual provides doctrine, tactics, techniques and procedures on how infantry rifle platoons and squads fight. This has been replaced with a newer version*

FO: *Forward Observer*

Frocked: *A commissioned or non-commissioned officer selected for promotion wearing the insignia of the higher grade before the official date of promotion*

GRID: *Also MGRS. Military Grid Reference System (MGRS) is the geocoordinate standard used by NATO for locating points on the earth*

Gucci Gear: *Slang for buying anything and everything to make you look awesome, super, serious and professional to a point of going overboard*

HHC: *Headquarters and Headquarters Company*

HLZ: *Helicopter Landing Zone*

HME: *Home Made Explosives*

HMFIC: *Head Motherfucker in Charge*

ICU: *Intensive Care Unit*

IED: *Improvised Explosive Device*

Joe: *Soldier (from GI Joe)*

JRTC: *Joint Readiness Training Center (Fort Polk, LA)*

Lickies and Chewies: *Junk food you pack up and store for a morale boost, including chips, dips, drinks, snacks, and whatever else you can carry, on top of what you have to take*

LtC: *Lieutenant Colonel*

Medivac: *Evacuation of Casualties*

MGRS: *Military Grid Reference System (See GRID)*

MICLIC: *Mine Clearing Line Charge*

MOS: *Military Occupational Specialty (US Army)*

MOUT: *Military Operation in Urban Terrain*

MRE: *Meal Ready to Eat*

MSg: *Master Sergeant*

NCO: *Non-commissioned Officer*

NOD: *Night Observation Device*

NTC: *National Training Center (CA)*

OC: *Observer Controller*

OER: *Officer Evaluation Report*

OJT: *On the Job Training*

Pax: *Passengers (in a military vehicle)*

POG (pogie): *People Other than Grunts*

PCC: *Pre Combat Check*

PCI: *Pre Combat Inspection*

PCS: *Permanent Change of Station*

Pfc: *Private First Class*

Plt: *Platoon*

PMCS: *Pre-Maintenance Checks and Services*

Psg: *Platoon Sergeant*

PT: *Physical Training*

PTSD: *Post Traumatic Stress Disorder*

P/X: *Post Exchange (see also B/X)*

QRF: *Quick Reaction Force*

RIP-ITS: *The national drink of war. An energy drink provided to service members*

Rotary Wing: *Helicopter*

RTO: *Radio Telephone Operator*

Selling Wolf Tickets: *Bragging about something that couldn't or didn't happen. Also known as lying*

S-shop: *Different sections, usually at Battalion level, that provide various types of support, logistics,* equipment, support, beans and bullets, wherever you are not in direct contact with the enemy. (Unless you get a mortar round lobbed in your direction in the middle of the night!)

SF: *Special Forces / Snake Eaters / Quiet Professionals; The Green Berets*

SFC: *Sergeant First Class*

SgM: *Sergeant Major*

Sgt: *Sergeant*

Sitrep: *Situation Report*

Soldier's Board: *This is where you are evaluated on your performance and knowledge. Most of the time it's where an enlisted Soldier goes to become an NCO/Sgt*

SOP: *Standard Operating Procedure*

SP: *Start Point*

Spc: *The rank of Specialist, grade E-4. They party Like Rock Stars! All are full members of the E-4 Mafia (Refer to fight club, they do everything). They know enough to be a Sgt, but love the middle. Eventually, they are the gate-keepers to turds who are not getting promoted. They are ranked high enough to not get stuck on crappy details. Usually they are put in charge of details or things needing to get done. They are cunning, ruthless, mean, nasty, and could probably end a war if left alone to handle business*

SSg: *Staff Sergeant*

Stryker: *An armored vehicle*

Terp: *Interpreter*

TIC: *Troops In Contact*

TOC: *Tactical Operations Center*

Turd Burglar: *Slang for a piece of shit*

VC: *Vehicle Commander*

West Point Prep: *United States Military Academy Preparatory School*

Wolf Tickets: *Stories or false tales*

Woobie: *A poncho liner. Even though it was created as an accessory to the poncho, it has become greater. It is the best invention, EVER!!! Bullets and bombs are in the same category as the woobie. Things that go BOOM! are cool, but besides that, there is nothing that can compare to the simplest, most wonderful invention known to a grunt*

XO: *Executive Officer*

Natividad "Shepherd" Ruiz
Master Sergeant, US Army (Ret.)

www.ingramcontent.com/pod-product-compliance
Lightning Source LLC
Chambersburg PA
CBHW052053110526
44591CB00013B/2186